ary

Life on a Plate

Life on a Plate

GREGG WALLACE

The right of Gregg Wallace to be identified as
the author of this work has been asserted by him in accordance with the
Copyright, Designs and Patents Act 1988.

This edition first published in Great Britain in 2012 by
Orion Books
an imprint of the Orion Publishing Group Ltd
Orion House, 5 Upper St Martin's Lane,
London WC2H 9EA
An Hachette UK Company

1 3 5 7 9 10 8 6 4 2

A CIP catalogue record for this book is available
from the British Library.

ISBN: 978 1 4091 4391 8

Printed in Great Britain by CPI Group (UK) Ltd, Croydon CR0 4YY

The Orion Publishing Group's policy is to use papers that are natural,
renewable and recyclable and made from wood grown in sustainable forests.
The logging and manufacturing processes are expected to conform to the
environmental regulations of the country of origin.

Every effort has been made to fulfil requirements with regard to
reproducing copyright material. The author and publisher will be glad to
rectify any omissions at the earliest opportunity.

www.orionbooks.co.uk

For my Mum

Contents

PHOTO CREDITS

Section 2

p.11: Me and Charlie Hicks © ITV/Rex Features

p.12: Fruit and veg © Oliver Lim/Evening Standard/Rex Features

p.12: Pasta © Rex Features

p.12: Pudding © Rex Features

p.13: Me and John in London © Neil Hall/Rex Features

p.13: Me and John on Daybreak © Steve Meddle/Rex Features

p.14: Rugby © Getty Images

p.14: John, Sir Terry and me © Yui Mok/PA Archive/Press Association Images

p.15: Michel, me, John and Monica © Ray Tang/Rex Features

CHAPTER 1

Milk

*T*here's always a brief lull before things kick off. And I usually find there's just me and John Torode when it happens. This time, we were all microphoned up, standing on the ramp near the stage door at London's Earl's Court. Music pumping, crowds of *MasterChef* fans cheering, and, for once, I was completely and utterly lost for words.

This was the first *MasterChef* live show, doing on-stage cooking. It was a sell-out and, despite everything – despite being a greengrocer by trade, being as passionate as ever about food and having already presented telly for the past eight years – nerves caught up with me.

'Thirty seconds to go,' I muttered to John.

I wiped a bead of sweat off my head and looked at my mate, who I'd first met twenty years previously while he worked as a young sous chef as I flogged him fruit and veg.

'It'll be all right,' he muttered softly. 'It will be OK. You'll be OK. OK?'

I nodded, grateful. 'OK.'

Then the cue was given and we marched on, crowds erupting, a sea of faces, some wearing 'Gregg and John' masks, thousands stretching as far as I could see ... Show time ... And I just thought: Wow!

For the next hour or so I cooked, just as I'd practised, my confidence gathering pace (I'm not a chef like John – it comes less naturally) and we joked and did what we do best: talk ... food, food, glorious food. And I couldn't help but think once again: blimey, just how far have I come from the Peckham days. And how had this happened?

Shortly afterwards, I found myself wandering around Earl's Court, alone among the crowds, wearing a 'Gregg Wallace' mask so that nobody knew it was me, and I spotted someone wearing a T-shirt with my name on too. As I smiled wistfully, I wondered what my lovely grandparents would've thought of that.

It was my grandfather, the one who lived in Wimbledon, who'd inspired the name 'Gregg'. He'd worked in the navy for years, from teenage stoker to warrant officer, and at one point he was stationed in the Falklands, where he met a local farmer called Gregg. Anyway, this farmer, Gregg, taught my Grandad W how to ride a horse – something he loved – and it was while out riding one day in the frozen fields, when he dismounted to open a fence, that Grandad W spotted something glittering in the mud and ice. It was a ring, a gold ring, and a perfect fit on his finger. As it was on Gregg's land, he took it to him, and Gregg laughed his head off when he realised it was one he'd lost ten years earlier.

'You can have it,' he said to Grandad W, who put it on his little finger and never took it off. The pair remained friends for a while and Mum remembers meeting the original (but not the best – sorry!) Gregg a few times. She always liked the name and voilà. It mightn't be one of the strangest stories of how someone's name was chosen but there you go. Years later after Grandad W died, I was given this ring and I still wear it every day. I feel I owe my grandparents on both sides a lot. And my mum. This is their story as much as mine.

When I hear what my poor mother had to go through to have me, my heart bleeds for her, not to mention having a desire to clamp my hands over my ears. This was 1964, Camberwell, London, and, God love nurses and all they do, but back then, there was plenty of tea but sympathy was in short supply. With no painkillers, and no husbands or family allowed to sit and hold your hand, the women were herded into a single room, all in different stages of labour, and left to get on with it.

Just as labour pains kicked off, Mum had been driven to hospital by her parents, my nan and grandad, who lived in Wimbledon. To make this story more complicated, I called both sets of grandparents 'Nan and Grandad', so I'll call these two Nan and Grandad W (for Wimbledon) – OK?

Pregnant with me, Mum had been staying with them for a few days, as they felt it was 'safer', which tells you a lot about what they thought of my dad, Allan, and the rented house Mum was sharing with her in-laws in Peckham.

Poor Mum. She'd married my dad, Allan Wallace, aged seventeen, after only a year of dating him. Quite the middle-class girl, she worked in the accounts offices of Bentalls, a department store in Kingston, and was the daughter of a naval officer. They'd met on the train on the way to work, where Dad was an electrician working in the building. A couple of years older, he'd quickly spotted this petite, brown-eyed girl with her beehive and mini-dress suit. I guess she fell for Dad's tall, dark good looks and his 'rough diamond' qualities. Anyway, off she trotted down the aisle when he asked her.

Of course she told Dad to ask Grandad W 'for permission' first. I'm sure he had his doubts about this south-east Londoner, a boy from the wrong side of the tracks in Peckham, who lived in a two-up two-down with his mum and dad still and who'd seemingly swept up Mum in some kind of whirlwind (and the problem with those is they tend to crash you back to earth).

'If this is what you want, I won't stand in your way,' Grandad W said, rather ominously.

Mum had a dream wedding in St Mary's Church in Merton with a white meringue dress, plenty of flowers, cake and a knees-up afterwards. The bride and groom were well toasted, everyone happy to see they'd found their 'ever after'. But after that, sadly, the dream ended. Almost as soon as her veil came off, so did Mum's rose-tinted specs about Dad.

Whisked away to begin her new life in Peckham, Mum already knew she'd be staying in a rented house, with her in-laws living in two rooms upstairs. She knew Dad liked a laugh in the pub. She knew life in deepest darkest Peckham compared to doiley-laced Wimbledon would be different. What she didn't know was that there wasn't an inside toilet and she'd be expected to pee in a bucket at night.

Yes, life in Peckham, where if it moved you ate it, if it didn't you nicked it, was going to be very different from the rolling lawns, neat houses and social niceties of Wimbledon. I need, at this point, to clarify what I mean about south

4

London. I actually mean south-east London. It is so very different to any other part. If people hear a working-class London accent, they think it belongs to an 'Eastender', but actually the accent of the south is different, albeit ever so slightly.

But south-east London is not 'south London': it's older, it's got more history. When London was just a city in the square mile, within the City walls, south-east London was the part people started to build on first. It had the first bridge going across to Southwark and to where Shakespeare's theatre and the like all sprang up. Peckham appears in the Domesday book as 'Pecheham'. It was on the Old Kent Road that produce was brought into the City, it boasted orchards, meadows and markets, and it was the place where farmers stopped to give their cattle a feed before reaching the City. In the eighteenth century it became a site of commerce, as rents were cheaper than in the City. And still today, south-east London is blue-collar-worker land, where the docks all kicked off, where breweries started ... all this happening long before things were built and took off in east London. South-east London has history, a sense of working self-respect that goes way, way back, and is something I take pride in today. In short, though, Mum felt like an alien dropped on to another planet. And planet Peckham was a galaxy away from Wimbledon, south-west London, where social climbing and middle-class suburbia were as alive in the 1960s as they are today.

Even the way she spoke was an issue. One of her neighbours, Mrs Dillon, overheard her talking in the garden once to another neighbour.

'Hello, how are yew doing?' Mum asked politely.

'Oi, you're a bit of posh girl, intcha?' Mrs Dillon said.

Very quickly Mum learned to drop a few vowel sounds

and not pronounce her haitches any more, along with trying to get her head around the rhyming slang and laughing along to the old music hall songs, the lyrics changed to set the most open-minded blushing – she so badly wanted to fit in.

Although how her accent was going down was soon to be the least of Mum's new worries. My nan had expected her to stop working and look after Dad full-time, but she carried on working, actually doing OK for herself: she got trained up on how to use the National Cash registers, the scary-looking machines that preceded computers and wouldn't have looked out of place in *Doctor Who*'s Tardis.

The problems started when she came to realise the 'temporary move' to rent the downstairs part of her in-laws' rented house was looking rather permanent. And then, to add the cherry to the top, she found out he was having an affair. A little Irish lady called Maria a few doors down told her quietly as she picked up some groceries one day.

'Did you know my Albert is out with your Allan every Friday night, trawling for a bit of skirt?' she said. 'And Allan is seein' one bit on the side in particular.'

Mum nearly dropped the loaf and milk she was carrying and ran home in tears.

In desperation, before she got pregnant with me, Mum swallowed her pride and begged Nanny W to let her come home.

'I've made a mistake, Mum,' she sobbed. 'I don't want to be married to this man. It's too hard. I didn't really know him.'

Now these days you live together first and thank God for that. If Mum had moved in with Dad, she'd probably have rented a flat, it wouldn't have worked and she'd have gone home again. Job done.

★

When I think of my own daughter, Libby, who is fourteen, I think that if this was her, now, I wouldn't be able to get her out of there fast enough. But this was 1960, and the scandal of having a daughter who walked out on her husband was too much for Nanny W and her values to bear.

'You made your bed when you said those vows, my girl,' came the stern response. 'Now you go back there and make the best of it, and we'll hear no more about it.'

Nan W never even told Grandad W (who'd have had her out of that house faster than you can say Jack Robinson) of their conversation. So Mum's bed was made, except she had to make it herself on the rickety pull-out sofa next to a bucket, often perilously close to overflowing. Years and years later, when Nan W was an old lady at the end of her life, she brought up all 'that business' and begged for Mum's forgiveness.

'I'm so sorry I made you stay,' she said.

'It was a different era,' Mum said. 'You did what you thought was right.'

Anyway, we've left poor Mum in labour, so let's get back to the story quick.

After arriving in the labour room, where mums-imminently-to-be were quite screaming their heads off in agony, my terrified mum found herself alone, writhing on a bed, joining in. Makes me wince just thinking about it.

The labour lasted for twelve hours and had Mum begging nurses for Nanny W to come and rescue her.

'I want my mum!' she screamed. 'Please!'

'She'll be no use to you now,' a prim nurse said with a shrug, eyeing the clock. 'Just get on with it and it'll soon be over.'

Finally, I arrived, on 17 October 1964, at 4.30 p.m., at St Giles' Hospital in Camberwell, weighing a respectable 6lb 9oz.

And despite the ordeal, Mum says she fell in love with me instantly. I was adorable, apparently.

She'd already chosen my name, and it was just her choice as well, as Dad had had nothing to do with her pregnancy, and had certainly not sat around discussing baby names. Mum had chosen Gregg Allan Wallace, an unusual spelling with a double 'G' now, let alone then in Peckham.

Mum says she was only allowed a few minutes with me before I was taken off by nurses and plonked in a cot with all the other newborns in the nursery. For the next forty-eight hours she was only allowed to hold me at feeding times, which were strictly only every four hours. Nurses would pick up the babies, hand them to the mothers for feeding and burping, and snatch them back to return them to their cots for a sleep, however much they screamed.

Mum says that in between feeds, lots of the mums would press their faces to the glass window of the nursery, to gaze at their new offspring, crying if they were crying, knowing they could only look on helplessly. Rules were rules in those days, though, and hospital rules were not ones to be broken.

As fast as possible, she got herself out of there and back home to Kincaid Road, Peckham. She went straight to bed, and Nanny W came over to care for her.

I had my other nan and grandad living upstairs, but let's just say mother-in-law and daughter-in-law didn't see eye to eye. Once, when Mum was ill, Nan made Mum a bowl of soup and then wrote out a bill for it afterwards. That says all you need to know about their relationship. My grandad, though, adored kids and was my hero. More about that lovely man later.

I managed a proper smile aged just three days old – so Nanny W swore. Very quickly I learned to talk, and I was always a good eater. Nothing much has changed. Mum said I was a bundle of energy: I always wanted to be the first, could never wait, and was desperate to see it all for myself. 'If you wanted to do something, then "bosh", you did it,' she said. This characteristic, though, could turn something like a nice Sunday stroll in the pushchair into a near-death experience within seconds. When I was old enough to walk, Nan W and Mum took me to a ravine on holiday for a breath of fresh air. After we'd arrived I shook Mum's hand off and raced to the water's edge. Blissfully unaware of the danger, I somehow ducked under the barrier like greased lightning, on to the other side where there was a sheer drop into the water around twenty feet below.

Mum said her heart was in her mouth as she started trembling and running towards me, but Nan W pulled her back, hissing, 'Sssshhh, don't shout, we mustn't startle him.'

Carefully edging forwards, Nan W very calmly approached me with all the swift calm movements of a bomb disposal expert. 'Ooh, hello, Gregg, what are you looking at, my love …?' Then she reached out an arm to grab my sleeve before I could panic and drop off the face of the earth.

Mum collapsed on to the grass bank and sobbed with utter relief. I am not surprised Nan W kept her cool and sorted this situation out. I mean, she was that kind of woman. Tall and elegant, she had long slim fingers and even when she was telling me off she'd be smiling. She just emanated warmth. Back in her house in Wimbledon, she was always doing something with her lovely hands – baking, sewing, mending, soothing me if I fell over. A lovely woman.

Soon after the ravine drama, Mum went to see a gypsy palm reader at a fair near Blackheath. She wheeled my pushchair into the small caravan where this gypsy lady was sitting and paid her a couple of pounds for a reading. Mum can't remember much of what was said about her, except that she suddenly pointed to me, sitting in my buggy.

'That little boy is going to go on and do great things,' she said. 'He's going to make you very proud.'

Mum laughed. It's what every mum wants to hear about their child but it was a story I grew up knowing. Took me a while to believe it was possible, though.

Apparently I always had my own way of doing things. Church and religion didn't feature big in our house, but we always turned up for weddings and funerals. The very first time I visited church as a toddler, to see a family friend get hitched, we were all asked to rise and sing the hymn. Wide-eyed and desperate to join in, I started loudly singing the only song I knew and blessed the whole congregation with a fine rendition of 'Hokey Cokey'.

CHAPTER 2

Chocolate Doings

*O*ne of my first memories is of me banging on Grandad's door upstairs. During the week, he was up before Nan, making a cup of tea, but at weekends, he'd have a lie-in. 'Hey now, Gregg,' he said. 'Come here and have a dip in the chocolate doings.'

Grandad, who loved kids, always had a big heavy tin filled with broken chocolate biscuits from the market (and if you were lucky sometimes Penguins) to dish out. He called all chocolate biscuits 'doings', whatever they were.

I'd put my arm up to my elbow in the jar to pick out a few chocolate digestives. Ah, the humble digestive, really not so humble in my opinion. So smooth on top and so satisfying for bite-mark effects.

With a cuppa, I liked to stack them up in a pile of four and wait until I'd drunk almost all my tea before I carefully angled the stack into the liquid. Sometimes I scraped off the edge of the biscuit in a straight line with my lower teeth or I tried to get the entire biscuit soaked without breaking it. Now that's an art, as you watch the golden-brown wheat darken with tea, but just the right shade, as otherwise it's too much and it falls into a sad mush. It can make biscuits last ages if you eat them this way.

Grandad didn't often have them but I loved choc-chip cookies too. Now they were a revelation, a real chap's biscuit. I didn't like any cream or goo in my biscuits, thank you. I loathed custard creams – stale, cardboard, synthetic-tasting things. And I'd pass on a Jammie Dodger. But I loved Wagon Wheels. Marshmallow, was it, inside? Or just sweet gunge? Who knew, but anything remotely crisp or crunchy that breaks into a bit of a chew is still right up my street.

That evening, I was back up there, squashed up next to Grandad's thigh as Nan hushed me quiet.

'High Why Five's on,' Grandad whispered, meaning *Hawaii Five-O*.

Our house was right in the heart of south-east London. It was pretty basic and we were poor. You don't realise you're poor as a kid; everyone seemed to be in the same boat. I don't want to lay this on too thick – there were a lot of families worse off than we were – but looking back without the benefit of a flat cap and a Yorkshire accent, we were poor.

Looking face on to our Edwardian three-bed terraced house, identical to all the others if you looked left or right, there was a low stone wall. The front door was to the left of a bay window, above which there was another one that matched it. There was a wrought-iron door knocker which you twisted to slide the latch across. In summer Mum put up some plastic strips so you could come in and out but neighbours couldn't see in. Across our road was the imposing Acorn estate. Its sprawling concrete metropolis always gave me the shivers a little, although Mum's best friend and my godmother, Margo, lived opposite it in another similar block, so I knew inside was nice. Her kitchen was deep orange and dark brown. Very modern. She seemed so much posher than us – she even had a bath in her house. Although everyone seemed posher than us, and to be fair they probably were.

Anything within a ten-minute walk was called 'around the corner' and our corner still had Second World War bomb sites. These were supposedly safely enclosed by fences and corrugated iron, but we boys were like rabbits, always finding a convenient hole or gap overlooked by the council. Running across the craters, shouting and playing with my mates, was fun, and it was even more fun when we spotted that the opening sequence of *The Sweeney* had been filmed on it. 'Round the corner' was also a house with a policeman standing outside it. Those were the days of the Krays' court cases and the whole neighbourhood was buzzing about them. This house with a copper on the doorstep belonged to some of the witnesses.

This was all before the age of The Supermarket, and Ted's corner shop mainly kept us all fed and watered. It was a magical place, full of shiny wrapped sweets for me and ready meals for Mum and our family. Its freezers were packed with Vesta meals, frozen pizzas, sausages, burgers and mince, just like the one in our house.

'Good morning, Gregg,' Ted would say, when I ran inside with a list from Mum.

'Good morning, Ted.' I would nod, in a way my four-year-old self had seen Grandad do.

Ted liked me. I was unusual, being one of the polite ones, and he'd point this out to the other kids.

'If you asked as nicely as Gregg it'd go a long way,' he'd say to any other little people in the vicinity, passing me Mum's Silk Cut and Dad's No. 6 Player's cigs, which I was entrusted to pick up. Once, after carefully stowing the fags, I spied a can of Tango on his shelf. The last one!

'Ted, could you please pass me the Tango too? Thank you very much,' I said, grinning.

I ran all the way home. Unable to wait, I tore off the ring and filled my mouth with the painful but syrupy fizz.

'Mum, look!' I grinned, as she sparked up a fag. 'I had the last Tango in Ted's!'

She fell about laughing.

Step over the Wallace threshold, straight ahead was the stairs. Immediately to your left was Mum and Dad's bedroom-cum-living room, with fold-up sofa bed for night-time. Mum's side was full of Agatha Christies and Dad's sci-fi novels were next to a bucket.

'Don't miss the island!' Grandad would say if I ever needed to use it. Our toilet was in the garden. I'd like to slap the man who invented Izal medicated toilet paper. Have any of you ever, how do I say, sampled it? Actually I don't want the start of this book to be about my bottom, but I just want to point out we were hard up.

The door of the toilet was about a foot off the ground, so come wind, rain, hail or snow, your knees bore the brunt. I loved sitting in there pretending it was an elevator, plunging downwards to the centre of the earth. It had a corrugated roof and years later I'd learn I could climb out of Nan and Grandad's window upstairs and leap on to it, driving Mum mental with worry.

Then there was my bedroom. It was very small: just a bed, wardrobe, walls of the inevitable chipboard wallpaper, and buckets and buckets of plastic cast green toy soldiers. Grandad loved spoiling me and bought me loads of them.

One day Mum decorated my room by replacing the yellowing chipboard wallpaper with more slightly less yellowy chipboard wallpaper. Grandad, who worked all his life as a handyman, taught her how to unfurl the rolls, line them up and slosh the paste on. They got on well, Mum and Grandad. She always said, 'He's a lovely man,' and he was.

At least a few times a year I'd be woken at night by the feel of tiny little claws flitting across my face.

'Muuuuuum!' I would scream, leaping from my bed, shaking the covers, as mice scattered on to the carpet.

No. 22 had more of these little critters in it than your average haystack. However many traps Mum laid out, the buggers still thought they ruled the place, scurrying around, climbing into food cupboards and nibbling away at packets of rice and flour or Angel Delight. Mum used to give the push-along Hoover a kick before she used it, as once she found one squashed between the rollers.

Once, slap bang in the middle of the hallway, slap bang in the middle of the day, a dirty great big brown rat waltzed in as if he owned the joint. I'd just got up from the TV to get a glass of Coca-Cola from the kitchen when we both froze, boy to rat, beady eye to frightened one, before I opened my gob again and screamed for Mum. I'd never seen anything move so fast. That included my poor mum, who echoed my scream as she ran towards it with a broom like a woman possessed. She chased it off.

Now the cupboard under the stairs was the 'food tin' cupboard and was also teeming with mice. From floor to the ceiling it was rammed. When it came to tins in shops Nan and Grandad were magnets to iron filings, quick to spot a bargain to add to the pile. Tins were never from Ted's corner shop, though. 'It's so dear in there,' Nan would tut.

The cupboard became a veritable teetering tower of metal-encased apricots, peaches, beans, rice pudding, custard, corned beef, sardines, mince, carrots, peas, pease pudding … A safety net of food, as much part of our house as the furniture. 'Just in case,' said Nan, although 'just in case' of what, who knew? Another war? A nuclear explosion? Armageddon? Or, more likely, it was just a simple insurance policy for two old people who knew what it was like to be hungry. Really, really hungry. I only ever got snippets of what life had been like in the 1930s, but once Grandad told me he'd watched fights at the East India Docks between men so desperate for a day's work they'd have a punch-up rather than see their families starve.

Next to the food cupboard you had the electric and gas meter, also always hungry – for shilling coins. That would've messed a soufflé up, wouldn't it: the gas oven switching off halfway through? Although this of course was a good few years before anyone in Peckham knew what a soufflé was.

Mum often found herself plunged into darkness watching *The Forsyte Saga* or Richard Dimbleby (her favourite) of an evening. And if she'd run out of change she'd have to sit in the dark and wait till Dad got back from the pub with some money to pop in. Often Grandad would nip downstairs and drop another coin in and pad back upstairs without saying a word.

Out the back was the parlour, complete with a fire, an armchair and a second-hand dining table of sorts. Later on, Mum got her hands on a chest freezer, as the tiny one above the fridge was always chock-a-block with her standby meals. Then there was the galley kitchen, which led to the back door to the garden. Ikea kitchen units would've looked Space Age in our sort of place. Masquerading as cabinets were shelves with a sheet of plastic on a wire, which you moved backwards and forwards until it tore. The kitchen, on the little table, was where Mum and I ate.

On the whole, food in our house was something to be ripped from a packet, heated up and slapped on the plate. Poor Mum was run ragged at work and never had much time. She often ate later than me, so I'd bolt down my re-heated food so that I could go upstairs to see Grandad or outside to play.

I always had to sit nicely to eat, holding my knife and fork properly, even if it was to eat something from the discounted frozen section. Mum can knock up good dishes now but when I was little, food was fuel in our house.

One of her specialities was chicken and rabbit stew. Salty, wet and rich in gravy, it was something you could eat quickly with a spoon, careful not to burn your tongue.

'Are the soft bits the rabbit's ears?' I'd enquire, poking my spoon around.

I was actually scared rigid of rabbits – nasty hoppy things. Mum always bought them from a tiny shop on Towerbridge Road. The window was filled with dead grey furry things on hooks. It was a popular place and I was happy to see them in the window. But in real life forget it. I think it started when I watched a horror film on a Saturday night and saw a giant rabbit as one of the monsters. Then I saw a wildlife programme about how a mummy rabbit eats her babies if a predator discovers their nest. Talk about reverse survival instincts – made me shudder! It confirmed my idea of a rabbit as the demon pet. Rabbit stew was the one of the few dishes Mum cooked from scratch. Boiled bacon and pease pudding heated from a can was another good standby. Fray Bentos pies, instant mash and tinned veg were standard fare. Meat pies and meat puddings were other stalwarts, straight from the butcher to be heated up. While the meat pies' pastry was always flaccid, soggy but somehow tasty, the puddings glistened in their creamy cloak of beef suet. Mum's curries and her chilli con carnes were exactly the same – mince, chillies, no sauce and boiled rice – except the con carnes had tinned kidney beans chucked in. I pointed it out once and she just laughed her head off.

Once I went to a second-hand shop with Mum to get our 'new sofa suite'. It was a second-hand job, of course, frayed, and the cushions sank a little lower than expected every time you sat in them, but their black-with-orange-and-green funky zigzag design had us all marvelling over them for weeks.

One day Grandad came home with a squashy orange cushion taken from a skip for a grey sofa he had upstairs in his room, to 'bolster' his own. It looked ridiculous, but there was no place for vanity in this house.

We washed at the kitchen sink: a strip wash a few times a week, a lick and a promise the other days. As for proper bathing, I don't remember what we did – sorry, Mum. I know I hated soap on my face. Mum coming towards me with a soggy flannel and bit of carbolic felt like a form of psychological torture when I was little.

Across the beige patterned carpet, you could walk back up the stairs, to where Nan and Grandad lived in two rooms with a tiny kitchen.

The first thing I always spotted was Grandad's big round smiling face. He'd be sitting on his cushion, always welcoming me in.

Now I can't wait to tell you about him, so here we go. Sidney James Wallace was a bald, short, squat man, with an open moon face and a big wide smile to match his waist. He called his nose 'my Wallace hook'. He was deaf as a post but wouldn't wear a hearing aid, as he thought it made him look stupid. But Grandad was anything but stupid.

Every day he wore the same outfit: a pair of trousers right up to his chest, a wide belt, a shirt and heavy brogue shoes with little bits of metal on the sole at the heel and toe. He often wore a tie, but you'd never see much of that, or for that matter his shirt, as his trousers covered most of his torso. He'd wear braces and a thick leather belt. It seemed to be the norm for men his age; maybe they all lived in dread that their trousers would fall down. He'd no reason to be scared, though. He wore long johns all year round. In winter he wore a cloth cap and an overcoat with a fly front covering the buttons and which ended below the knee.

This was the uniform of every man over the age of thirty-five in our area. The men'd walk almost in unison, in long lines – hats on, coats buttoned, all in the same style but maybe in slightly different shades of black, grey or beige, faces down against the wind or rain, like Lowry figures, to go and see Millwall play.

As summer turned to autumn Grandad always said to Nan, 'Winter drawers on, Mum.' I never knew if this was an observation or instruction but it made her laugh. He cleaned his teeth with a piece of rag dipped in salt and he told me and Mum you shouldn't wash too much and 'do away with your natural oils'. He only washed once a week, on a Friday. He never smoked, or drank, or gambled. Suffering so much in the 1930s had seen to that: they were unnecessary luxuries. Grandad lived for his family, for me, for football. I'd watch him most mornings shaving at his tiny sink upstairs, singing silly songs which neither made sense nor probably ever existed, and looking at me out of the corner of his eye to see if I was giggling, which I usually was.

They almost worked; they almost had a tune.

> 'If you were the one
> Then you would be just yooooooooou and meeeeeee
> We'd be the twooooooooo
> Forever yoooooooooooou . . .'

There were variations on this theme but you get the picture.

He often said, 'Money speaks all languages, boy.' Something he knew not much about. As a man without a trade to his name his whole life, Grandad knew of real hardship. Although he worked at the Strand Palace Hotel (SPH) for twenty-odd years, it was pure chance he got the job in the first place. As a consequence he nagged his son, my dad, to 'find a trade' and was thrilled when he found an apprenticeship as an electrician.

Grandad's family were from Stornoway and moved down when he was a kid, looking for work. He'd had no formal education, my grandad. I don't know much of what he did before the hotel – just factory work of a sort. I don't know why he didn't go to war either; perhaps it was something to do with being deaf. He played his part, though, in the fire service, fighting fires, sometimes for three days at a time.

He was there when the Woolwich Arsenal went up in 1940, the site of munition factories. Grandad helped battle against the blaze. He told Mum how he spotted an orphanage nearby. 'I'd so badly wanted to go and pick up all those kids and put them in my pocket and take them home,' he remembered. 'They must've been petrified.'

Anyway pre-war London had very few jobs for men like him

and Grandad'd heard of an interview for a general dogsbody, so he queued with all the other men, and there were plenty. This was 1930s, the Great Depression, and work was scarce.

As he shuffled along the queue, a man emerged with a loud voice.

'Sorry, fellahs, go home, time to go. Positions filled.'

Poor Grandad was in despair. He sank down on the steps and put his head in his hands. It was all he could do to stop himself from sobbing. He had a family to support.

Then another fella poked him in the ribs. 'No good sitting here, mate,' he said. 'You need to pull yourself together. Whatcha think you're doing?'

Sympathy in those times for working men was in short supply.

Grandad quickly got up, put his cap back on and brushed himself down. Always a proud man, he'd just forgotten himself for a minute.

'Yep, I'm gone,' he said.

'Where you heading?' the man asked.

'Peckham,' he said.

'Same here. Let's grab the tram together, eh?'

The two of them went off, and got chatting. Turned out this fella was the foreman for the SPH and he took a real shine to my grandad, who after a five-minute chat with anyone could charm the birds out of the trees.

As he jumped off at his stop this foreman yelled to him, 'Come back to the hotel tomorrow, Sidney.' He did and the foreman gave him his much wanted job.

Grandad spent the rest of his working life at SPH, only leaving briefly to help during the war as a fireman. Everything in our house had SPH written on it: bars of soap, coat hangers, bed sheets. Grandad was no villain, but he was a bit of a tea

21

leaf, according to Mum. If he saw something nobody would miss he'd take it. 'It's just a bit of bunce. Goes with the job, innit,' he'd say with a wink.

Nan was a different kettle of fish. She'd worked in a factory before she got married and then like most women of her generation immediately gave up work. I don't know what she did. I do know her sister Daisy used to clean railway carriages for a living, but we rarely saw her. But Nan didn't see herself as much of a housewife either.

I mean, she did the cooking, but mainly out of tins, and she did the washing and ironing. But she expected Grandad to keep her company at all times. He took her shopping every Saturday. He took her to the launderette. He'd make her cups of tea and wash up afterwards. But he'd married her and a marriage was for life, however bad it got. And that, in Kincaid Road, was the mantra of our house.

CHAPTER 3

Caramel

It made perfect sense to me at the time, I thought: Grandad and Nan W should get together. The two nicest people in our family: what a great couple they'd make. But when I ran this idea past Mum she laughed and shook her head. 'No way!' she cried.

My two sets of grandparents never mixed. Not even at Christmas. I can remember once my two grandads meeting briefly when Grandad W came to pick us up. 'Give my regards to your good lady wife,' said Grandad with a nod of his head, as if he was addressing dignitaries. That didn't sound like Grandad – not the one I knew. Now I am older, of course I can see how absolutely different they were. The worlds of Peckham and Wimbledon definitely didn't collide. Even when I very young, I knew they liked eating different things, for a start. Grandad in Peckham had a long list of 'urgh' food including coffee and pepper, and when garlic hit our streets, both Dad and Grandad were incensed.

Slight digression here but once, when I was sixteen, I took them to a new local café on Peckham Rye, and they were serving garlic bread. The stink the pair of them kicked up overpowered any wafts of the bulb.

'Oi, boy, watcha brought us in here for?' Grandad cried. 'They do that blemmin' garlic in here!'

'They don't, do they?' chipped in Dad, a face on him as if they were serving rat poison. 'Blimey, what's the world coming to?'

'Sorry,' I said, sighing. 'I didn't know, did I?'

Compared to Grandad's traditional ideas about food, Mum's seemed positively cutting edge. As I've said, on the whole convenience foods were the way of life downstairs. Mashed potato was always Cadbury's Smash. This was the age of convenience food and anyone who didn't use it for their convenience was decried on the telly adverts as stupid. What was it those Smash Martians laughed at us for? Us earthlings for being primitive and peeling potatoes.

On the whole I hated veg. Perhaps because it was mainly tinned, and boiled to the point of soggy disintegration. I hated Brussels sprouts. Mum had a ploy, though. She'd put one on my plate and I'd munch it fast without breathing through my nose to minimise the bitter taste, barely tolerating the dry, chewy insides. Then the next time she'd put two on, and then the next, three.

'Mum!' I would cry. 'That's not fair!' As if I wouldn't notice!

Although Mum mustered about as much enthusiasm for cooking as she did origami, she always, always said to me, 'You can't say you don't like it till you try it, Gregg,' and she made me as adventurous as she was. Even if it was at the local Chinese or trying every single Vesta meal in the range.

Beef curry and risotto, chicken supreme and rice, chow mien and crispy noodles, sweet and sour – any flavour Mum could lay her hands on we tried. For us, like many people in the 1970s, these dishes were our first taste of foreign food, all conveniently packaged and ready to chuck in the oven or stir on the hob. Scalded taste buds were par for the course, as they emerged with their boiling neon or mucky-brown glutinous sauces, with pasta and rice with the texture of pieces of plastic. The flavourings always knocked your socks off, though, once you'd managed to 'fuuuuff' the steam off the fork enough to dare try a mouthful.

Looking back, I had eclectic tastes as a very young kid, thanks to Mum and her hurried ready meals. When a Chinese finally opened nearby, and I got the real McCoy, a proper chow mein, it was less exotic to me than to some, although the MSG almost blew my tastebuds out of my mouth. It was Mum's and my treat now and again. Prawn balls, dripping in radioactive coloured sweet and sour sauce, crunchy wet bean sprouts you could eat by the fistful straight from a plastic bag – a whole world away from Spam fritters and fish and chips.

Like Grandad, Dad always turned his nose up, though. 'Urgh, keep that away from me,' he'd say, flaring his nostrils and raising his upper lip. Like his father, but not like his son.

Mum was a grafter. As I said, she had to be. She was always getting ready for work or coming home from work, it seemed. I saw her briefly in the mornings and then we'd sit and have tea. A few times Mum was home early from work and you could tell by the food presentation. A big mound of mash with four sausages sticking out of it and a sea of peas below was Mum's 'I've got time' speciality. 'Mash hedgehog sitting on grass,' she'd say proudly.

Our other top treat was a steak from the butcher's. Or

chops. Drizzled with vegetable oil and stuck under the grill to spit until brown. Mum would make home-made chips too. If it was a special dinner we'd sit and eat together, if she had time. Dad's would sit on a plate, on top of a saucepan of simmering water, going slowly soggy with condensation, waiting for him to return from the pub, which often he never did.

Desserts went down easily. Especially Mum's Angel Delight. If it came out of a packet, Mum could cook it, and butterscotch and chocolate powder whisked with milk was our mainstay for dessert. Mum would plonk a big bowl in front of me, barely set after being hurriedly made up after work and shoved in the fridge for the minimal length of time, and I'd say, 'Thank you' and carefully take my spoon while surveying the edges.

There is only one way to eat a big bowl of this stuff of childhood legend: as an intrepid explorer. Chipping down the sides to try and create a tunnel to infiltrate the other side of the bowl was my preferred method. The tunnel would always collapse but that never stopped me from trying. Prisoners escaping from Stalag Luft III had nothing on this kid with a spoon and a tub of brown fluff. Even now I think the best milk puddings have to be brown to be good ones: caramel, chocolate, sticky toffee, butterscotch. I could happily live in a sticky toffee pudding. Anything with fruit in and milk doesn't work for me. Strawberry, banana, pineapple – urgh, no thanks.

Caramel cups were sometimes on hand in our fridge if there was no time for Angel Delight. Mum would upturn hers and tap it politely until it slid out, wet and wobbly, like a smooth beige tower of jelly, the 'sauce' – always too thin for my liking actually to be called a genuine 'sauce', but tasty nonetheless – gathering as a pool at the base.

I never upturned mine. I liked the runny burnt-sugar liquid

at the bottom too much. I've always liked to save the best till last.

Mum didn't have a sweet tooth. So she often ended dinners with cheese, waxy pillar-box-red-sided slabs of Edam, plain Cheddar and a few times, if she could afford it, brie, a new-fangled cheese from France from Sainsbury's. 'Posh foreign stuff,' said Grandad.

On special occasions, if there was time, out came the Wall's Viennetta: the queen of puddings. Now that layered, strange cake of synthetic chocolate that crackled so delightfully under a knife and that creamy smooth but cardboardy-tasting ice cream was a big, big indulgence we only tasted on bank holidays or birthdays. And that, for our table in Peckham, was about as indulgent as it got. No, for indulgence and home-cooked food, Wimbledon was the place to be. With my Grandad and Nan W, around their table for Sunday lunch.

Sundays were a time when we left the chaos of Peckham behind and immersed ourselves in a different way of life. The hour-and-a-half trip seemed like a million-mile journey away from Kincaid Road. It was quite a jaunt for a small lad. We'd get a bus to Vauxhall and then a train to Wimbledon, the red-bricked houses all becoming neater and cleaner as we wound our way en route. We'd pass a working Battersea power station too, with thick billowing smoke emerging from the towers. Eventually, as money became tighter, Grandad would drive to Peckham and pick us up and then drop us home again.

Dad came when I was very small, but one day he stopped. It was after a heated discussion with Grandad W as Nan spooned out the spuds.

'The Tories stink and you know it,' growled Dad, stabbing at his roast chicken as if it were about to run off his plate. 'I mean, do you seriously think we should stand for the nonsense? The working man!'

Grandad sighed, calmly chewing in thought. He was a staunch Tory; Dad was a staunch Labour man, a union man. Both worked for the Civil Service, Grandad W by now as a clerk in the MoD, Dad down the road in Whitehall fixing the plugs, but they couldn't have been further apart.

'Well, what do you think?' Dad cried, rising tension wobbling his lower lip.

'I think we should have a second helping,' Grandad said. He was a wise man and he'd never enter into an argument, especially not with someone like Dad. The next Sunday and the ones for ever after Dad's seat at the table was empty.

Nanny and Grandad W were Wilf and Lily Springette, and compared to my Peckham grandparents, they were very, very posh. They'd moved from Plymouth after the war and had three kids: my Uncle Wilf, Aunt Hazel and Mum, Mary, the youngest. They remained in the family home after Mum had moved out, and to me it was like a palace.

Their house in the Quadrant had a low stone wall and a proper front garden, but the *pièce de résistance* was the amazing glass sliding doors, in place of an ordinary front door. How groovy were they?

Inside was just as luxurious. The carpet was thick, the wallpaper lush, flocked even, and not only did they have a living room for the sole purpose of sitting in, but they even had a dining room. Out the back they had a big garden, with its own tiny tree about thigh high, with orange leaves, which had grown many years earlier from a peach stone buried by my mum as an experiment. Behind that were rose bushes and even a shed. And beyond the back gate was an alleyway, an exciting place with a railway embankment I was forbidden to go anywhere near. I used to love climbing Nan W's apple tree, though. I used to get covered in filth, which was especially annoying for Mum who had few clothes for me.

'Look at the state of you,' she would say, frowning, as I came in for lunch.

'It's not me,' I would say. 'It's your trees. They're dirty.'

Now when I think of Nanny W, I think of an elegant lady and I think of food. She appeared to be a natural cook, although Mum tells me she was quite a basic cook; I thought she was an incredible one at the time. I lived for her Sunday lunches. And for the first time in my life, I was allowed to help prepare them – well, a bit. It was my job to pick the green spearmint leaves from the disused kitchen sink outside where it used to grow. I'd carefully pull up a handful and then rinse them in the sink, before Nanny W got out her little chopping knife and turned it into confetti the colour of a football pitch.

'Oooh, smell that?' she'd always say, inhaling a few inches above the chopping board. 'Beautiful.'

I knew it would taste even better once it had made its way on to that lamb.

My other job was to ring a little ornamental bell to 'announce lunch'. As I say, it was posh.

Even now I can sit back, close my eyes and taste her joints of lamb: they were so deeply rich, succulent, moist and stunningly tender that they fell off the bone and melted in your mouth like butter. They were always served with a fantastically sharp mint sauce, giving them a refreshing edge. Her roast potatoes were unbelievable and I have never ever tasted anything like them since. I don't know how she did them and neither does Mum. Their tops were so crispy and almost black; they sat like hats on top of the spuds and you could literally lift them off intact. The rest of the potato underneath would fall apart and was fluffy as mash. Incredible.

Her veg were even lovely too, and I hated veg back then. The whole thing lay on their nice bone china plates, swamped in well-seasoned gravy, just dripping. Just how I like my savoury dishes to be today: wet, rich, comforting and moreish. From then on, brown and wet food was always my preferred choice. I stand by that today.

I would always eat my lunch using the 'worst first' system with which I tackled most plates of food. That meant downing the greens or the carrots at once. Then, in the case of my Nan's roasts, I could polish off the rest quite happily. I'd savour the glorious meat, and then finish with those legendary potatoes, spiking them with my fork and listening to the crackle as I wedged it in. Oh God, it was good.

The best thing was, we could always go back for seconds too. Something unheard of in our house. Or even thirds. Can you imagine!

Only once was there a disaster on my plate, when I spotted an unusual-looking more elongated browned potato. When I happily picked it up to munch it, I found my mouth turning with distaste as I was hit with an awful spongy, dry, oddly chewy texture and a sickly sweet taste. It was years before I was brave enough to try a parsnip again.

After our roasts came our desserts, something we often went without in Peckham. Nanny W loved her puddings. Her strawberry jam was red, daring, glistening and so sweet it made your lips pucker. Her brandy snaps were sticky, chewy horns of delight, and made the most satisfying cracking noise when you got your side teeth around them (front teeth wouldn't always do the job). When these were filled with cream, the table became a chorus of 'hmmm' as we polished them off.

My firm favourite, though, was Nan W's 'Crackalaks', a

sweet she named herself and which you couldn't say without smiling. The simple recipe worked perfectly. Cornflakes were put in a bowl. Then she reached for a tin of treacle, wedged it open with a spoon and dipped a generous-sized tablespoon in. Twisting it round and round quickly, like a professional glassblower, to stop any stray curls of stickiness escaping, she'd hold it high and pour it on top of the cornflakes. Then, using a fresh spoon, she'd mix it up by making wide circles, coating every single flake and crunching a few along the way. Then it was swiftly transferred to a baking tray, squashed down neatly as possible and baked until golden.

The saltiness and crunch of the cereal along with the cloying sweetness of the treacle was absolutely delicious, however young or old you were.

Her trifles were legendary. Vast glass bowls filled with perfect layers, tinned fruit at the bottom, sherry sponge and strawberry jelly, then dollops of snowy-white cream topped off with a shake of hundreds of thousands, like a rainbow wave, always done at the last possible minute before serving so that the colours didn't seep in.

She wasn't too keen on baking cakes, but we did get gingerbread now and then – something I was less keen on. It made my throat itch a little, its sticky, gooey crust always coating my fingers however hard I sucked them.

Tinned fruit and Carnation cream was another standby pud. Soft fruit, simple cream. Brilliant.

'Would you like an apricot?' Nan always asked, offering peaches.

'It's a peach, Nan.'

'Oh, is it? Would you like one anyway?'

After dinner, we'd sit and chat – something else that didn't happen much at home. And my grandmother's strong

Plymouth accent was a source of wonderment. She pronounced 'Co-op' as 'Kwop' and called her daughters her 'maids', and 'boy' sounded like 'bye'.

Nanny was a great cook, and she was also a great dressmaker and seemed to know exactly what to do if anyone got ill. In fact she could probably bring small family pets back from the dead, but she didn't pass any of these skills on to her daughter. This must've been typical, as after the war American-style labour-saving devices became all the rage and passing down the skills of housework, or drudgery, wasn't something mums wanted to do.

Grandad W still had the air of a naval man. He was very strict about good manners – something Mum instilled in me anyway. Although he wasn't like Grandad from Peckham, I knew he liked me. He 'didn't suffer fools gladly' and would rant and rave about stories from his naval days.

'Those above really thought they knew what was what, but my God, did many not know their arses from their elbows.'

'Well, if you'd kept your mouth shut,' Nan would say, 'you'd have done a lot better as well.'

She meant it in a light-hearted way, but I wonder now if there was a grain of truth in it. Grandad W was a clever man and he never made it to the top. Perhaps it was easier to say, 'I was never promoted because they were fools' rather than try to get along with people. Like a lot of young men from Plymouth, Grandad W had joined the navy after a few years working as a very young man on the docks. He'd actually joined the Marines first but after discovering the navy had a better signing-on fee, switched. The Marines came after him too, and it was lucky he didn't end up in prison.

Originally Grandad was due to come out of the navy in 1936, and Nan was looking forward to having her husband back home, to start their family and set up their home. But on leave for what Nan hoped was the last time, Grandad had some news.

'I've signed up for another term,' he said.

Nan was devastated and wholly disappointed in him. 'But you promised!' she cried. 'We were planning a new life, a new home.'

Grandad explained his decision. 'It's in the wind there will be another war in Germany. If war breaks out I'll be pulled back in the navy again and if I stay in, the navy will expand and I could get promoted.'

He did go back, Britain did go to war with Germany for a second time and he did get a rapid promotion. Three years before war had broken out, interestingly the Royal Navy had taken the conflict as a foregone conclusion and had given sound advice to the men.

Nanny W was a woman with a big heart, not just for herself but for everyone. A story she told me about the war showed this very essence of her. She lived through most of the war in north Devon, where she evacuated with Mum, who was a baby, Hazel, then five, and Wilf, aged ten. She heard on the radio how Plymouth was a prime target for the Luftwaffe (who tore the place to pieces in over fifty-nine terrifying raids: the royal docks at HMNB Devonport were the main target but over 1,500 people were killed and nearly 4,500 injured – horrific) and all she could do was listen.

At the turn of the war, though, in 1944, Nan W returned to her native Plymouth, as it was deemed safe enough, although Mum clearly remembers that Christmas, sitting in her high chair, and the sound of bombs nearby. Nan W made a rugby tackle for the sugar bowl on the kitchen table as the house shook. Never mind about anything else: sugar was expensive and they'd been looking forward to a treat.

Soon after arriving home one evening, Nan and her neighbours ran outside as the skies darkened with shadows and the menacing rumbling of engines could be heard. It was American and British bombers joining forces to fly to Germany to take out their cities and infrastructure. Now my grandmother had suffered many stressful, frightened, sleepless nights during that time. She'd no idea what political correctness was, but she said she felt an overwhelming sadness. She went back into her house and gathered her children to her – 'Gregg, your mum was a small babe,' she said to me – and all she could think of were the German women in their homes with their own children, completely unaware of what was coming. She said that if she'd had the power to stop them, she would've done.

Gosh, some of these memories even get me today. The strong sense of family, the values they had, the pride I feel, the taste of that food, even the smell of pipe smoke brings it back. Thank you, Nan and Grandad W. Sometimes I can feel you watching me. Am I doing OK?

CHAPTER 4

Custard Tarts

As on ours downstairs, on Nan and Grandad's floor there were three rooms – one for sleeping in, with a bed taking up the entire room, one for watching telly in – and a little tiny kitchen. The walls were covered in cupboards, filled with all kinds of bric-a-brac and materials, like bedding, hand and tea towels, pillowcases, things for a rainy day. One wall was painted in orange, and the gas mantels they still had on the walls were painted blue. 'Takes the dairy off,' Grandad said. Nope, neither Mum nor I knew what he meant either.

The pair would sit every evening, side by side, in silence watching a dusty telly on a screen with a giant perspex 'magnifying' glass on it.

The room was littered with packets of Rennies and glasses – glasses for reading and others specs for 'telly'. Neither ever had indigestion and they took so many of the chalky tablets immediately after any meal 'just in case' they were never likely to either.

Nan had her own ways of dealing with sore throats too. Mum came down with a terribly hoarse throat during a cold once and Nan was happy to impart her advice.

'What ya need is a pair of old socks wrapped around it over-night,' Nan said, nodding wisely. 'It'll be gone by the morning.'

'You're all right, Win,' said Mum, eyeing Grandad's holey socks resting on the table as he watched telly.

Although Nan and Grandad were Dad's parents, Dad was like the cheese to his own father's chalk. They couldn't have been more different. But his parents adored him. They lent him money; Nan made him dinners if Mum hadn't. Dad would disappear upstairs and then go out again, food in his belly, a few extra notes in his pocket for more beer. They never said a bad word about my dad. He could do no wrong. Even if there wasn't much right either.

At weekends, Grandad didn't go to work, so Nan got up and made tea and Grandad stayed in bed, but it wouldn't be long before I appeared after a quick breakfast. Breakfast was toast, and maybe a boiled egg or cereal. I couldn't stand the dry, 'claggy' mush of most brands, but I'd happily chew away at a packet of Sugar Puffs or Frosties, that extra coating of sugar on every puff and flake keeping me sweet too.

Every Saturday, the three of us would troop up Rye Lane, with Nan's shopping trolley. We'd walk in a crocodile line on the bustling pavement, soaking up the atmosphere, a vague smell of fish, apples and fags clinging in the air, always taking the same route, from one end to the other, with them stopping to chat to neighbours on the way.

'Awright, Sid? How's the boy doing?'

'Your Gregg's getting big now. Can't Adam and Eve it.'

'They've got nice strawberries in up the road.'

Everyone said hello to everyone, as we marched on. Grandad was the one with the shopping list in his hand, the shopping carefully budgeted for. I loved crossing the threshold of the baker's – the yeasty warm smell of fresh bread was fabulous. Grandad would get a few cobs or a tinned loaf and then we'd both eye the custard tarts.

'You want one, boy?' he would say with a wink, bending down to my ear.

'Yeah, please.' I would laugh. He knew I'd never say no. They were whoppers, flaky puff pastry, about the size of my head and dashed with cinnamon. Mmm ... Now the smell of cinnamon, I think, is the closest smell you'll get to a cuddle. Like someone with really soft knitwear on a cold winter's day.

It was on these trips that I was introduced to the delights of rum and raisin ice cream in Jones & Higgins department store, where Nan would pick up wool and patterns for her knitting. Smooth ice cream with a little kick at the back of the throat from the rum – such an unusual flavour for a little boy. I loved picking out the plump juicy raisins with my fingers. It's still a favourite now.

Grandad would happily watch 'his boy' eat sticky clouds of candy floss, or sticky buns that made your mouth turn gummy. No wonder I grew up with a sweet tooth!

Then we'd pass the fishmonger's, and watch as the helpless eels from the Thames whipped around in their watery coffins.

'Love a duck! Look at that one,' Grandad would say, jiggling his finger in the water. 'Go on, give him a stroke.'

Flinching a little, I'd tickle their heads, feeling both exhilarated and repulsed by their slimy, slippery bodies. They'd soon find themselves jellied or stewed and sold in a tub or in the pie and mash shop nearby.

Sainsbury's was another 'must stop' shop. Nothing like the huge commercial giant it is today. This was a tiled shop, quite grand, and airy, where ladies in overalls and hairnets with serious faces sliced and wrapped ham and cheese.

At the top of Rye Lane were markets run by West Indians. When Mum went with us she would be enthralled by what they sold: piles of pinky odd-looking sweet potatoes, yams, plantain. 'Look at that, Gregg,' she would say, handling a knobbly long root. 'I wouldn't know what to do with that!' She liked the new population, though. 'We need 'em,' she said. 'After the war, we're short of people. It isn't out of the goodness of our hearts the government has let them in. It's because we need them and I am glad they're here.'

Funny how back then, you always ate fruit and veg in season, as there was nothing else in the shops. Nan wasn't mad about food, but she loved strawberries, as we all did. When they appeared in the market, hordes would gather to ferry home as many punnets as they could balance on the back of their pull-along trollies.

Nan would gather as many as they could afford and take them back for our first 'strawberry tea' of the year. She'd treat us to scones, clotted cream and tea.

It was Grandad's and my job to pull the flat green stalky leaves off. 'Shuuuuush,' Grandad would say, grinning, as more went in our mouths than the bowl.

Like Mum, Nan wasn't much of a cook and heated up everything from tins, always careful to replace any used from below the stairs. One thing she did make from scratch, though, was a good mince and onion pie, even rolling her own pastry. All served with boiled potatoes and peas.

'Handsome,' Grandad would say, describing it through a mouthful. Sometimes he paused to pick out budgie feathers.

Billy, their budgie, would every so often have a funny five minutes and flap wildly, sending bluey-yellow fluffy feathers all over the place.

I never ate with Grandad, though. We ate separately in our house. Mum and me downstairs, and Dad when he was about; Nan and Grandad upstairs.

Most evenings I'd watch TV snuggled against my grandad's knee and elbow. We'd watch *Hawaii Five-0* or *Star Trek* or *Match of the Day*. When I started school, one boy with a colour TV shocked me when he explained Spock was actually green. I hadn't had a clue because I'd only seen him in black and white. War films were another favourite. Grandad would say, pointing at the screen, 'See them: that was my old lot. I was with them in the war. My old firm, that was.'

'Wow, really, Grandad!' I'd reply, eyes like saucers. I could imagine Grandad dodging bullets and having his hair slicked back and shiny, although I never knew him to have a hair on his head.

As I grew older, though, I started to question Grandad's wild stories a little.

'Hang on, Grandad,' I said, as we watched some Romans charging on chariots and horses. 'They are Romans!'

'Yep,' he nodded, in all seriousness, eyes not flickering from the screen. 'They were definitely my lot.'

Next time, I laughed. 'But Grandad, they are Red Indians.'

'Oh yes,' he said, sagely. 'Like I say, my lot all right.'

One thing he'd say if I played up that'd send me mad with frustration was, 'If you keep that up, you'll end up where our Herbert is.'

'Where's our Herbert?' I'd ask.

And every single time he'd reply deadpan, 'Well, you'll find out if you carry on like that.'

As I said, Grandad was my hero. A war hero, nonetheless, although the war was something he never talked about and I never asked. Grandad'd tell me stories of knights in castles, Romans, Vikings and battles, reeling off answers as fast as I asked them, firing my imagination and inspiring in me a lifelong love of history.

Afterwards, we'd maybe have a game of football or cricket in the hallway.

'On your head, son!' Grandad would joke, chucking at my bonce. Then we'd take it in turns to kick the ball up the stairs and take it in turns to try to control it as it came bouncing back.

With Grandad and me playing or all cuddled up on the couch, Nan didn't get much of a look-in. But she also didn't seem to want to either.

Once, though, when we were playing dominoes at the table, unexpectedly she joined in. As I matched up my dots, carefully counting them with my index finger, she let out a big sigh.

'It's three and six, Gregg,' she said impatiently.

'All right, he's just counting them, aren't you, Gregg?' Grandad soothed.

That was the difference: Grandad waited, Nan didn't.

I'd be up there all evening until Grandad stamped his feet suddenly. It took me years to realise this was a sign to Dad to take me back down.

Because my mum worked, I was 'looked after'. Me and a little West Indian lad called Terry St John were left in the care of a childminder called Alice. I don't remember much about Alice, but I do about Terry. He was a stronger, bigger kid than me. But we formed a good bond, always playing with our Airfix soldiers together or Action Men. Everything was about Action Men, fighting, tanks, guns.

It never ever occurred to me that Terry was 'different'

because he was black. We were all the same. Funny, really, because there must've been tensions at the time.

Terry and I would hang out outside whenever possible, kicking a ball, or lining our soldiers up in snaking lines to prepare them for battle. The days would fly by till our mums came to pick us up.

My dad's best mate, Scott, was West Indian too. I also became friends with a Polish boy called Jan.

Being poor to me was more noticeable than the colour of my skin or where people 'came' from. It was only later, at school, that my classmates pointed out just how little we had.

'I can't believe you live in that house, Gregg,' said one little girl, when she saw me wave goodbye outside No. 22. I turned to look at our shabby door, open with the yellowing plastic strips fluttering in the breeze, and the net curtains hung with safety pins in the window, and my smile sort of faded a little. I loved this house, because of Mum and Grandad, and I didn't like the idea that someone could say anything bad about it.

What football team you supported seemed to me, as a young boy, a more defining feature than skin colour or amount in your wage packet. Grandad was a passionate Millwall supporter and had been going down the Den since the 1930s. He went with Dad and Uncle Ted (Grandad's brother), and then me from the age of five. As I say, all streaming down there, a sea of flat caps and coats and boots, all puffing like dragons on their No. 6 Player's hanging off the corner of their lips.

Grandad sold Millwall lottery tickets and when he got older and wanted to sit down he saved up and bought us season tickets every year.

Nan would prepare the same 'sustenance': a flask of stewed PG Tips, a cheese sarnie (always Cheddar or red Leicester – no 'fancy' muck) on pappy Mothers Pride bread and a paper bagful of toffees.

41

We'd set off, down our road, past the gasworks, across the Old Kent Road, picking up Uncle Ted on the way.

Ted was a gruff geezer. Never had much to do with me either really. He lived with his sister, my auntie, who I just remember for having rotten teeth. A lifelong bachelor, Ted had served in the army, under Montgomery, but that was all I knew. He cared for his sister when she got ill. Then she died and he got a dog, and then the dog died too.

Dad bought Ted another dog and I had to look after it for a few days at first. I called it Terry, after my friend Terry St John. The name stuck and Ted and Terry became inseparable. Ted's house was tiny, with bayonets and swords on the walls. But we didn't stop long: he'd grab his coat and we'd carry on with our journey, down into the long straight road to the Ilderton Road entrance, past the deserted greyhound track and under the railway bridge.

I loved this bit. As we marched under the bridge the buzz, the cheers, the rising excitement engulfed your senses like an all-consuming wave as they echoed against the old Victorian brick walls and steel girders above.

'Go on, you lions!' I'd shout, sometimes jiggling up and down if Dad had put me on his shoulders.

Then we were on to the terraces and waiting tensely for the match to start. We kids would sit on the concrete base of the floodlights, munching our way through bags and bags of Percy Dalton's Monkey Nuts and giggling at the bad language. Even from a very young age, it gave me a wonderful sense of belonging. It felt tribal, everyone tight with anticipation.

And then, and then, the players would emerge, one by one, jogging on to the turf, with pressed, clean tops and white shorts, all eager, faces as full of concentration and hope as ours, some giving cheeky waves, and we just let rip. They were

our heroes, our soldiers. The cheers rose, as did our sense of
being as one. And if someone scored, all hell broke loose and
we'd jump up and down like mentalists, thrilled to be part of
this, the taste of victory in the air. This was a stadium full of
people, good, honest, working people who in so many respects
felt outcast and alienated from the world at large. Who grafted
for a living, who understood what it was to be a south-east
Londoner. It was about shared memories, upbringing and a
love of something maybe a little bit broken. We were always
the underdogs, we always lived on the edge of glory, maybe as
we did in our own lives. Millwall was not one of the sides to
follow. They only made it to the First Division once and even
then it was only for two seasons. But we're proud of our club
– we're south-east Londoners and that club represents us.
'There is always hope,' Dad or Grandad sometimes said with
a watery smile, after we lost another game. And this, for them,
was a very optimistic statement. Millwall somehow gave us
that sense of hope, something to strive for, and the idea that
one day maybe all our dreams would come true.

At every game there was an old boy outside the ground
selling peanuts, and when we were in the second division, he'd
shout, 'First division peanuts' and when were in third division,
he'd shout, 'Second division peanuts!'

One of Grandad's old mates would always be sitting on the
same bench, in the same place, every Saturday, with his bull
terrier, before and after the game.

'How did Millwall get on, Sid?' he'd ask Grandad.

And he'd be informed whether they won or lost. He must've
known already, though, as he was only a ten-minute walk from
the grounds.

I grew up loving Millwall as much as Grandad did. And he
did, all his life. So much so that when I got into a bit of trouble

later on accidentally and had to go to court, he turned up to support me, proudly wearing a Millwall tie, and paid my fine for me.

Going to football with Grandad was also practically the only thing I did with Dad, apart from the occasional spot of fishing. We would take the bus from Peckham to Crystal Palace, picking up a box of maggots on the way. I loved lifting the lid off the box to look at the wiggling mass. No need for an XBox in those days when a small lad had a box of maggots to mess about with.

Once, I don't know how, we got on the wrong bus.

'Dad,' I said, as unfamiliar buildings emerged into view, 'I think it's going the wrong way.'

'Sssh,' Dad said, his cheeks reddening. He looked embarrassed.

'Should you ask the driver which way it is?' I suggested.

Dad's face was shaking a bit. 'I dunno,' he said in confusion, quietly. 'No, it'll be OK. No need to ask anyone.'

We sat in silence as the bus took us even further away from Crystal Palace.

'You sure, Dad?' I whispered, as it took another turn into a traffic jam.

'Can you go and ask for me?' he said, finally. Dad hated asking anyone for anything.

Fishing was a form of meditation to Dad. He sat in silence, staring out at the water.

'Can I go and get lunch?' I would beg, when boredom kicked in after a few minutes. He let me set off up the road alone, to buy a pie. Dad always loved a pie. He couldn't ever shovel it in quick enough, burping afterwards, before he lit up yet another No. 6 – beer and fags, an acrid smell, permanently hung on Dad's breath. We were always, always back in time for tea, although often Dad missed his and went to the pub instead.

For me, tea was sometimes a sauce sandwich. Tangy Daddies sauce slathered on one side of pappy white bread, ketchup from Heinz on the other, and eaten as fast as you could. As long as I didn't eat with my mouth open. Fish finger sandwiches were another firm favourite and is a thing of absolute perfection. Mum would chip open the tiny freezer above the fridge, tear open the cardboard box and line up the fingers on the grill until they hissed and spat and oozed fiercely with white juice. Their crusty orange crumb cases the same colour as Margo's bathroom, they were lined up like railway sleepers on white Mother's pride bread and perfect with something tangy like Daddies sauce or ketchup maybe, and cut in half horizontally. I'd polish one off within a minute.

Bacon was as easy. Cheap cuts from the butcher's, slapped between two slices of bread with brown sauce again to finish off. Made in seconds, eaten in seconds. I loved Alphabetti Spaghetti too. Now if that blew up in a microwave it could spell 'disaster' (sorry).

CHAPTER 5

Meat Pies

*O*n Saturdays, if we weren't going to football, we'd go to Rye Lane, as I've mentioned. And afterwards, if Grandad and Nan hadn't taken me there already, sometimes Mum'd ask if I wanted to go to the pie and mash shop.

Oh, and the answer would always, always be a resounding: 'Yes!'

M. Manze's, on the Peckham Park Road, was a joy for this little boy's eyes, not to mention his stomach. It opened in 1902 and it was the McDonald's of my grandparents' era. The menu wasn't extensive: either pie and mash or eels, jellied or stewed. And nobody knew what meat was in the pie. Just brown, tender bits of joints from unidentifiable animals. What was in it was not important. Taste was everything.

For half a crown you'd get a steaming meat pie, and the softest, fluffiest mash blobbed next to it with a green 'liquor', delicious parsley sauce, smothered over the top.

We were always served by fat jolly waitresses, who dumped plates on our marble table with a clatter and a toothy smile. The cold marble was used for tabletops because it took the heat out of the plates quickly, making people eat faster, so more customers could pile in.

The mash (not Smash) was always scooped from a giant vat behind the counter and was slid unceremoniously on to the plate in one swift motion with a big metal spoon and knife, looking like a ski slope. Copying most customers in the shop, I always turned the pie top face down, with the soggier side of pastry base standing up. The top always had a wide base, so your liquor'd splash all over the place, and turning it over was the trick. Presentation wasn't top priority in this gaff anyway, but you'd never get away with it in a restaurant today. These plates of ultimate comfort food were served in a setting of black-and-white tiled walls and sawdust on the floor. You got in, ordered, ate and then you were out, stuffed to the gunnels.

I'd bounce like a Labrador over the threshold, and Mum would always ask for the same, but one without the liquor for her. 'It looks like something you'd scooped out of a pond,' she'd half grumble. You could take the girl out of Wimbledon …

Then we'd sit, and I'd reach for the chilli vinegar and the pepper to coat the top of my pie, and I'd eat it, mash first, pie next, savouring every salty, chewy, mouthful. Then I'd slump back in our hard wooden seats with a little round belly, feeling deliciously warm and satisfied.

The owners today are the grandchildren of the original owners. They still use the same recipes. Nothing has changed. It hasn't needed to. Pie and mash can be appreciated by everyone, whatever the generation, because you can't beat it. A pie and mash, for me, never fails to hit the spot. Yes, I loved our little pie and mash visits. Not least because I got Mum completely to myself.

I knew even then that Mum was a very pretty lady. She was fashionable too. Although Nan disapproved of a new mother still 'dressing up', having a child (me) hadn't stopped Mum enjoying her clothes and the fashions of the time.

She'd pick up very cheap knock-offs, from the market or a shop where her mate Pat worked called Candy Fashions, the equivalent of a Primark. Her favourite outfit was her mini dress, copied from Mary Quant, teamed with a pair of white plastic knee-high boots. Go, Mum! She bought bits of material and asked Nan W to knock up mini skirts too. Back in the day, Nan W had been a dressmaker and was only too happy to.

Mum loved wearing huge spidery fake eyelashes big enough to give Dusty Springfield a run for her money. Her hair was a huge beehive à la Amy Winehouse, which she'd pull out every few days into a frizzy Afro big and wild enough to scare the neighbours. Her hair was constantly changing colour too, from dark to red, to blonde to dark again, although she cried 'I look like a banana!' when the bleach was washed out. Nan W would say, 'You'll be bald by the time you're thirty,' but it never stopped her. And she'd do all this standing over our kitchen sink, hoping for the best. Yes, although Mum had reluctantly made her home with her husband and adopted a bit of a south-east London twang to fit in, she was still determined to enjoy herself and make the most of being young. She was 'lying in the bed she'd made', as Nan W had told her to, but she'd managed to make the most of it.

Despite her more genteel upbringing she quickly took the blue-collar side of life to heart, even finding herself learning and laughing at the naughty songs everyone knew.

'I painted her' was one everyone round our way knew. I

mean, at this point I didn't, but as soon as I was old enough I did. 'I painted her up the belly, down the back, in the hole and every crack.'

Rhyming slang is part and parcel of life in south-east London. It's not just a gimmick, or a novelty, or put on for tourists: people really did use it in everyday life like a secret code.

Grandad used it every day. 'Where are my almond rocks and dickie dirt?' he'd ask Nan, looking for his socks and shirt. And he never went out without his 'tit fer' (tit for tat means hat) and his daisy roots (boots). 'Is your boat clean, boy?' he'd say before dinner to see if I'd washed my face. Dad often would say he was going out for a 'pig's ear', when he was going for his pint of beer. Mum would have a sneaky 'Vera Lynn' or gin.

After we'd let our food go down, Mum might do a bit of shopping herself, to catch up before she had to go back to work on the Monday. She always popped into Kennedy's, the butcher's. She liked to pick up cheap cuts from there, carefully waiting as they were weighed out. Sometimes she got liver and bacon or some ham. The next stop was the rabbit shop, where, as I said, I was happy enough to see them, all silently swaying on hooks.

I loved spending that time when it was just me and Mum. Even though I was like Grandad's shadow at home, it always felt wonderful to be just us two.

Saturday evenings were party time. By now Mum had lived in Peckham for almost a decade and she'd made some close friends. Once she'd been accepted she said she felt 'safe', because in that community everyone looked out for everyone else. She may've been a 'posh bird' but she was also 'Awright, intcha'.

There were four main friends. Margo, my godmum, was a self-made lady who'd been brought up in the roughest of tenements in Camberwell. She worked 'damn hard' alongside Mum in accounts, where they met, and got herself a new council flat opposite the Acorn estate. Always well spoken, she seemed posh to me; even the name 'Margo' was so upmarket. A natural redhead, she had creamy pale skin and huge beautiful eyes that bulged a little because she suffered from thyroid problems.

Margo needed to work, because she was married to Steve, a lifelong dreamer, whose latest 'get rich quick' scheme didn't always work out. He was a second-hand car tyre dealer, but he was best mates with a wheeler-dealer, who was usually the brains behind the latest venture.

Once the pair managed to get squatting rights for a piece of wasteland in Camberwell and sold illegal goods off it. They did all right and Steve boasted, 'I'm one of the missing millions' – he never paid a penny in income tax or VAT. Eventually the wheeler-dealer managed to march down to the town hall and claim the legal rights to the land, and the pair were made. Well, he took the biggest cut. I think Steve ended up running a fishing tackle stall, and it was always thanks to Margo they never went under. Long-suffering Margo never approved. 'If you break your leg you'll be the first to be rushing down the hospital,' she would say with a sniff, over-pronouncing the aitch in 'hospital'. 'And whose paying for that, eh? Muggins here.' She stuck by him, though.

Then there was Eileen, a single lady who lived in Bermondsey and loved to dance, and Christine, a married woman with a few kids.

Mum says they were like *Loose Change*, a popular mini series in the late 1970s about a group of girlfriends from the sixties all leading different lives but bonding together. She says she wouldn't have survived all those difficult years with my dad unless she'd had them to sound off to. All they needed was a few bottles of Mateus Rosé and a few Helen Reddy numbers, and a party could be had. I loved all the old tunes: Barry White, Burt Bacharach, with Dionne Warwick, Frankie Valli and the Four Seasons, Roger Whittaker. I have 'Last Farewell' and 'I am Gonna Leave Old Durham Town' on my iPod today.

With Dad safely away in the pub, Mum would crank up the volume and we'd roll back the carpet and all dance around the living room. We kids would snack on crisps and big bottle of Coke for a treat, and then eventually go off one by one and fall asleep in my bed or on the sofa.

For ages actually we had stacks of Coca-Cola, thanks to Mum opening a bottle one day and finding a lump of glass in it.

'Gordon Bennett!' she exclaimed. 'I'm not having that.' So at work she typed up a letter of complaint to Coca-Cola HQ. No idea where she got the address from. It must have somehow made its way to the top, though, as a few days later two men in suits landed on our doorstep, causing a few curtains to twitch on our street. They apologised and handed Mum a cheque for £100 and gave her crates and crates of free drinks. We had so much that I actually used it to swill my mouth out in the kitchen sink after cleaning my teeth, slightly defeating the object.

I don't know what Mum talked about but there was always gossip going on. You'd hear snatches of it as you reached for more glasses of Coke as they sat around at the end of the night.

'Did you hear of so and so's new baby?' said Eileen one evening.

The other three gasped in unison.

'Noooo,' said Christine. 'Tell us!'

'Weeeell,' Eileen continued. The four heads leaned forward as they oh-ed and ah-ed and shook their heads.

'And the worst thing was the look on her husband's face afterwards. There was no hiding it, though, with the colour of the baby's skin.'

Babies out of wedlock was something absolutely frowned upon still, but, Mum said, affairs went on left, right and centre. She once said she reckoned most families had a baby not belonging to the dad of the household.

And with the influx of the black community in Brixton, and with more and more Turkish Cypriots moving here because of the problems in Cyprus, some women had an affair with a man of a different race. Still, it was deemed better back then to have a slightly different-coloured baby 'with' your husband than a white baby as an unmarried mum. There was a man who called himself a herbalist on the Walworth Road who could provide a concoction for any woman who found herself in a bit of trouble, but it was seen as a last resort.

Eileen's dad was a big drinker too, and she'd often tell the girls of the latest events in her house, where she lived with her mum.

'Last night Mum swore she wasn't gonna open the door for him,' she said. "I've 'ad enough!" she insisted. But Dad came down the street after midnight to find the door locked and do you know what he shouted?'

'What?' said Christine, stifling a giggle.

'He yelled, "Annie, if you don't let me in I am gonna shit myself!" and I've never seen Mum move so fast, in case the neighbours heard.'

They all fell about laughing.

Once, I came back into the living room because I couldn't sleep and I'd run out of Coke. The records were slow songs now, and the lights were dimmed. A few of Mum's friends were nattering on the carpet, a fug of smoke hanging over the living room lampshade from their fags.

'And he said … and then she said …'

Mum wasn't there. So I peered into the gloomy hallway, where I saw Mum's legs, entwined a little with another pair, belonging to a man and his shoes were different to Dad's. They were sitting on the stairs, heads bowed, deep in conversation.

Mum glanced up, wiping her mouth lightly with the back of her hand, while the strange man with dark hair did a double take as he saw me.

'C'mon, Gregg, shall we take you back to bed?' she said softly.

Before long I was off to start 'big school', otherwise known as Peckham Park primary.

I was keen on trying to read from a young age, thanks to Grandad W and Mum always reading to me. I used to write down a series of letters and then look at Mum.

'What does this say?' I would ask.

She would screw her eyes up as she 'read' them, as if she was thinking.

'It says "My name is Gregg and I am a lovely polite little boy",' she would say, with a laugh.

When the words did make sense we raced through *Winnie-the-Pooh*, my favourite. Sometimes for a game Mum used to say, 'Every word beginning with an "s" say "sausage" and every word beginning with an "m" say "mash",' and I'd double over with laughter every time.

On my first day at school, I couldn't wait to get stuck into that sandpit. The sand felt so cool and nice in between my fingers. School had such exciting things we didn't have at home: sand, paints, more toys.

One kid brought in a little truck and I was so envious of it as he pushed it around making 'brrmmmmmm' noises. When no one was looking I swiped it and stuck it my schoolbag.

I did it so fast, without thinking, but it didn't take long for a sickening guilt to creep in. It was out of character for a boy like me.

Luckily the little boy hadn't seemed to notice and nobody spotted me. So I walked home with it and got it out in the garden.

'Where's that from?' Mum asked, as I 'brum brummed' it around on my hands and knees.

'Oh, they were giving them away,' I lied. 'Everyone got a lorry today, er, for being good.'

What a whopper that was! Blood whooshed to my ears as I turned my face so that she never saw my cheeks burn. Suddenly I didn't want to play with it any more. Now I'd lied and stolen, all in one day.

Mum insisted on walking me to and from school, even though it was only about five minutes away, after a vicious bout of hair brushing. 'Gerroff!' I'd shout, as she caught my ears for the umpteenth time. I swear that's the reason I went bald.

I hated all the 'fussing' Mum did. She'd lick the edge of her hankie to wipe away a smudge on my face if I'd missed a bit. But the most humiliating thing was having to stand with my arms raised as if in surrender while she 'tucked me in'. What is it with mums and their tucking in? As if the quality of my education and her reputation as a mother hinged on my vest being 'tucked' perfectly into my pants. Being 'all rucked up' was the biggest no-no. Of course I'd twist my torso impatiently and almost immediately become untucked two seconds later in the playground. And Mum knew this. But still she'd do it. I needed a good tucking in before the school gates every single morning. Nothing but ritual humiliation in front of my mates.

At lunchtime I'd race home, starving, from school if Mum was in. But often she wasn't, so school dinners were the order of the day. Now, looking back, I think the food was probably hideous, but I was a famished growing lad, so it all went down rather well. I loved the chicken and tomato stew, lapping up a creamy dollop on my plate. And if chocolate sponge custard was on the menu, I was happy. Approaching the dinner ladies as they stood, mucky aprons and hairnets on, sweating with the heat and the ordeal of cooking for two hundred kids, I always put on my best smile.

'Do you mind if I have a corner bit, please?' I would ask in my politest voice, eyeing the light brown goo – probably Bird's Eye instant powder.

The corner of the sponge meant you got more, and I could inhale the custard on top, so it was worth a try. It was creamy, sweet, with a powdery cocoa edge; I didn't even mind the skin.

Suddenly how I spoke and pronounced my words, now I was going to big school, was more important to Mum. 'It's not "fink", Gregg, it's "Thhhhhh-ink",' she said, one of her many corrections, sounding like the woman who read the news. Vowels become more important. 'It's "a-bowt",' she said. 'Not "abaht".'

I started to be much more careful about how I spoke at home – well, apart from upstairs watching telly with Grandad, who didn't know what all the fuss was abaht.

Now, many of you may not know downtown Peckham, but let me tell you, one of the keys to survival is not to sound like a Radio Four announcer, even a little one with a woolly jumper and shorts. So the inevitable happened and I ended up with two accents, like a vocal chameleon: one for home and one for school. Devilishly tricky at home time at school in the playground when Mum picked me up and I was saying goodbye to my mates. 'See ya! Oh, hell-oh, Mum.'

My first class teacher was a lady with a mesmerising amount of tumbling blonde curls. I'd never seen a lady round our way with hair like that. Mum told me one evening it was probably a wig, so I promptly tapped my teacher on the arm the next day to parrot the observation.

I loved some of the teachers at that school. Like Mr Roseman, a West Indian who would organise enormous games of cricket at playtimes, about twenty aside, to keep us out of trouble.

'Have you got any kids?' one kid asked one day.

'Yes!' he cried, throwing out his arms and gesturing to the whole playground. 'About two hundred of them!'

Another character was Mr Donahue, our headmaster. He was a mysterious and austere man, who always wore a monocle. He'd served in the RAF with the head of the London Nautical School, Blackfriars, which was lucky for many of the kids, who went on there. He was a scary man to a five-year-old, but I soon grew to like him. Especially when I whacked my head playing a piggie-back race and was out cold. I came to in his office, with him telling me stories about the planes he used to fly as he checked my lines of vision by holding fingers up.

In the dinner hall, though, he definitely did not look approachable. He'd sit chewing ferociously, on his own, staring into space with a far, far-away look. I wondered where he was then – probably on night raids over Dresden.

We had a Mr Edwards, who was like the school's gatekeeper

of books, as he kept the key to the library and organised the school's recommended reading list. If you read every book you got your name on a plaque on the wall. I wasn't too bothered about this, until I heard of some bright girl in the class getting one and then I wanted one.

Once you'd read a book, you had to have a 'chat' with Mr Edwards, who quizzed you on the story content to check there was no skim reading going on. I stuck with it, though, and managed to get my name up in lights (well, on the plaque). Oh yes. I was so proud, and so were Mum and Grandad.

A few weeks in someone threw some sand from the pit and it landed straight in my eye.

I screamed the class down, and Mum was called. She arrived, eyebrows knotted with worry, demanding to know what had happened. All that did happen was that I wasn't allowed to play in the sand pit again. Gutted.

I was always getting into scrapes, always a bit clumsy. I fell down three stone steps leading to the playground soon afterwards and badly sprained my ankle. That meant a few days off school, with Grandad holding a bag of frozen peas on it to help.

Another time I was racing someone, tripped and skidded, scraping my face across the tarmac. I ended up looking as though I had tyre tracks over my cheeks.

'Urgh, it looks burned off,' said my mate Robin. He was a short, fat kid with hair the colour of carrot soup and he loved Elvis. Not a winning combination when you're under ten.

I grinned back proudly.

Grandad saw me right, though. He'd often come and pick me up from primary school and we'd stop in the sweet shop on the way home.

I called it the sweet shop, Grandad called it the paper shop and Dad called it the newsagent's. Past the threshold you always caught a faint whiff of brown paper, mixed with tobacco and vanilla, and it had a machine of magic: a Mr Whippy machine – you didn't even need a van for it. You could fill up a cup with swirls of snowy-white ice cream or with lemon ice, Grandad's favourite.

I often dithered between the two, so Grandad would kneel down to aid my decision.

'How 'bout you have a bit of each, boy?' he'd suggest.

Usually I hate fruity milky things, but the soft airiness of the vanilla ice cream teamed with the almost eye-watering bite of the lemon was something I adored. I used to carefully swirl my flat plastic blue spoon around the cup edge, to glean a layer of both. Hmmm, I can taste it now.

On colder days (and there were many of them) I settled for sweets instead. Grandad seemed to love spending his meagre pension on me, treating me to a constant supply … Probably it's thanks to him I developed the sweet tooth I did.

 Oh God, now this takes me back. Black Jacks were top of the list. I absolutely loved the stick-in-your-canines, chew-till-your-jaw-ached deliciousness, getting my aniseed hit. Looking in a mirror or asking an adult to 'see how black my tongue is' was part of the thrill. The more obscenely black (as if you'd contracted a medieval illness), the better.

Fruit Salads were next, their wrappers just as painstakingly tricky to peel off, thanks to my nails being nibbled. I sucked or chewed depending on my mood. Golden Cups were up there too. I could never get their crinkly, golden foil off fast enough. The hit of the oozing caramel and smooth, slightly stale-tasting but sweet chocolate never failed to win me over. That caramel chocolate combo still has that effect.

If I didn't get an ice cream with Grandad, in the summer months I could always trust a van to turn up outside. As soon as we heard the plinkety-plink of the van's siren all the kids would make a run for it, to be the first in the queue.

First of all, though, I'd have to rifle through the pockets of Dad's coat or ask for Mum's purse.

'Mum, can I have 50p, please?'

'Go on, then, it's on the side.'

I mastered the art of having that conversation, grabbing the change and legging out of the front door in a few seconds flat to be first in the queue.

I always opted for the same: 'A-Flake-99-please-with-chocolate-sauce-and-nuts.'

We didn't often have nuts in our house. Too expensive. I loved the mixture of the slightly salty nut, heavily glooped in the sickly syrup, and the cold of the cream of Mr Whippy. Good old Mr Whippy. None of us knew then its main ingredient is vegetable oil: that's why it's so creamy. Even if we did know we wouldn't have cared.

CHAPTER 6

Battenberg

*A*s I've said, how much money we did or didn't have was
something I only cottoned on to at big school, where everyone was tearing around in fabulous nylon *Star Trek* T-shirts.
They were V-necked and tight, with a raised *Star Trek* badge,
and came in reds, greens, blues and yellows. It meant that
when people played 'Beam me up, Scotty' and we signalled
with the Vulcan sign under the desk during a lesson, if you
wore the uniform too you looked the business. I never had
one, despite pester power: Mum said patiently, many times,
'We can't afford it, Gregg.' Later, I managed to persuade
Mum to buy me a parka coat, though, a big green number
with a hood that made it spectacularly dangerous to cross the
road in when it was pulled up. No wonder kids needed extra
help with the Green Cross Code back then. I think maybe
Nan W bought it. I also got bumper boots, something else to
help me fit in: canvas shoes with a rubber sole that laced up

past the instep. Now they were cool. Sometimes I knew exactly how to wind Mum around my little finger, but at the same time it was her opinion that mattered the most.

For a little boy who always ate like the proverbial horse, I certainly didn't look well fed. Mum was so worried about me. Nowadays I fight a constant battle against the size of my belly, but back then I was like a walking broom handle. With a big mop of curly long hair on top.

She took me to the doctors about my concave belly. She pulled up my top and pointed to my ribs, poking through my chest.

'I am so worried about him,' she said to our GP. 'He's just so thin, however much I feed him.'

He laughed when he saw me. 'At last,' he said, giving me a little prod with his cold hands. 'One healthy little boy in front of me, a wonderful sight around here.'

He assured her there was nothing wrong and I got to happily munch another Mars bar on the way home.

From a worryingly skinny kid with way too much curly hair to a worryingly portly baldy: is there no justice?

When I was about six, Mum told me one weekend she had a friend visiting.

'He's called Dave,' she said. 'And he's taking us out in his car. Be nice to him, Gregg.'

Nice? Wasn't I always nice?

Dave had a very big, very flash sports car and tooted round the corner from our house. Mum looked right and then left again, before she opened the door and I was ushered into the back of the car. The seats were polished leather, and slippery. Mum didn't stop smiling the whole time she was in the car, Dave brushing her knee while he changed the gears. We drove and drove, until the houses turned into rolling countryside, and then Dave put his foot down on the winding country roads, Mum giggling and laughing.

'Do you want to look out the sun roof, Gregg, eh?' Dave was eyeing me in the rear-view mirror.

'Yeah, OK!' I said.

He winked at Mum and with one hand wound it open. My hair started blowing everywhere and I couldn't help but smile.

'Stand up, lad,' said Dave.

Holding on to the head rests, I stood up, as he slowed down a bit and then, there I was riding high and fast, down the country lanes, my breath being snatched away by the wind. Cool! We stopped in a small country café, where Mum had a ham salad and Dave had something called a ploughman's while I ate just chips.

Afterwards, back home, Mum didn't say anything to Dad or Nan and Grandad about where we'd been. Then, as she tucked me into bed, she tutted a bit at me.

'I think you should make more effort to be friendly to Dave,' she murmured. 'Maybe show him some of your toys or something next time.'

Two weeks later, we saw Dave again. I'd brought my yellow Tonka truck, a 'big' birthday present from last year, to show him. He was standing with his hands in his pockets in a pub, jangling his loose change, waiting to get a drink for Mum after another drive. I walked up to him with my truck feeling heavy and clumsy in my hand, knocking at my knees.

I didn't know what to say, so I just raised it up to my eye level as I stared at him, as if proffering a gift.

'Did you say you wanted an orange cordial with your crisps?' he asked impatiently, completely missing my Tonka-holding hand of friendship.

I never told Grandad and Nan W either about Dave and the

pub visits. Something automatically made me think they wouldn't want to know. Although their house was a place where generally I always felt heard.

Sometimes I stayed there for the whole weekend, and it was always a huge treat. Padding around on their luxurious soft-pile carpet, lovely smells always coming from the kitchen, lots of books in the house, lots of smiles, lots of delicious home-cooked food.

As I said, Nan W was always creating. She even loved making wine – Château du Lil, Grandad called it. The wine-making kit sat like the strange glass contraption it was on the sideboard, bubbling away, looking as if it was something with which to make Frankenstein. Nan W allowed me a sip once and I screwed my face up.

'I think I prefer your dinners,' I admitted as she laughed.

Grandad W may've been strict but he never failed to take an interest in me, taking me for trips to the library or reading to me. He devoured books and I'd sit on his lap while he read stories like *Treasure Island* and help me read them back. Once he played a word game with me and my cousins, Mark and Steve (the kids of Wilf, Mum's brother), and he marvelled when I won. 'You're clever, you are,' he said, winking at me.

Everybody smoked back then. All the adults in my life smoked cigarettes as if their last breath depended on it, but Grandad W's choice was a tobacco pipe.

It was such a mysterious-looking implement. As a child I loved watching him get out his yellow Golden Virginia tobacco pouch, and pull off sweet strands pinched in between his finger and thumb, before packing them into the pipe bowl. He could do this contentedly on his own, or while having a conversation or watching the TV, his hands working automatically, as if his pipe was another limb. Then he'd strike a Swan match, always flaring it first time, and hold the flame over his packed bowl for the exact required time. He'd half puff and suck on the stick end, causing a comforting red glow to light up the end, until the whole thing erupted into plumes of smoke and we'd all get a punch in our nostrils too. It was a fuggy, very sweet, comforting smell. His coat pockets were often full of tiny moth-like burned holes caused by him putting away his pipe before it was out properly. The smell of pipe smoke still reminds me of him today. Nanny W said Grandad W had no sense of smell because of 'that pipe', and he did put salt and pepper on his food by the bucketful.

Half a mile away lived the rest of the family, all in one house: Mum's sister Hazel and her husband Ron downstairs and Wilfred and Shirley upstairs.

Uncle Wilf and Shirley were hard for me to comprehend as a kid. Poor Wilf developed Parkinson's disease at the age of forty, and at the same time had what we'd know now as a nervous breakdown. Each time we saw them, he seemed to have deteriorated even further. Once, while I was staying for a weekend, Nan opened the door to find him soaking wet, in heavy rain.

'All right,' he said, barging past her. He stood in the smart hallway, shaking from head to toe and unbuttoning his duffle coat to reveal he was wearing nothing but a pair of trousers underneath. Nan W ushered him in and got him a shirt to wear, saying nothing.

Over tea, he sat in silence; then suddenly he entered the conversation.

'Last night,' he barked, 'I had a dream I was Jesus and a man punched me in the face.' He screwed his eyes up as he spoke, rocking a bit.

'That's nice,' said Nan W. 'Would you like another slice of Battenberg?'

Another time, Uncle Wilf was slurping his peaches when Nan asked if I wanted any more apricots.

'Oh, yes please,' I said, eyeing the bowl of syrup.

'Oh sorry,' she said, after nipping into the kitchen, 'we've actually run out.'

Wilf looked up, pulling a spoon out of his mouth. 'Oh, you can have mine, then!' he said. He chased a slithery peach on to his spoon. 'Here, have the last one.'

His hand was shaking slightly as the spoon came towards me. The peach, mixed, I imagined, with a lot of Wilf's spit, suddenly looked like poison. I felt hot and sick. I didn't want any peaches now. Not off Uncle Wilf's spoon.

I knew it was rude, but needs must. I held my hand up. 'You're all right, Uncle Wilf,' I said.

He made a 'harummphing' sound in the back of his throat. 'All the children think I am *mad*,' he cried.

I was the only child in the room and I just looked at my hands.

On the way home I wondered out loud if I was going to get Parkinson's like Wilf.

'No, don't be silly,' soothed Mum. 'You'll be fine.'

Auntie Shirley was none too sympathetic to her husband. A churchgoing woman, she was keener on seeing her boys attend Sunday school than go to their nan's. Years later she finally ran off with a girlfriend. We were all amazed, especially Nanny W, who swore blind lesbians didn't exist in her day.

They didn't join us for Sunday lunch but would come round for tea, something we often stayed for too, whether I was sleeping over or not.

This was always the same: sandwiches, cakes and salads. Now salads in those days could be one thing and one thing only. Oh, how the salad world has progressed, with our rocket and fancy pea shoots. But back then we'd have lettuce, always iceberg, for super crunch, carefully washed, dried and placed at the bottom of a glass dish. Then Nan quartered tomatoes, placed them around the edge and cut up transparently thin slices of cucumber to join them. Then out came the dreaded jars of eye-wateringly sharp pickled beetroot. Nan would spend a few minutes dancing a fork around in order to stab one of the tricky blighters and once she'd got a firm hit she'd lift it up and out as fast as lightning so it didn't 'splatter', marking the worktops with its hideous purple stains.

Once safely in the bowl the beetroot would be chopped a little, or left whole, to bleed its red spiky vinegar over anything and everything it touched. And as if that wasn't sharp enough the Heinz salad cream came out 'if anyone wants it'. Nobody ever did, except me and Grandad (who added some pepper for extra measure – as I say, very different from Peckham).

The horror of the beetroot was long forgotten, though, once we'd chomped through the salad and reached our tea pudding.

Whenever I spied the unmistakable long cuboid shape of the Battenberg packet it was enough to make my mouth water. This really was the stuff of legend. I'd eye everyone's plates, hoping I'd got the most generous slice: it was such a treat. You couldn't help but sit and stare for a moment at the prettiness of the alternate yellow and pink squares, the delicate line of sweet unidentifiable jam spread so thinly to stick them together. Then I'd set to work, and there is only one way to eat a piece of Battenberg as far as I'm concerned, so let me explain.

First, I'd delicately peel off the lightly dusted yellow marzipan and leave it on the side of my plate, saving the best till last as usual. Next I'd pull apart the squares as if I was a forensic scientist looking for clues to a crime. Then, one by one, pink first and then yellow, I'd pop the squares in my mouth, the spongy sweetness quickly dissolving into a ball in my mouth. Finally came the almondy, sugary, cloying strips of marzipan, sticky on my fingers. I still adore anything marzipan, or with almonds or amaretto. Funny how some childhood tastes remain. I even had a tier of Battenberg on my wedding cake.

So escaping to Wimbledon was wonderful. But even better were our seaside adventures. Although we had so little money, Mum always made sure she could afford a holiday every year in Margate. Mum would pay for a room for us to share, with Nan and Grandad W in the one next door. For twenty quid you could get full board and lodging: a bargain.

We'd spend the days walking down the promenade, cooing at the sea, everywhere we went the sounds of other workers' twangs in the salty air.

Once a week, Grandad would take me to the American-style amusement park. Dreamland was about as exciting a place as any boy from Peckham could imagine. I'd queue for ages for the Scenic Railway, a mile-long Victorian wooden rickety roller coaster that had us all screaming like banshees. Next minute I'd be tearing around the dodgems and then begging Grandad to please buy me another candy floss. I loved watching them shake the lurid pink sugar into the spinning machine and the smell of burned sugar. I'd marvel at how the stick held the wobbling hair-like ball of fluff. Being careful it didn't blow away in the wind, I'd stick out my tongue to turn it red and soggy. Then I'd pull the fluff off with my fingers, patting it down into a papery mash of cotton wool. Finally I'd take the biggest chunk I could and open my jaw wide, always wondering how much I could stuff in there without it melting (but it always melted faster than I could stuff). There are so many ways to enjoy candy floss.

Some days for tea, Grandad would treat me to a hot dog. The smell of frying onions was all too tempting. It was heaven to me. The white fluffy bun encasing a steaming sausage: who knew what was in it? Who cared! This, teamed with the sweet crunch of translucent and black badly fried onions, all washed down with a bucketful of ketchup: wow! Do you know what – I could eat one now!

Something about the atmosphere of the fun fair, with all those lights, sounds and energy to watch while you ate it, made it something special. Not that I ever went hungry with Grandad around. He constantly had a bag of toffees with him wherever he went, handing them out whenever I asked and struggling to slurp and suck them himself, minding his dentures as he did.

On the way back to the hotel, high on the sugar rush, I'd want to go back on the trampoline. Bouncing up and down, so high it was a wonder I didn't go into orbit, I felt so excited and free; it was the nearest thing to flying. I'd stop for a little breath and then reach out my hand and start begging Mum to join me.

'Go on! Come on with me!' I'd shout as she rolled her eyes.

But if she was wearing jeans she'd hop on and we'd hold hands and jump, or I'd show off and bounce even harder.

I always hankered after a Knickerbocker Glory too, something that was mainly sold in cafés by the sea. A pudding to end all puddings, with custard, jelly, ice cream and sponge, topped with synthetic cream and a cherry on top. Its name alone sounded exciting, exotic, a bit naughty. It was so high that I needed to stand on a chair to reach the long 'special' spoon to the bottom.

'Mind it don't eat you, Gregg,' Grandad would say, laughing, as I licked my lips.

That excited feeling of pushing my spoon inside, trying to

reach the bottom and chase as many flavours as I could fit into one mouthful, giving me a slight pain in my temple as the freezing ice cream slipped down my throat, is one I'll never forget.

I managed it, though, and victoriously polished it off, scraping that long spoon up and down till my arm ached and the glass became transparent again. As the café erupted into a round of applause, I realised I'd had an audience.

''E's got hollow legs,' Grandad said, winking.

Eating a Knickerbocker Glory wasn't just pudding: it could be an Olympic event.

Back at the hotel, we'd go in to the smoky lounge, where parents sat and compared their sunburn, drinking beer and lemonade, and the kids flew around like blue bottles, until the games started. For every single one, my hand flew up: I couldn't wait to enter.

Then before we knew it, seven days were over and it was time to repack, find the tickets and be on our way – a sad day.

On the train on the way home, Mum bought me crisps. I always went for the same: salt 'n' vinegar. And if we found Hula Hoops I was happy. The short hollow cylinders quickly found their way on to my fingers and I'd munch them greedily at speed. The beef flavour was strangely more salty than the salt 'n' vinegar. I'd no time for Quavers – processed, cheesey, powdery mush. Later on I also loathed Monster Munch: they were too sharp and made my mouth hurt. Crisps shouldn't cause pain.

The natural feeling of holiday blues was always compounded by a huge barney once we got through the door at Kincaid Road. Before the suitcase was even opened, Dad would be back in the pub. He'd disappear for longer these days and sometimes I caught Mum's eyes filling. She always blinked them away from me, but I knew – I just knew.

One afternoon I got home from school to find Mum red-faced and brandishing a piece of paper in the air at him.

'You what?' she cried. 'How much do you earn? Is that really how much you're spending? In that boozer? Can this be right!'

Dad was holding his head in his hands. He looked like a little boy, lost, broken. Then within the blink of an eye, this meek boy's face screwed up with rage.

'I'm getting my coat,' he shouted, pushing back his chair violently. I only just stepped out of his way in time as the door slammed again, leaving Mum sighing with fury in his wake.

I slipped upstairs, unnoticed, and knocked on Grandad's door.

'Do you want to come and watch some telly, son?' he said quietly.

It must've been around this time that Mum's friends Jenny and Alex came over to take me out one Saturday. I liked this pair: they were young, trendy, just married, always made a fuss of me and were just so easy going and full of laughter. Jenny was a lively blonde who liked to spoil me rotten.

'C'mon, we'll take you up to Higgins,' Jenny said.

Jones & Higgins was a department store selling everything from furniture to haberdashery stuff, toys and of course my rum and raisin ice cream, and we could never ever afford anything much from it. It seemed to be posh for Peckham, but actually when it was built in Victorian times Peckham was, like Brixton, still a fairly well-to-do suburb that boasted a high street. Mum used to do her 'window shopping' there. Only once do I remember her buying something – some material with which Nan W knocked up some curtains.

Now Jenny took me to the toy department and asked if I wanted anything. I was amazed: this felt like such a treat.

I picked another Action Man to add to the collection, and

we went home, Jenny having me in fits with some joke or other. It felt so easy, so relaxed. 'I wish you were my mum,' I suddenly blurted out.

She shot me a wide smile and ruffled my hair. 'You're a good kid, Gregg,' she said.

Back indoors, she made a joke to Mum about what I'd said and although Mum seemed to laugh it off, afterwards she turned to me all seriously.

'Gregg, is it true? Do you really wish Jenny was your mum?'

'No!' I gasped. 'Of course I don't!'

Mum's trips in Dave's car became less frequent and then one weekend they stopped. And Mum seemed to stop with them. She walked around that weekend looking as though lead weights had been attached to her ankles. Her eyes looked puffy. She stopped making butterscotch Angel Delight after dinner. I slid upstairs to see Grandad and we played snap for a bit.

Later on, I went to bed, while Mum was on the phone to her friend Pat. When I woke up, the sun was streaming through my curtains and Grandad was standing over me.

'Nothing to worry about, lad, but Mum's not well and she'll be back from hospital in the afternoon,' he said, shaking his head. 'Nothing to worry about.'

Mum did come back and went straight to bed. It was odd, Mum being in bed in the middle of the day. I wondered if maybe that was a fun thing to do, so I went in to see her. She was lying on her back, in her nightie, pale and half dozing. I climbed on to the bed, and thought I might jump on her and surprise her, but Dad caught me.

'What you think you're doing?' he whispered harshly. 'Leave her be.'

Later on Mum told me she'd sat at the kitchen table with

several packets of paracetamol and methodically downed them with a glass of water. Dave had dumped her, she'd had enough and couldn't stand any more life as it was in Kincaid Road. It was thanks to her friend Pat and her husband, who'd she'd spoken to earlier, thinking something was amiss and came round after having a 'feeling'. He picked Mum up, carried her to their car and whisked her to hospital where her stomach was pumped. Suicide was a criminal offence so she got short shrift from nurses and was sent home with a flea in her ear.

Mum told me afterwards this was a turning point for her. She'd never meant to kill herself, it was a cry for help. But it gave her a tougher veneer, for better or for worse.

Dad didn't mention 'the carry on', nobody did. His attitude was as long as nobody blamed him and he could continue in his own sweet way, then nothing else mattered.

Around this time, I got a new babysitter. Mum'd decided Nanny Alice wasn't 'good enough' after she'd moved flat. Once I came home and said, 'Now we have to eat our dinner standing at her kitchen worktop in case we mess up the carpet,' and Mum said I wasn't going back.

This new babysitter was called Bernie and she lived up the road from the Acorn estate. Bernie seemed a kindly woman. She was always busy in the kitchen, knocking up snacks for us hungry kids she picked up from school to 'look after' while parents were working.

Her husband, George, was often there too, a tall scrawny man in his sixties, who chain-smoked roll-ups – his fingertips were permanently yellow. He loved watching us play our soldier games and some of the other little lads who came and went. And we spent hours talking about wars, Action Men, guns. He had a cannon that fired matchsticks.

'Look, Gregg,' he said, bending down to my eye level. 'If you get the spring and pull the lever as far back as possible, you can ping it right across the carpet. See?'

He showed me a few times, and then gave me a go.

My matchstick hit the wall on the other side of the room.

'Whoa, that was a good 'un,' George said, grinning and clapping excitedly.

I loved all war stuff. Grandad used to take me to the Imperial War Museum at Elephant and Castle sometimes during the holidays. We'd always head for his favourite picture first: a large painting of the Blitz in front of St Paul's, the whole place a raging inferno, aside from Christopher Wren's masterpiece.

'This is how it really was, lad,' he said every time.

Then he'd stand, lost in thought, scratching his nose. It was broken with blood vessels. To a stranger in the street he looked like a boozer, except he'd acquired that complexion while he was fighting those infernos as a fireman.

'Sometimes it'd take three days and nights,' he said. 'The power of them hoses, the water – whoa, I'll never forget it.'

While in front of that picture he'd tell me how he'd lost his friends. His hands would be in his pockets, rummaging in his paper bag of toffees.

'Do you want one?' he'd ask, changing the subject.

We'd saunter round the exhibits, always a little disappointed that all the tanks were roped off. I loved musing over the maps, models, old uniforms.

Grandad would talk me through artillery or battles – whatever he'd picked up by reading about them. He brought romance to history, sparking my imagination and a need to understand completely how battles were fought. Whenever I see a meadow or open space now I'm never just admiring the beautiful landscape. I find myself plotting where I'd position my artillery, infantry and calvary, thanks to Grandad.

After Mum came out of hospital she seemed different. She didn't stand up to Dad any more; when he left for the pub she just sighed. She didn't mention money any more either. Her mouth was always set in the same grim line. She set her alarm clock earlier and went to bed earlier. She never ever mentioned Dave's name again.

A general air of heaviness lingered.

One evening after the news came on all the adults seemed annoyed.

'In this day and age an' all!' Grandad said to Dad, who was stabbing a finger into his newspaper, the *Sun*.

'He's got a bloody cheek,' Dad said, nodding. 'Switching us all off, for that long!'

'I am going to get some more candles in,' Mum said, sighing. 'I'll visit Ted's for tea stuff earlier too.'

The three-day week was upon us, thanks to the brainwave of the Conservative government, who were trying to limit electricity use following the miners' strike.

I liked candles, playing with the melted wax on top when Mum wasn't looking. The candlelight made our house look even cosier somehow, though to be honest, I never really noticed the wallpaper peeling or holes in the carpet anyway. But I did notice something in the candle holder.

'Mum, what's that?' I shuddered as I felt something dark and furry huddled in the base of the candlestick. It didn't take long to realise it was a dead mouse.

Shortly after the lights came back on, we started having

butterscotch Angel Delight again, and Mum had news. She sat me down and was smiling.

'How would you feel about being a big brother?' she asked, a light shining from her eyes. I looked at her and her tummy. Always a slim lady, she'd grown a pot belly, and she looked happy – well, happier. If it made her happy, then it made me happy.

'Great!' I said.

Mum carried on working and looked more tired than usual every evening as the months sped by. She rubbed her back as she stirred in the boiling water for the Smash one evening.

'It won't be long now,' she said, sighing as she sat down.

Then on New Year's Day, 1972, Mum was driven off to hospital by Grandad W in his car, with a little bag, and the next day Grandad told me I was going to meet the baby.

'Exciting, isn't it?' he said, beaming. He wanted to comfort me because he thought I might be jealous but really, I wondered, I hoped, that this baby would be a good thing. After all, everyone seemed quite happy about it. Maybe even Mum and Dad would stop rowing.

Grandad held my hand as we wandered down the long squeaky hospital corridors of King's College Hospital. My hand always seemed to fit perfectly in his big warm one. If he smelt of anything, it was of the colour brown, of chocolate digestives and warm hugs – much nicer than the breeze of disinfectant that hit us as we walked in.

Mum was in bed, looking drained and tired, as if she had flu. A few curls of her hair clung slightly damp on her forehead. Her face lit up, though, and I was swept into a hug.

'Gregg,' she grinned, kissing my head, 'look what the baby has bought you.'

I tore open a paper box to find an electronic robot inside.

'Whoah!' I cried. 'That's brilliant.'

It had batteries and moved and everything. A real proper expensive present.

While I was on a high from my gift, Mum pointed out the baby, sleeping in the cot next to her. I peered in. He looked like a pink marshmallow with arms and legs and a mop of dark hair. As I stared, he opened his eyes. They were bluey green, like Dad's, huge and glowing like an owl's.

'Your baby brother,' Mum said. 'We've called him Paul.'

'Hello, Paul,' I said. Then I turned back to the serious business of speeding my robot along the squeaky floor of the hospital, probably driving all the nurses mad.

After a bit Dad came from the pub. He said hello to Mum and then started looking in the cot too. I watched as he held out his little finger to try it get Paul to curl his fingers around it.

'He's so beautiful,' he cooed, his eyes crinkling in the corners in a way I'd never ever seen before.

CHAPTER 7

Cadbury's Caramel Bunny

Mum came home soon afterwards. She looked more tired than ever and talked about 'going back to work soon' every day. Dad didn't seem to notice how tired she was, or help with the nappies and what not. Grandad would jiggle Paul to sleep or sing him a silly song and Dad would smile.

Once a bottle of Lucozade appeared to help Mum with how she was feeling. If you were ever ill or run down in our house, the large, imposing scarily neon orange bottle appeared like a sentry guard by your bedside. The Lucozade's bubbles were the nearest thing to champagne we'd ever get in Peckham. It was always bought from the chemist's, the only place you could get it, the glass bottle wrapped in plastic, feeling very sticky. I'd quite like to meet the marketing men from back then to ask why they advertised quite a decent product solely to ill people –'Lucozade aids recovery' – even though it made a nice sweet drink too.

When Paul was just three months old Mum started 'asking round' to see if anyone could childmind him while she went back to work. But Grandad stepped in. He'd retired by now from his job at the SPH. There was no golden handshake or gold carriage clock as a goodbye present. He just left one day and that was that. Now he was a pensioner and would have to eke out his money on a state pension. But he had free time and he was happy to pitch in. Far more so than Dad.

It suited me fine. I liked having Grandad round more and it meant I could spend less time at Bertie's and I could run home from school to spend more time with him too. He was soon known as 'Grandad' by others too. He used to take Paul to the Peckham play centre off the Old Kent Road during the summer holidays, and get invites to parties addressed 'To Paul and Grandad'. A few times I joined them for walks near the pond in Peckham Rye. One winter we had loads of fun throwing breadcrumbs on to the frozen pond and watching ducks do a Superman dive to try to eat them. They'd jump, land on their feathered bums and slide a fair few yards as they scrabbled to eat the bread. It was one of the funniest things, as an eight-year-old, I've ever seen.

Reminds me of a joke. When it snowed we went bob-sleighing and one week we managed to kill ten bobs.

I soon wished Grandad could look after me all the time, but I was still going to Bernie's after school – something I now dreaded. Since just after Paul was born, George had been spending loads of time with me, with our cannon matchsticks, and I was more than happy to spend time with him, until one rainy Monday afternoon.

Bernie was out collecting some other kids, when George beckoned me away from the TV.

'Gregg, come here and I'll teach you what happens when you get a girlfriend,' he said.

Bit strange, as George didn't have a girlfriend, he had Bernie as a wife, but George knew a lot about stuff. I went over to him and he knelt down, and before I had a chance to ask him what he was on about his hot stinking tobacco breath was in my face, his lips were stuck on mine and he was poking his tongue into my mouth. My arms turned to jelly and felt limp, as I stood there, unable to move. I was in a state of total confusion. I'd no idea what had happened; I knew nothing about sex or relationships or anything. He was staring at me intently, his face different from when we fired matchsticks.

'Well done, Gregg,' he said. 'Now I need to show you what the girlfriend does to you. Give me your hand.'

I didn't move my hands. I just looked down at them, wondering what I should do. Wondering what the hell George was doing. This didn't seem like a game, or if it was, I'd not had a chance to catch up. He wasn't smiling. He grabbed my right hand tightly and then, in one swift movement, shoved it down his pants.

George closed his eyes. 'There,' he gasped, pulling a weird face.

He loosened his grip on my hand slightly, so I wriggled it out, my heart beating like a drum. I felt utterly baffled. What on earth had happened?

'Don't you dare tell anyone, now,' he said, his face falling seriously. 'I mean, you don't want to cause trouble for me, do you now? Do you?'

I shook my head, as he ruffled my hair, his face brightening again. I ran back downstairs as Bernie arrived with more kids and some sweets. But I wasn't hungry.

A few days later Bernie popped to the shops again and I

was on my own in the living room when George appeared at the door.

'I'm going upstairs to lie down,' he said. 'Come up with me, Gregg.' Then he disappeared.

I didn't move. I just kept watching the telly, but not hearing the sounds or really seeing the pictures. I felt frozen to the sofa.

Later on Bernie came back, and George caught me on my own for a few seconds. His face was dark.

'You've let me down there, you know, Gregg,' he said grimly. I blinked away some hot, unexpected tears. I never asked to play with the matchstick cannon again.

I never did tell Mum, or anyone else. I didn't really understand what had happened, and somehow I also knew he'd be in really big trouble if I did, and I had an overriding sense that I didn't want to get George into trouble. After all, he had been so lovely to me for months and months before this and he was Bernie's husband. I didn't, until I got older, consider myself a victim. Instead, I felt ashamed of what had happened, as if I was complicit. I should have told somebody; something should have been done about it. He should have been in trouble; moreover, it may well have protected other children from similar assault. It's a horrendous thing to happen to a child. Things that happen when you're a kid stay with you and it feels natural to blame yourself.

He didn't need to worry about me telling anyone anyway. Most times I opened my mouth by now, I seemed to be drowned out by the sound of a baby crying or Mum and Dad bickering. Mum was very busy with being kept awake by my new baby brother – who was growing cuter by the minute – and working all hours during the day. Dad was coming home earlier these days, though, to kneel down on the carpet and chase Paul. He used to always run into things and could be a real ruffian as he started to walk.

'He's always biffing stuff,' I said, laughing, to Mum one day, as he knocked over yet another tower of bricks I'd built for him.

And the name stuck: Biffo.

At first I hadn't taken much notice of my baby brother. I mean, he couldn't walk or talk, so I couldn't play with him much. But as he grew into a quiet, thoughtful little chap who loved to eat anything he laid his hands on, I really started to love him.

Once when I got home I laughed as Paul started chucking his cars in a bucket and then toddled over to me.

He handed me his bucket proudly. 'Cars!' he babbled.

'Aw, thanks, mate,' I said, taking them from him. He could be so sweet.

'Look how clever he is,' Dad quipped. 'He's bringing you something to Shut You Up, to make you Go Away.'

Something caught in my throat. I dropped the bucket and ran upstairs to Grandad.

When I wasn't avoiding my father, I was hearing Mum ridiculing him. It was so easy to; I didn't blame her. Dad wasn't only useless with money and helping out in any way, but he always got things wrong. He used to get his words mixed up all the time, but not in funny way, just in a silly, irritating manner, and the more she lost respect for him, so did I.

It sounds petty but living with someone who was so demanding but sometimes thick was difficult for us all. Mum used to sometimes get irritated too by some of his cockney speak.

'It's not "your royal higher-ness". It's "highness" she'd say, sighing. 'It's not "laun-der-rette". It's "laundrette".'

He never helped around the house unless Mum nagged and

cajoled for weeks. For example, Mum wanted a chain on the door. I hoped it wouldn't turn out like the memorable fiasco of the broken lamp in the living room, when I came downstairs to find Mum standing over Dad and pointing at his handy work.

'What's this?' she raged. 'You've just stuck two matchsticks into the wall to hold the wires in. It's so bloody dangerous.'

This time, Mum had to ask the usual ten or twenty times for Dad to help.

'It's for extra security,' she said. 'Everyone round here has one. We should have one too.'

Dad always shrugged, or changed the subject, or just appeared not to hear if DIY was mentioned. Then Mum went to the hardware store and bought one.

'Right,' she said, slamming it on the table so the salt and pepper pots skittled together. 'Can you please put this up now, Allan?'

He took half an hour. 'It's up,' he said, grabbing his coat to go out.

Mum went to view his handiwork and started sighing loudly with exasperation.

'Blinking heck, is there nothing this man can do properly? Nothing?'

I went to look. Dad had screwed just two screws in the sliding part of the chain door, instead of four.

Some nights I'd get in from school and he'd be sitting at the kitchen table, downing a pint of beer in three giant gulps, not noticing if he spilt it, foam dripping off the edge of the table and reminding me of the shoreline we sometimes saw in Margate.

Now there were four of us living in two rooms, there was even less space, what with Biff's toys too. A new regular row cropped up. Mum wanted to move on, get their own place and a mortgage. When she'd moved in over fifteen years earlier, she was a teenager who'd thought it was a temporary place to stay with her in-laws until her husband found his feet and sorted out a proper home. Now she had a drunk for a husband and two kids in tow with very little space, and was having to work all hours to throw money away on rent.

'We both earn enough to get a mortgage,' she argued. 'With your salary too we can do this. We need to get on the property ladder. Get somewhere cheap. We can't keep on living like this. It's not fair on the kids. It's not fair on me.'

She said that a lot these days – 'living like this'.

The rows would end with Dad storming to the pub for an extra-heavy session and Mum just going to bed early, probably to cry.

I went to bed that night earlier, as Biff was now sharing my room. We'd had another drama recently, as I'd been scooting Biff around on a tray for a laugh in the front room. He loved it, but his head had gashed on the cabinet, causing floods of tears, from both sides, and a mad dash to A&E. I felt so guilty. But it proved to me how much this little kid meant to me now.

One time of year when a ceasefire seemed to descend was during Christmas. It was pure magic. We always opened our presents first at Kincaid Road, and I always felt spoiled rotten, especially by Grandad. Then we'd hop in the car and drive to Wimbledon, and every year Grandad W would dress up as Father Christmas. Nan W, being a good seamstress, knocked up a fantastic outfit for him. He'd go outside just after we arrived and then knock on the door and come in, with a sack full of wrapped presents. Every time I thought I'd wet myself with excitement. Then he'd disappear as quickly and seemingly as mysteriously as he'd arrived, and I'd bomb upstairs.

'Grandad! Grandad! You missed 'im!' I'd scream, tugging at his hand.

'Oh no!' Grandad W would cry, pulling a genuinely miffed face. 'You're joking! Not again. Where was he?'

I still don't know how he made it back indoors and up those stairs so fast, unseen.

We always had the actual Christmas dinner at Nan W's. Although I loved Nan W's Christmas dinners, especially the vast quantities of gravy she served, in proper gravy boats too, I hated being made to sit at a separate table to the adults with my cousins Mark and Steven. I sat with the grown-ups every Sunday lunch, so why should Christmas be any different?

Although we always celebrated Christmas and Easter, Mum and Dad weren't in the least bit religious. Nan P had a small picture of a big blond Jesus surrounded by lots of little kids from different races and nationalities following behind him like the Pied Piper, but nobody spoke about God or beliefs. Although Mum never ever wrote or said the word 'Xmas': she thought it disrespectful.

CHAPTER 8

Hot Cocoa

One New Year, Mum told me we were going to see a fella called Gerry. He'd been a vague family friend and I'd over-heard Mum bandy his name around at some of her parties and things. But now she was smiling and saying it was time for me to meet him.

He lived out in Sydenham in a 1970s new-build open-plan house with polished wooden floorboards, which looked absolutely gigantic compared to ours. There was no place for lino in this gaff.

What really blew me away, though, was the onyx ashtray. Very 1974. Smooth, polished and black. I couldn't believe something so posh was used to drop something like ash in.

Gerry seemed a lovely man, short and bald, with a big belly that the belt on his trousers struggled to contain. (His father was a publican and had done quite well as a cabinetmaker before that. He had been a Barnado's child and was married to an East End Jewish lady called Rosa. I know all this from filming BBC's *Who Do You Think You Are?*, but at this point in the story, I didn't actually know who I was, without realising it. Anyway, I won't spoil the plot.)

So we started to see Gerry every now and then. He continued to be a sort of a shadowy family friend, I suppose, a nice enough guy. Except I started to get £5 or £10 notes or vouchers in birthday and Christmas cards from him – huge sums of money.

I asked Mum why he sent me so much and she just smiled.

'He's just a nice man who must like you, Gregg,' she said.

Seemed a bit weird. I mean, my own dad didn't give me that much, so why did this guy? But when you're young you only really give such a thing a thought for about twenty seconds before you get to the shops to splash out.

Thankfully, I had a great school trip to get me out of the war zone that my home had become. To the Isle of Wight – a massive adventure. Mr Edwards found quite a remarkable way to get us there too. He'd got an ex-London bus and painted it bright canary yellow. I shared a room with my best mate at the time, Robin, whose dad ran a corner shop.

Our few days on the Isle of Wight were magical. We had mass games of Twister, wandered for long walks by Freshwater Bay and marvelled at all the souvenir tat, although I never saw it as tat then. The glass lighthouses you could fill yourself with different colours of sand were a source of wonderment. I witnessed my first snog on this trip too. It was between Caroline Simmons and Simon Evans. They did it in front of a crowd of us, tongues and everything. We all sat, staring, suddenly silent, as they kept going, probably a bit longer than was needed to get our attention.

Another naughty kid called Micky Bachelor grabbed the

hotel waitresses by the bum and we all fell about in fits. A big lump of plaster also came down in the hotel dining hall, because of the amount of jumping about from a big group of boys in the room above. We must've wrecked the place.

On the last night, I had some unexpected news. I was due to go to secondary school the following year but I didn't know which one I'd get into. There were only a couple in the area, including Peckham Manor, a big comp with a bad rep, which terrified me, but the London Nautical School was the big one and it wasn't a local school, which made it all the more special. It was a grammar school then, founded in 1915 after the *Titanic* sank, and had a nautical theme. You wore a sailor's uniform and those who went there were expected to join the navy afterwards: that was the deal. Anyway, on this school trip we were all in our pyjamas and drinking cocoa, feeling rather cosy, when Mr Edwards called out some names, including mine, and asked those named to leave the room.

Then he gave a big grin and said: 'Congratulations: all of you have been accepted into your chosen schools.'

I nearly choked on my cocoa. My head was spinning and fit to burst. I couldn't believe I had got into the London Nautical School. I already knew we'd passed our eleven plus, but that didn't mean much unless you got to the grammar school.

'Wow! Wait till I tell Mum and Grandad,' I cried to Robin. I was made up. I couldn't believe someone like me was going to join a school as grand as that. Suddenly I felt as if I was part of an elite.

Months earlier Mum had taken me along for an interview to see if I stood a chance of getting a place. It was on the cards, but no way a done deal.

In the interview I'd sat politely agreeing like a nodding dog to everything the head teacher said. He asked me a few questions about books and words.

'Do you know what the word "jinx" means?' he asked suddenly. It was in a passage of a book I'd had to read.

I bit my lip and looked out the window.

'Umm, it means it's like a curse, sir,' I said politely.

He nodded as I'd got it correct.

'Would you like to join the navy?' he asked sternly, peering over his glasses.

I looked at Mum's face, all expectant. Cripes, I'd no idea what I wanted to do when I left school but yes, a life at sea might be exciting. I nodded firmly, knowing this was what he wanted to hear.

Back home, I saw Mum, who'd already heard the news, and she wrapped me in a hug.

'Oo, you clever boy,' she gasped.

Grandad was pleased as punch too. But I overheard him later say to Mum, 'Don't say it to him too much. We don't want it going to his head.' That was the thing: 'ideas above your station' weren't on.

Grandad W almost danced a jig when I told him, the navy being his vocation and all. Mum took me down there the following Sunday after I'd got my new uniform. As I told him all about it, I watched his face break into the proudest smile. That was it really: I just wanted everyone to be happy.

The uniform jacket was battle dress. It finished at the waist, and buttoned on to the trousers. It had two breast pockets, the buttons on the pockets and the jacket were gold, and it was topped off with a peaked cap with a white cap cover. At £26 Mum had to go to a specialised shop in Tottenham Court Road and save for weeks to buy it, no doubt going without things she needed for herself.

On the first day at the Nautical School I couldn't wait to get dropped off. The vest-tucking days were long gone, and although I knew I'd miss my cosy primary, where I was top dog, I was ready for the challenge. I also had a briefcase to take instead of a satchel. I'd fill it with papers and flick it open, looking this way and that, pretending to be a spy with secret documents on a mission. When I started school, though, the briefcase soon got filled up with all kinds of books and sports stuff.

I was one of three Peckham Park boys who attended that year: me, Allan Miller and Mark Jones. Allan had a brother called Chris, who was in the year above. Years later I bumped into Chris in the fruit and veg trade.

To begin with, faced with the new school and all these rough boys, I felt quite timid. I wasn't particularly big then, and never grew to be over 5 feet 8 inches tall. But I taught myself to be tough in a boisterous school, which was full of boys with various levels of testosterone; you had to know how to handle yourself, and someone like me, who had a fairly laid-back nature, had to learn fast.

The first time was in the playground over football. A boy called Follet, a tall lad, who was actually all right, had the ball and I went in for a hard tackle. I followed him, and went in for the kill, sliding my right foot forward and churning up a bit of gravel at his feet so that he lost balance.

'Oi, Wallace, you dick!' he yelled, slipping up as if on ice, his calves scraped with blood. He regained his balance in a split second and squared up to me. 'What was that supposed to be?'

I pulled myself to my full height and pushed my nose to his. 'You just lost it, Follet,' I snarled.

We probably gave ourselves just milliseconds of eyeballing before his right hook came towards me and I sailed half backwards, raising my own fists to meet his, blow for blow.

'Fight, fight . . .' The chant only had time to begin before our PE teacher pulled us apart with threats of detention.

I didn't let my stare waver from Follet's as we were sent off to calm down. The next day I had a cracking black eye, but also new-found confidence.

The sport of choice for lessons at this school, though, was rugby, a sport I'd never seen or heard much of – it wasn't on telly at the time and nobody I knew played it. The school didn't play football but I never left Millwall behind. However, learning the art of rugby triggered in me a lifelong love of the game. I have to say, I was rubbish at it; I wasn't fast enough on the pitch. But I loved the etiquette, the rules, the way you shook everyone's hand while walking up and down a tunnel of players before and after every single game. It was a gentleman's sport, but also a very rough one, rougher than football, and so complex. You had to give an attitude, try to overcome the fear of the other player. As someone who couldn't keep up much, I still admired everyone else.

Because we were a nautical school we had the usual compulsory lessons of English, maths and RE but also seamanship and navigation. I was always hopeless at maths, so navigation for me was a real struggle. Longitude, latitude, dead reckoning – it was all Greek to me. I was – excuse me – all at sea. They also expected us to learn Morse code and semaphore.

I loved going out on boats, though. Can you imagine? Instead of sitting behind a desk we'd head off to the East India Docks and climb down ladders to get into a rowing boat, bobbing on the Thames. To this day I have no idea what we were supposed to be taught, but whatever it was, it was really good fun.

'Right, lads, one by one, careful now, no rocking,' said our teacher for the day, an old naval boy.

We'd all get in and then take up the oars, dissolving into laughter as we went round in a circle till we got going. Then we'd row up and then back down again. Not really achieving a whole lot, but having a lot of fun. My favourite command was 'Stow your rollocks' – good advice for any young man. A rollock is the U-shaped device your oar sits in. There was a motorboat as well, moored up somewhere, that took us right out on to the open sea. It slept about four people but there were about twelve of us on it, with sleeping bags and smuggled alcohol – well, someone usually did.

Retired naval officers used to take us out on these trips, bless them. I heard later that the bloke who took us lot had a nervous breakdown at one point, which was hardly surprising. Once we found ourselves in a pub right up a river. Can't recall where, but then I doubt many people would recall much about that 'lesson', as we were all, the teachers as well as the pupils, rolling drunk by the end of the day in a lock-in.

Strange times.

We were cheeky when we could get away with it. This was a time where puberty was striking, boys becoming men, and finding their voices, myself included.

Once we had a stand-in teacher for registration.

'Keep quiet,' he snapped, trying to exert some control from the beginning. A good attempt, but hopeless when it came to my class. Despite our school's good discipline, he was a rookie, so we couldn't let him off.

'I said: quiet!' he shouted.

Then he changed tactic. 'The problem here, lads, is not so much the noise you are making but the shape of the room we are in. You see, it's domed and therefore causes an echo, so I'd appreciate it if you could try harder to keep the noise down.'

It was a nice try. But this was too much for us to resist. A few crafty glances around the room later meant we all knew what to do.

When he called the next name we were ready.

'Bell,' he said.

'Ell … ell … ell … ell … elll,' we all murmured.

'Yes, very funny,' he snapped.

'Unny … unny … unnny,' we continued.

'That's enough!'

'Ough … ough … ough … ough …'

You get the picture.

I am guessing I always felt a little out of place, a little lost, but sometimes you find a sense of belonging from unexpected sources and in my case, I discovered I could sing. My form teacher, Mr Cook, was also the music teacher and he got us all to sing scales. As I did so, giving it my all, unbeknown to me he was auditioning for the choir.

'Gregg, I'd like you join in,' he said.

I couldn't believe it. Me in the choir! I grew to love Mr Cook and his teaching style.

'Sing as if you have a hole in the middle of your head and are releasing the pressure,' he suggested. And he's absolutely right: that is the way to sing.

We sang in the Royal Festival Hall and I did a duet at the Greenwich naval base. Grandad W's face wibbled with pride in the audience as I sang my diaphragm out. We sang Christmas carols that year at Southwark Cathedral too. It was one of the few times I set foot in a church, apart from weddings and funerals. I loved weddings. Everyone made a fuss of you and (when I was a bit younger) you got to eat under a trestle table and were allowed to run around. Sometimes I overheard Dad or Grandad making a fuss over the food, though. 'What's this spicy potatoes larkin?' asked Dad one time. 'Why can't they just mash 'em?' Mum sighed and explained people did special things with food on special occasions.

Lunchtimes at school used to really annoy me. There was a 'system' whereby classes were called one by one, the eldest first, and alphabetically within classes. So the younger you were, the longer you waited. And as well as being in the youngest class, being a 'Wallace' I was obviously listed last alphabetically too. There was a 'Winter' after me, but essentially I was almost always the very last to be served in the entire school and I felt light-headed with hunger by the time I was served.

I soon wised up and got a job as a staff steward. This role was basically as a waiter to the teachers in their own dining room. One of the dinner ladies wheeled in steaming food servers on a portable hotplate and we'd have to ferry plates to the staff. It was easy as pie and the best thing was you got lots of the food. We had unlimited access to everything. I especially loved the piles of crusty golden chips and creamy, sharp coleslaw, and I'd always finish with the biggest helping of pudding I could muster, often going back for thirds and even fourths.

Not sure why but one day I ended up going to work with Dad. Maybe school was closed for the day and there was no childcare – not sure, but what an insight!

By now Dad had been promoted to a charge hand and seemed quite chipper about having me tag along. We arrived to find teams of electricians going out on their jobs, dealing with the Whitehall area. Another bloke was wearing a proper suit and looked incredibly smart, with a pressed shirt and tie. He chatted to Dad for a bit and walked off efficiently with a clipboard.

'Is he your boss, Dad?' I asked.

'No, Gregg, I'm his superior,' he replied. I looked at Dad's tieless shirt hanging out of the back of his trousers and wondered what was going on. At lunchtime he took me down to a tea hut at the bottom of Westminster Bridge.

'You'll never believe what they have there,' Dad said, his voice full of intrigue. 'There's a thing called a microwave, a special electronic oven, and it heats food from the inside out.'

'Nah!' I cried. 'Really?'

We bought cold meat pies and the lady behind the counter heated them up. Sure as eggs our pies emerged steaming. The pastry was now flatter and had a soggy, slightly damp, rubbery consistency, but actually it'd worked. Heated in sixty seconds flat – a minor miracle if ever I saw one. The boiling insides were hot enough to scald your tongue but could be scooped quite happily with a spoon. And I've always loved any food I could eat with a spoon.

Despite Dad's indifference or even belligerence towards Mum getting our housing situation sorted, she ignored his panicking and excuses, visited a bank herself, did the paperwork, cajoled him into signing and clinched a deal for a mortgage. Finally, after over fifteen years of roughing it with her in-laws in their rented house, she was a homeowner.

Before we set off, leaving Kincaid Road for good, I slipped upstairs, to find Grandad sitting on the sofa, the telly off.

'I'm going now, Grandad,' I said, quietly.

'Right-o, Gregg,' he said, clapping in between my shoulders. 'I'll see you soon, won't I?'

'Course!'

Briefly, I put my head on his shoulder, and he clapped me on the back again, this time a bit harder.

'Chocolate doings and a cup of tea always waiting here for you, boy,' he said. 'You know that.'

So 55a Ivydale Road, Nunhead, became home. Ivydale is a long curving suburban road, sweeping uphill from Nunhead station and carrying on for what must be over a mile past the Waverley pub and Ivydale school, and almost reaching Peckham Rye. Hundreds of terraced houses lined up either side, the line only broken on the left-hand side by a number of prefabricated houses. Our flat was a conversion job, a downstairs garden part of Ivydale House, and it wasn't a great deal bigger than the space we'd left behind in Kincaid Road. Yet it had something my mother had lived without for a long time: a bathroom and indoor toilet. The days of the bucket were over. Now Mum had her 'own home' she was determined it would improve all our lives. She even gave up her beloved Silk Cuts to save extra dosh for central heating and a basic fitted kitchen, the first she'd had since marrying Dad.

What proved much better living conditions for us, though, proved disastrous for her marriage. The thought of being 'saddled' with the debt of a mortgage worried my dad so much he started downing more beer than ever. Once I came home from school to see Dad hunched over the bars of the gas fire in the living room, one arm on the top as if to steady himself. He looked spooked and was shaking.

'You all right, Dad?' I asked.

He turned and looked at me, a haunted look in his face. He looked like a cadaver: he'd lost weight recently and his work shirt hung off him.

'Hmm,' he grunted, unable even to speak.

Later on, Mum came back from work. 'Whatever is wrong, Allan?' she said with a sigh.

'I miss Mum and Dad,' he moaned and started sobbing.

That was it really: one minute he was crying, the next he

95

was shouting and stomping around like an irritable old man. Soon after Mum got the heating put in and we were all sitting watching telly, Dad came home looking even more unsteady than usual. He crashed around in the kitchen for a bit and then stood, looking a bit lost, staring at me, Biff and Mum on the sofa together.

He held up his hand against the doorway, to try to steady himself, raising his beer to the TV.

'Whatcha watchin', then?' he said, with a fake joviality.

'*Doctor Who*,' I said, although it was obvious with Daleks on the screen.

CHAPTER 9

Roast Lamb

S ince our move to Ivydale, Mum had started to go out more in the evenings, usually after dinner for a few hours so Dad would stay in to 'look after' us. Sometimes he'd randomly ask me to play chess with him. I'd no idea why; if he played with anyone, it'd usually be with Biff, but even that was less often nowadays. I'd sit and start a game with him, but sometimes he'd just start knocking over the figures, as the drink took hold. Biff would look on, bored.

'What's up with Dad?' he whispered once as Dad knocked over all the pawns.

'Dunno,' I lied. 'He's just tired.'

One night when Mum was home and Dad went out, she put a litre bottle of Olde English cider on the table and a glass. By the end of the night she'd got through two bottles. I was used to seeing Dad drunk. But Mum just grew quieter and her eyelids flickered, and she slid off to bed. It became a common occurrence, but I didn't twig that anything was massively wrong. I just knew, somehow, slowly and very definitely, that things were starting to properly fall apart.

Thankfully our Sunday lunch trips to Nanny and Grandad W were still something to look forward to. Now, though, Mum started to drive us. She'd recently bought a Mini from someone at work. Her learning to drive was a big thing. She'd been inspired by someone at work who'd lost her husband tragically at thirty-two and decided she'd take the reins and learn to drive herself. She'd had to take her test three times before she passed and was as nervous as hell about trying to work out the clutch when she was on her own in the car with us. And whenever she got to a hectic junction with other cars and lorries steaming past she visibly tightened her hands on the wheel.

'Hush up in the back,' she'd hiss at me and Biff as we set off. 'I need to concentrate.'

I felt so proud of Mum. Not many mums could drive at the time: it was usually the dads. But, as ever, my dad didn't bother even to learn, and he couldn't afford a car. He wasn't in a frame of mind for congratulating her about her success either.

'You saddled me with this,' he'd screamed at Mum the night before. 'The mortgage, the house, the kids. Everything!'

Mum was incensed. 'And you're supposed to be a *man*?' she asked. 'You can't even look after yourself, let alone a family.'

I went to my room and held the pillow over my head. That night I could've done with a hand in Grandad's chocolate doings jar more than ever.

I'd settled into a new routine. I'd get up on my own in the morning, polish off a bowl of Coco Pops, never waiting long enough to hear the snap, crackle and pop before shovelling them in, and listening to Graham Dean on Capital Radio, then get my school books together and pop into Dad's room to find some money for lunch from his trousers at the end of the bed.

Lots of things were being forgotten now. Like Mum and my visits to the pie and mash shop, like the Angel Delight, like being taken to see Grandad at Kincaid Road (I had to take myself). Mum and Dad seemed to move around like ghosts, and when one appeared the other vanished.

I knew Mum still loved me, but our impenetrable bond, the one that had felt like an invisible iron string between our hearts, had somehow thinned and disappeared. Maybe it was because Mum was constantly going out now. Maybe it was because she'd retreated to a place she could exist in by herself now.

I suppose you could say I was looking for something then and our Indian physics teacher, who happened also to be a Catholic, seemed to agree with me.

He was a nice guy and ran an electronics club, a group who met during lunchtime. This teacher, Mr Singh, took a shine to me, and we spent more time sitting around talking about life than the finer points of the circuit board. He was so much fun that when he told me he was to start taking separate assemblies from the usual ones for Catholic pupils, I asked if I could come.

Now, religion aside, Mr Singh's assemblies involved a lot less standing and sitting than the dull Church of England school ones. About thirty of us, some new converts from the electronic club, got to sit about in a classroom, nattering with Mr Singh. No hymns, no sermons, just a bit of God talk and then a catch-up about the week.

After a few months, Mr Singh suggested I join him for mass

at a church in Waterloo after school, so I went along to see what the fuss was about.

I wasn't sure about the rosary beads and the confession (blimey, I'd be in that box all day and wouldn't know where to start), but I enjoyed being in a peaceful church and hearing about Mr Singh's view on the world. I'd been christened at six months old, like everyone around our way, but that's pretty much where my religious life had begun and ended.

Mum told me how in Peckham, after you'd had a baby, you were expected to be 'churched'. 'A woman was seen as "unclean" unless she'd been "churched" apparently,' she explained. 'After I had you, a few people came up to me. I went into a pub shortly afterwards, and I literally saw someone elbowing ribs, whispering, "Oh her, she's not been churched." I'd no idea what they were on about! I think it was something like the vicar giving you a blessing, but I was having none of it. As for calling me "unclean" – well, they could naff off!'

After one lesson Mr Singh said: 'Mr Wallace, you have been chosen by God. I don't know why or what for but you have been chosen.'

I'd no idea either but it sounded nice. So when he suggested I get baptised, I thought it sounded like a cool idea. I went home full of enthusiasm. I wonder now if I was inspired by a sense of belonging really. Sadly, though, Mum and Dad had different ideas. Faster than you could say 'Hail Mary', Dad went off like a rocket.

'I ain't having no bloody priest preaching round *this* house,' he bawled, screwing up the letter Mr Singh had passed on.

Mum backed him up on this. 'He's a vulnerable teenager,' I overheard her say. 'I don't want him growing up with the fear of God in him. I mean, what about Susan a few doors down? Poor girl. She nearly wets herself if she hears the priest is coming. I don't want that for Gregg.'

So that was that. My brush with God got the brush-off.

I'd started to struggle to concentrate at school. I was playing about at lessons and backchatting to teachers. Nobody seemed to care as much at home, so I didn't see why I should bother.

'Wallace, will you sit still and read the passage you've just been asked to look at?' my teacher, Mr Brooks, yelled one day.

I just looked at him and sniggered. For some reason it seemed crazy to be told what to do now. I could do what I liked; after all, nobody at home seemed to notice what I did any more. And although I'd been top of the class at primary, this school was full of clever boys and nobody noticed if I kept up or not.

On another occasion we had another old navy boy, Captain Madge, as a stand-in for a geography lesson. The rule of the school was to call him by his official title of 'Captain', but as he marched into class, looking officious, a file tucked under his arm, I said very loudly: 'Good morning, Mr Captain Madge, sir!'

He paused at my desk and turned slowly to see who'd dared shoot out such a patronising remark.

'Get out of my class, Wallace, and go and see the deputy *now!*' he screamed in my face.

I trotted out, feeling all thirty pairs of eyes boring into my back. I was for it now, but actually it didn't feel like it. I just resisted the urge to laugh. Funny how along with pimples arriving and my voice breaking, many aspects of school I'd once enjoyed suddenly seemed almost ludicrous. The marching from the playground into class, the whistles and bells we had to respond to, the whole naval ethos: it was like a silly game.

Mum first found out when the school told her at a parents' evening that I was 'slipping'.

'What's going on, Gregg?' she quizzed me. 'What are you playing at?'

I rolled my eyes.

'I'll tell you what your problem is,' she snapped. 'You've got no respect. For anyone.'

Saturday evenings were the times of the week I looked forward to now. Mum and Dad would go out and see their friends in the Clarkson Arms, on the Acorn estate, their local, and we'd be dropped off with Nan and Grandad in Peckham.

I was so happy to be back there. The downstairs was back being used as Grandad and Nan's living room, as it had been before Mum and Dad got hitched.

Biffo and I would watch telly with Nan and Grandad, and then Nan would yawn loudly while Grandad and I switched to *Match of the Day*, sharing the 'doings' and endless cups of tea. I was almost a teenager but still the apple of Grandad's eye.

Then Mum and Dad would knock and have a mini cab running outside, so it was a quick kiss and cuddle to say bye and we were off back home, the frosty atmosphere in the taxi such a stark contrast to the cheers in front of the TV. Sometimes Mum or Dad would have a bottle of Scotch on their lap. The pub was full of characters who could 'get you anything', from bedding to tobacco or alcohol, and occasionally the temptation to buy a knock-off was too great. Biffo and I'd go straight to bed and pull the covers up to our necks as we listened for the latest onslaught of rowing. Then peace would descend and I'd try to drop off too, my stomach twitching with feelings I didn't understand.

That Christmas summed up for me how I didn't know who I was or where I belonged any more. But although things were falling apart at home, thankfully my grandparents still carried on all the usual routines. One of these was Nanny W taking us to Wimbledon Theatre every year to watch the panto. I saw Basil Brush and Emu and Bruce Forsyth there. That year, the audience was asked to sing a song and Widow Twanky said: 'Right, first we'll have all the little boys and girls singing it,' and I didn't sing because I knew I was no longer little. Then it was the turn of the mums and dads, but I didn't sing with them either. And I loved singing. I'd entered an awkward age and, to be honest, I still don't think I've come out of it.

Aside from the awkwardness, turning thirteen was a revelation for many reasons. First I got a digital alarm clock, which seemed positively Space Age back then. How the numbers glowed and how it switched itself on when the alarm went off to provide a radio just blew my mind.

I discovered something else to blow my mind, well, a bit further down. It was a time of thinking of girls a lot and some nights I found myself overwhelmed with feelings as I rocked on my pillow, until one evening my toes curled suddenly and it felt as if my head was exploding. I mean, I'd grown up knowing the facts of life from Mum, but her approach was 'I will answer any question you have simply . . .' and she'd never gone into details.

I picked up Mum's technique for my own kids. If they've ever asked a question I've answered it. 'Where did I come from?' 'Your mummy's tummy.' 'How did I get out?' 'Through the lady's front bottom.' You get the picture. Except as a single dad I found that, having been so open with my kids, in later years I was being asked: 'What's S&M, Dad?' 'What's a tranny?' when they were about twelve!

Anyway, poor Mum must've known about my pillow episodes, as I started to go to bed earlier and earlier. 'Who is your pillow going to be tonight?' she asked cheekily one evening as I tiptoed to my room.

With hormones raging, it was little wonder I felt the rising tension. Watching TV one evening, I turned to see the door open and Dad standing in the living room, swaying slightly as usual, struggling to open his tin. Mum emerged, and the look on her face told me to get out of the room, but I was trapped.

It seemed strange at first to see my gentle mum, raising her tightly held fist. Then came the first blow, and the second and the third, as Dad ducked and dived, shouldering some of the punches.

'You fecking bastard,' she screamed. 'You *bast-ard.*'

Nobody swore in our house – well, not much. I never once heard either Grandad or Nan swear. Oh, Grandad, if only I could slip upstairs to squeeze on the sofa with him now . . .

I'd no idea this time what Dad had done or not done, but I just stood, like a lemon, wishing that somehow the lino would swallow me up.

It was only a few nights later that I started on my dad myself. You never remember how all the most ghastly rows begin, as the end result overshadows them, but this was a humdinger.

'Get off me,' I shouted in Dad's face, as he blocked the doorway. People talk about red mist; this was a slow-motion car crash in crimson. The glass door between the kitchen and living room became a wet paper bag as my fist flew directly through it.

'Gaaaaah,' I screamed, clutching my wrist. Blood was dripping down my trousers, as Mum grabbed my shoulders.

'Oh, Gregg, what did you do that for?' she asked, shepherding me away from the shards at my socks. Hot tears dripped off my chin, as fast as the blood streamed down my front.

'What's he doing?' Dad shouted at Mum.

'I don't effing know, do I?' she yelled back. 'But look at the state of Gregg! He needs someone seeing to him . . .'

Dad grabbed his coat. 'You, in the car. Now.'

We drove in silence to the hospital. A&E nurses patched me up as I trembled, the adrenalin long gone.

'And it'll cost a pretty penny to get that effing glass sorted too,' Dad grumbled afterwards.

CHAPTER 10

Fish & Chips

I didn't go to school on the Monday with a bandage on my hand. I didn't want people asking questions. Moreover, I couldn't be bothered. So I just got up as usual, put my uniform on and took myself off for the day.

I wandered round Waterloo, looking for somewhere to go, and decided to head to the Imperial War Museum, though I missed Grandad. Wandering around all the big tanks and artillery, reading about the shell fire and how the soldiers lived, I felt that I was learning more than I ever did in the classroom. But in fairness I wasn't there to learn. I just wanted to keep out of the rain and be warm and entertained for the day. It was fun, and I vowed to do it again.

Interestingly there was no phone call from the school, and Mum and Dad obviously didn't have a clue, so I knew I was safe to do it again some day. That was the thing about a grammar school. They were only interested in helping the boys who wanted to learn. If you didn't, they didn't bother chasing you.

The only subject I really loved at school was English. We had some great teachers too, usually women. But then one came along and he almost ruined it. He was a fat lazy lump of a man who obviously couldn't stand kids. It was amazing how many teachers couldn't. He used to photocopy text and get us to write it out again, as he sat, picking his fingernails at the desk.

A few teachers were brilliant, though. One Mr Evans took us for social studies and even I found it more interesting thanks to him. Once he asked me to defend football hooliganism in a debate, and lent me a book of political cartoons, 'as long as you don't show anyone else'.

He seemed to engage with the person I really was. 'Mr Wallace,' he once said, 'you were born in the wrong era. You'd have so much fun with me and my mates putting flowers in the guns of policemen in San Francisco.' I couldn't help but smile. He made me feel bright, as though I had something to offer.

Once he handed us a report written by a scientist.

'Now this ground-breaking report suggests a link between children's behaviour and their diet,' he announced. 'And I'd like you all to have a look at it.'

We all fell about laughing. 'Don't be crazy, sir,' was the general consensus. This was the late seventies and it just didn't seem credible back then.

At this point I didn't dare bunk school all the time; I just went in often enough so nobody said anything. Even though I'd been going for a year or two now, I'd not made any firm friends. I tended to put more energy into making new mates near Ivydale.

Les was a boy I discovered skateboarding nearby. He was an only child who lived in his parents' very smart house up the road. Like me, he spent lots of time alone, and was constantly being sent up to his room 'to play', which really meant 'get out of our hair', by his parents, who seemed more interested in their jobs and pubs than their son.

We hit it off, and Les certainly seemed like a man of the world. He bought some lager and invited me over to play music, along with a few other mates. He had a girlfriend called Anne, who at fourteen seemed like a grown-up. She had big tits too, something we all appreciated.

'Do you fancy snogging Anne, then?' Les asked one day after she had left.

'Cor, you sure?' I asked.

'I'll arrange it,' he said, winking.

How he did this I'll never know, but I found myself sitting on his bed a few days later with Anne next to me, Les the other side with another girl, and she was totally up for it.

'Go on then, Gregg,' she said, grinning and puckering up.

I clamped my mouth on hers, as though I was a pro, thinking of all the films I'd watched with snogging in and reminding myself to pretend it was easy. When I finally pulled away, she didn't look too offended, so I decided 'in for a penny' and managed to slip my hand up her acrylic shirt too. Talk about all your Christmases, birthdays and pool-winning days coming at once.

I really didn't have much clue about it at all, aside from a few fumblings with Clare, Margo's daughter, when we were messing around. (We used to play a game: guess what body part this is ... One person had to close their eyes and the other guided the hand. It started off with an elbow or earlobe, say, and, well, we always ended up laughing our heads off ... Sorry, Clare, for telling the world.)

My biggest crush by then, though, had been on the

Cadbury's Caramel Bunny – that West Country accent, those long legs, that pert fluffy tail …

Later, a few doors up from mine I bumped into Graham Breen. He'd been born in his house and knew everyone in the area, so was a good kid to know. Nan W had bought me a cool skateboard with mahogany strips the previous Christmas and Graham told me to bring it round the next time. 'I'll show you how to use it,' he said when I admitted I hadn't mastered it.

I was still rubbish weeks later, but Graham organised the dangerous pursuit of forming a 'catamaran' with the others. This involves sitting on your board with your feet on the board of the fella opposite you, and he of course does the same. Once you've got this basic structure, you can enlarge the vessel with other boarders all hanging on, kneeling or standing on their boards, while somehow linking to you. Once we were all tightly knotted we set off sometimes in two catamaran races in the middle of the road at the top of the hill that joined Ivydale Road.

Hurtling down at breakneck speed in your wobbly human frame was about as thrilling as it got, the only options being to sail serenely into the traffic or capsise your board, risking tarmac or gravel burns. Back home when Mum caught my arms and legs with so many cuts, scrapes and bruises, she wondered what I'd been doing.

While I wasn't busy getting myself into scrapes and being a boy, albeit rather a rough one now, I was hankering after my first big crush since the Cadbury's Caramel Bunny: Rose Hatfield. She had long thick brown hair and creamy white skin, was a little bit older than me, and could cut down a man in seconds, being a brown belt in the judo club I'd just enrolled in.

Every time she flitted across the room, in her baggy white judo kit, with that belt squeezed tightly round her waist, I felt as if the heavens had opened and were sprinkling sparks across my eyes.

Quickly I made her laugh and caught her eye. I always hankered after her, but though she found me to be cheeky and fun, sadly I was firmly ticked in the 'friends only' box.

She invited me over, though. She had two older brothers and just a mum, as her dad had died. They all lived in the upstairs of a crammed house, but there was a lot of laughter in there. Being poor didn't matter to them, unlike, it seemed, in my house. I was grateful to find myself invited over for lots of meals.

I soon found out why Rose wasn't interested. She had the hots for Doug, our married judo instructor, who was a good few years older. Eventually they got together when Rose was eighteen and they are still going strong today. Well, I wouldn't have wanted to get in the way of a good love story, after all, would I?

Aside from judo and skateboarding, activities that took me out of the house, where at this point I was more than happy to be, I joined the Ivydale Youth Club, another initiative to keep us kids off the streets.

It was held in the local school hall and we did stuff like play pool and hang out. One evening a skinny lad called Andrew Dyne came in. He was tall and gangly, as though his six-foot frame didn't fit into his fifteen-year-old body. We hit it off, both not really knowing what direction our lives were heading in and always up for a bit of fun.

One afternoon one of the younger lads started having a go at Andrew and then this lad's friends joined in.

'Whatcha looking at?' Andrew snapped, squaring up to him.

Within seconds the atmosphere changed. Andrew stood his full height and they started circling. Without thinking, I went and stood next to Andrew to even things up a bit. 'Thanks, mate,' Andrew muttered as we stalked off, the youth leaders all hopping around like cats on tin roofs.

Turned out Andrew's dad owned Dynes car hire in Peckham Rye and they were the richest family around our way. The Dynes lived upstairs too but in a huge Victorian four-storey house, and ran their business from downstairs. On the first floor was a lounge/games room with a record player, pool table, table tennis table and the very first games console I ever saw.

'Whoa!' I cried, as Andrew showed me how a joystick worked. 'It beats skateboarding.'

Andrew's parents, Maggie and Allan, were a kind couple who took me under their wing a few years later ... but that's all to come.

As far as I was concerned Ivydale Road was somewhere I came home to from school, where I bolted down my tea in record time; then I bolted straight back out again. Later I came home and just conked out in bed. I rarely found myself on my own home sofa these days. Nobody asked where I was going or when I'd be back.

But despite my visits home being fly-by-night, I couldn't avoid the crossfire.

'Who is he?' Dad spat once as Mum came in. 'Tell me!'

'What I do and who I see is none of your business!' Mum screamed back.

I flinched. Dad had accused Mum before of seeing another man, but he was insistent this time. I quickly stuffed my sauce sandwich in my mouth and shot away from the table.

I'd just turned fourteen, but sometimes felt heavy with the

weight of the world on my shoulders. School was rubbish and I missed it whenever I could. I hated being at home just as much. Thank God I had Andrew's games room to take my mind off it. My world sitting watching telly on Grandad's sofa, my hand in the chocolate doings, seemed a million light years ago. I still went and visited, but it wasn't the same. Nothing was the same.

Another welcome diversion was the school camping trip. Mr Scrivener, one of the teachers who actually seemed to love teaching, organised it.

'It's called "bivouacking",' he said. 'You're all to be dropped off in a forest and you have to fend for yourselves.'

I was used to doing that at home, but with my mates in a woodland? Now you're talking.

So off we went in a coach all the way out in the sticks somewhere. In those days, health and safety being at the bottom of the list of priorities, we were sent off with tents, but first we were asked to make a weatherproof shelter from twigs and leaves. All this was so exciting to me and I felt a long-forgotten enthusiasm rekindling. These kind of lessons, along with English lessons, were the only ones that seemed relevant to me.

The teachers made assault courses, with things like beer barrels to be navigated, and we did 'team building' exercises in the dark, which quickly deteriorated into dirty great punch-ups. The next day we were put into a little boat and rowed to a remote island where nobody lived to pitch a tent on a fell, almost at 45 degrees. Amid the gales of laughter we barely noticed the real gales swirling around us. One afternoon we all went horse riding and one kid, John Heffernan, got thrown right off.

'You all right, mate?' someone yelled as we all trotted on.

'Nah!' he cried. 'My leg's caught on some barbed wire.'

The teachers took him seriously then and someone had to drive up and take him to hospital for stitches. Everyone just laughed about it, though.

One evening we were pitched in a field when a crazed bull knocked open the gate and barged in.

'Go to your tents,' yelled Scrivener. It was the first time I saw him agitated too.

I was very much an urban kid, though, and I didn't reckon a flimsy tent was going to be much cop at keeping out a tonne-weight beast.

'Wallace, what the hell are you doing?' Scrivener screamed as I pegged it across the field, feeling like an extra in one of the Wild West movies I'd watched with Grandad.

A few weeks after Dad started banging on about Mum's 'affair' I started to lose my own rag about it. Surely she wouldn't, would she? I remembered Dave, but that all seemed quite innocent in a way. I couldn't imagine Mum having a 'fancy man', as Dad called him. Not Mum.

Mum was sprinkling some salt on her chips for dinner, and Dad was refilling his beer glass, making more barbed comments about men and Mum keeping her knickers on, when I couldn't stand it any longer.

'If there is another man,' I snarled at her, 'I'm gonna beat him up.'

'Don't you dare . . .' Mum gasped. As soon as the words left her mouth, we sat and stared at each other. It was out. There was someone, after all. I pushed my chair from behind me violently, and slammed the door as hard as I could, Dad style. I had to go somewhere, anywhere.

Later on, I skulked in, to find Mum calmly sitting watching telly. Dad was out.

'His name is Gerry. It's Gerry,' she said, her eyes not moving from *Coronation Street*. I sat next to her, I suppose in a way relieved. In a funny way, I couldn't blame her for meeting another man, not when she was trapped in a marriage like the one she had, but I'd never had an inkling it was Gerry. That bald guy with the pot belly.

I felt a bit sick, as I thought of the birthday cards with the money inside. He still did that. A shadowy family friend, he felt like, not Mum's lover.

'What's going to happen next?' I asked, suddenly.

Mum shrugged. 'I just don't know, Gregg.'

She must've had an idea, though, as things moved pretty damn fast after that.

Mum was out for most of the next day with Biff and I had to make my own lunch and dinner. She came back late, looking tired.

'Gerry says he quite understands if you want to punch his lights out, but don't expect him to hit you back.'

I didn't know what to say to that. So, as usual, I said nothing.

As these things tend to, everything came at once. I'd started bunking school again, just for the heck of it really. I'd lost interest in so much and had recently been banned by my geography teacher from lessons.

I'd walked in one day, albeit reluctantly and without any of my homework done, and she opened the door and pointed to it.

'Out, Wallace,' she said, smirking. 'We've had a class vote and nobody wants you in here.'

'You what?' I spluttered.

Apparently this teacher, who prided herself on being a bit New Age, had asked the class if anyone would like anything changed and some smart ass had voted for me to be banned, for being 'disruptive'.

'You heard,' she said. 'An education is wasted on the likes of you.'

Cheers, miss.

I left and walked straight out, nobody stopping me. I mooched round Waterloo for a bit and found myself in the Greater London Assembly canteen. Don't ask me how, but I'd heard they did nice food, and cheap too. Even though the discount was for staff, nobody checked if you were general public, so I just took off my blazer and went and got myself a massive portion of fish and chips for 50p. Very nice they were too.

Around this time I became firm friends with a lad called Allan, who'd also been at my primary school. I totally wanted to join his gang, and when I heard that Allan's brother Chris and his mates worked in part-time jobs after school at the Royal Festival Hall, a ten-minute walk from school, my ears pricked up.

They all worked in the canteen there. It was a huge, chaotic self-service affair on the ground floor. They cleared tables and did 'pot wash' or washing up.

'Can I join you one day if you need extra help?' I asked. And they said I could. It was hard, boring work, but good fun messing with the lads, especially having water fights. I became a dab hand at clearing trays on to trolleys and then wiping the tables clean. Then I'd rattle the heaving great trolleys into an enormous dishwasher, as someone else checked the cutlery and plates were clean on the other side. For our hard work we earned a few quid at the end of the week, but what a princely sum! For a lad with little in the way of a decent wardrobe, suddenly I had money for clothes and records. Things that made me cool.

The extra dosh gave me some identity for the first time, as I decided to become a mod just as Allan already was. It's tribal, I suppose. You wear the same clothes, you listen to the same music, you're one of them whether you're a mod, skinhead, punk or rockabilly. It's important to be someone when you're trying to work out who you really are.

My other mate, Les, was still on the scene around this time, and after watching *Quadrophenia* we went out and bought a couple of green parka jackets the same as that of the character Jimmy Cooper in the film to feel in the zone.

Next came the desert shoes, the prerequisite Ben Sherman shirt and Sta Press trousers. Oh, how good did I feel in all my get-up! I added the *Quadraphenia* album to my collection along with *Secret Affair* and *All Mod Cons* by the Jam. And Paul Weller, well, he appeared to have the same energy and anger we felt too. Thanks to Mum's parties I'd always loved 1960s pop, soul and beat, and this added to the repertoire.

Allan, four or five other lads from school and I started seeking out all the mod nights in the local pubs, and if we could afford it we'd go to gigs too. After school we'd join the other mod lads to watch bands play at the Marquee in Wardour Street, Soho, bands like Secret Affair and the Lambrettas, Long Tall Shorty and my all-time favourite, the Q-Tips, even though they didn't dress like mods, so weren't seen as cool. I never understood why mods didn't follow them, but maybe mods are just easily fooled.

Since I had a bit of extra money now, I was able to buy a few things for myself here and there. I bought a really nice jumper once only to come home one night to find Dad wearing it, all stretched out and about three sizes too big for me.

Thoughts about my own situation didn't last long, though, as Mum was busy packing. She was humming to herself as Biffo watched TV, lost in his own world.

'Where you going?' I asked.

'I am leaving, Gregg,' she said softly. 'Me and Biffo are moving into Gerry's place in Sydenham.'

'Whaaaat?'

CHAPTER 11

Ice Cream

*M*um sighed heavily as she stopped folding her dresses and sat down on the bed.

'Listen,' she said. 'I want you to come and live with us. I mean, you can come down and visit Gerry's, and then see what you think and if you could settle there. Dad is staying here.'

Well, what a pickle, but I definitely wanted to stay with Mum, so I didn't hesitate to say yes. So I packed up my room, helped Mum pack up some cardboard boxes, and we said goodbye to Ivydale. Dad wasn't in, as he was in the pub.

I didn't really discuss the move with anyone and later on there wasn't anyone to discuss it with anyway. As soon as Grandad heard Mum was leaving Dad for another man, he refused to speak to her and didn't really want to talk about it. I'd heard him and Nan raging upstairs about 'marriage being for life' and the word 'she' was now bandied a lot – 'she' being Mum.

So I jumped in the car, with Gerry at the wheel, and he turned and smiled. 'All set?' he said.

Gerry's flat was like a showroom compared to our house. I couldn't believe how smooth the floors were, how tidy the work surfaces looked. Everything was shiny, flat, dark wood and fake marble.

I hovered on the wide, expansive, light brown sofa, feeling as if just being there would cause a stain. Biffo was excited, though. He ran around, arms out like an aeroplane, saying how great it was to have room. My room was the spare room and I shared it with Biff.

That night I lay on my bed and struggled to drop off. I could hear Mum giggling next door with Gerry. Finally I fell asleep and woke up feeling confused. The clean white walls and the starchy sheets didn't feel right. I had to admit, though, I admired Gerry. He was a bookkeeper by trade. He liked nice things – smart suits, crisp white shirts, shiny black shoes. He had stainless-steel cutlery, and pillowcases and duvets that matched. He knew who he was, what he wanted and where he was going, well, on holiday at least – and he could afford regular trips abroad.

In almost every respect, Gerry was the polar opposite of my own dad.

For a while I found myself dreaming of the same aspirations. I mean, this middle-class malarkey didn't look like a bad gig to me really. It meant you knew what you were worth, could look forward to things, have a pension and hold your own in arguments about stuff. He talked of savings, of security, of being 'comfortable', and how attractive was that? I even quizzed him about his background in Judaism. About the Jewish culture. It seemed a solid heritage to have.

Nan and Grandad, Peckham. I loved him so much, such a great man.

My mum looks fantastic. She had no idea what she was letting herself in for.

Nan and Grandad at Wimbledon. The house seemed so posh to me, it was like a palace!

Grandad Wimbledon, a strict Navy man. He had a lot of time for me, and I admire him a lot for that.

Me and my godmother, Margo, very chic in her shades.

Me and my cousin Mark. More than anything, this shows off my grandmother's dressmaking skills.

Love mum's hairdo!

Mum holding me with her mate Jenny beside her. Mum's friend at work said what a lovely looking boy, such a shame about his legs!

Now that's more like it! At a restaurant with a big bottle of wine.

What a hippy, look at that hair! Where did it all go?

The whole family on a cruise ship. That's my little brother Biffo there, we're very close now.

Hard to believe that this small child was going to develop an enormous belly.

Me and Biffo in Nunhead. Not a happy place for me.

Three brothers: Biffo, me and Adam. I'm the only one who's changed, the others look exactly the same.

The Wallaces all together. I think this was our last holiday as a family.

Mum and Gerry's wedding day. I'm wearing a Beatles suit – don't ask.

The first day of possibly the shortest marriage in the world! Me and my first wife, Christine.

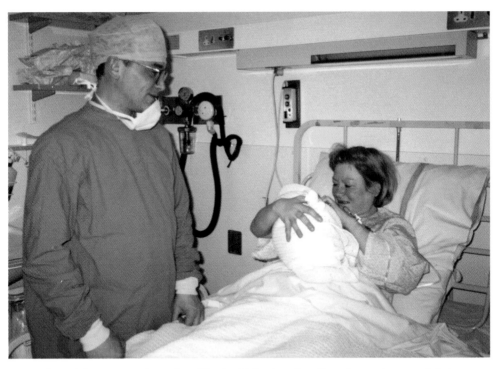

One of the greatest days of my life, the birth of my boy, Tom. I'm such a proud dad.

My brother has been working with me by my side for 20 years from fruit and veg to the restaurants. Love you Biff.

Hello Nan, I loved you very much.

Grew up big, didn't he? My brother Biffo.

'Do you think I could maybe join as well?' I asked one day. I knew he didn't go to the synagogue or practise much, but he spoke about it with pride.

'Er,' he said, 'well, if you'd really like to, I suppose I could introduce you to people.'

He never did, though, and I never asked about it again. I think perhaps it just seemed like a good place to belong to at the time. And I was still looking for something to sign up to.

Gerry was always OK to me. I mean, he never lost his temper and he tried politely to encourage me not to drop my haitches, but it proved pretty fruitless really. He was a jovial, happy sort, I suppose, and I learned to rub along, keep my head down, go out a lot.

One evening, though, a few months after we'd moved in, Gerry brought out his 'family album'. Mum was nodding and smiling enthusiastically as he flicked through the grey, black and white snaps of various camping holidays and school pics. Gerry had lots of hair then, thick curly hair. I wasn't expecting it, as he was bald as a coot.

Then he stopped at a page where he was about the same age as me, smiling into the camera on holiday somewhere.

'Have a look at this, Gregg,' said Gerry. Both he and Mum were looking at me intently. As if they were waiting.

I took the album and held it closer to my face. Then I realised. Looking at Gerry's picture was like looking in the mirror. The face in the snapshot staring back had the same shape, the same nose, the same curly hair. I looked up. Mum, a watery smile on her face, shot an almost imperceptible look at Gerry.

'Is there something you want to tell me?' I asked, putting down the album on the coffee table.

I knew then. All that birthday money, the heavy hints. It was a Luke Skywalker/Darth Vader moment.

'Are you,' I said slowly to Gerry, 'my real dad?'

Mum was beaming, but a flash of anxiety knotted her brow. I suddenly feared they were both going to start hugging me. Gerry nodded, looking like the cat who'd got the cream.

'And how do you feel about this?' Mum asked.

I blew out my cheeks and laughed. It was crazy. Gerry was my dad!

I stared at him. God, I could see it now: we looked so very much alike. The same round faces, the same dimples, the same height. And then it made so much sense. Dad had never been interested in me. He doted on Biffo, though, his real, biological child. A strange sense of relief also flooded over me. Dad was a useless dithering drunk really, a weak man. I'd never held Allan in high regard. Look at Gerry and his lovely flat and generous nature. If I could've chosen, I suppose I would've chosen him, although I sensed he looked down his nose at our life in Peckham, the life I'd grown up in.

'Great!' I said finally. 'You owe me fourteen years' pocket money, though, Gerry.'

Gerry laughed as Mum seemed to wilt with relief.

'I'm sure I can help you out when you need it now,' he said, winking.

Looking back it was funny how fast I accepted it. No counselling or handwringing or navel gazing in those days. It was just life.

The whole story came pouring out. Mum had had a fling with Gerry when she worked as an accounts manager in one of her temping jobs. He was her boss. The two of them hit it off, and Mum, being in a loveless marriage as she was, started an affair.

Three years into her marriage, Mum found out she was pregnant with me.

Now as I've said, Mum reckoned that in those days, half of the babies born in Peckham weren't the 'father of the house's' because everyone was at it. So many marriages happened too fast and too young, but nobody could afford or manage the scandal of divorce. So you put up and shut up. Or, more likely, just shut up.

But poor Mum could've picked a better bet than Gerry to have an affair with. He was a single man who was living with his mum and dad, but when Mum fell for him he was having a relationship with a divorced woman with two children. When it came to the crunch, he picked the other lady and not Mum. After Mum fell pregnant, his parents, who ran a pub, retired and he needed to find somewhere else to live, so he didn't hesitate to shack up with his divorced lady. He ended up marrying her, but she left him for another man. (Are you keeping up with this?) So Mum was pregnant, but the father wasn't her husband. But also her husband didn't seem to even care. To her credit, she chose to be open with my dad. He was having affairs left, right and centre anyway, so she matter-of-factly told him over their toast one morning.

'I am pregnant, Allan, but it's not yours and I am keeping it, and that's that,' she'd said.

Who needed *EastEnders* in those days?

Dad just carried on sipping his tea as if Mum had been talking about the weather. 'Well,' he said, after a moment, 'you're married to me and you'll just have to bring the baby home and we'll carry on as we are.'

And he asked her to pass the butter.

That was Dad all over: as long as it affected him in the most minimal way possible, he was all right. Essentially if he was all right, everything was all right – stuff the rest of us. He wanted to be able to just continue with his own merry life, or what he thought he could get away with, drinking in the boozer, working to pay for it and getting looked after by everyone else. Why rock the boat when it was one that kept him perfectly afloat (and his beer cold)?

Mum also told Gerry she was having his baby. He, having chosen to be with his divorced woman, told her he'd chip in financially for the little blighter. Except Mum was a proud woman and refused. Well, he set up a bank account and put money in every month, but after taking about a tenner out of it, Mum decided to put her pride first.

'If you don't want me or our baby, then I don't want your filthy money,' she snapped. And so Gerry disappeared and I arrived, becoming the apple of my mum's and my grandad's eyes.

Fast-forward ten years and Mum was out with Margo one evening at their local when Gerry walked in. He was working for a loan club at the time, giving punters the chance to put a few bob aside every week for a big pay-off at Christmas. For many hard-up people with no bank account it was their only chance of saving. Gobsmacked at Mum meeting Gerry again, Margo disappeared and left the two to speak.

'How are you?' Mum found herself saying. Gerry smiled and straight away the pair knew the spark was still there. By now Gerry had split with his divorced woman and he asked for Mum's number. A new friendship kicked off between them and the rest became history.

When she settled in Sydenham, overnight Mum seemed to morph into the posh genteel girl she once was from Wimbledon. After all, now she was with Gerry, who was as middle class as they come, she didn't have to keep up with the Peckham twang any longer.

Adapting to a new home can be tricky anyway, but seeing your mum switch identity too was unsettling, to say the least.

One evening, as she was wiping up after dinner, I wondered what was for afters.

'Whatcha got for pudding?' I asked.

Mum didn't reply straight away. Instead she turned to look at me, throwing the tea towel down on the side. We had colour-coordinated tea towels now.

'Gerry asked why your speech is so bad,' she said.

It felt as though she'd punched me in the guts. 'Well, you didn't say anything about it while we were in Nunhead, Mum,' I said sadly.

'Well, now you need to make more of an effort,' she continued.

Before I could snatch them back, angry words poured out my mouth. 'Just a month ago, you were a Peckham tart like all the rest of them, Mum!' I yelled.

And yep, I probably deserved it: Mum went up like a bomb. I went and hid in my room to wait for the storm to die down.

Later that evening, I watched as she tutted, busying herself in the kitchen, tidying away the plates in the neat kitchen cupboards. I stood there feeling like a dirty plate she couldn't put away. I loved my mum, but suddenly I realised she was a strong character – she'd had to be, it's what'd kept her going – but at the same time I couldn't be managed and controlled like a child any more. I had my own money, a circle of friends and an identity, and not only were they not part of the Sydenham world, but they actually clashed with it. Now even the way I spoke naturally didn't fit in. With each dig, my aspirations to a middle-class life soon vanished.

To top it off, it was a much longer journey from Sydenham to school in Blackfriars, which didn't make turning up any easier.

I started doing more shifts at the Festival Hall; after all, I longed to be out more than ever now. Being with the lads, earning dosh, listening to music, drinking lager, chatting up girls – life outside my family was on the up. Then things got even better. I met Tracy.

I was out with the lads one night to watch the Lambrettas' gig somewhere in north London, when one beautiful blonde landed right on my lap – well, at my elbow. She smiled. I smiled and offered her a drink.

Tracy was absolutely beautiful, very clever, doing lots of O-levels, unlike the dropout I was, and a bit older. All the ingredients to set the pulses of most fifteen-year-olds racing. She lived with her sister and mum in the upstairs of a big house near Clapton Pond in Hackney. The top deck of the 38 bus to and from there became my second home, Tracy's being my first. I loved going there. I also fancied Tracy's mum, who was an older version of her, all wide hips, round bum and brassy blonde. We went to concerts together, to the cinema, we hit the all-you-can-eat salad bar in Pizza Hut and her mum let me stay there overnight. We went to mod pubs, drank lager, danced a lot. I fell in love.

Until Andrea came along. I bumped into her at the Festival Hall when Allan brought her along as his date. Instantly there was an attraction and although Allan had her first he seemed to be fine with us making a play for each other – the attraction was that instant. Another mod (of course), she was the opposite of Tracy. Dark and fiery, with curly brown hair and brown eyes, she spoke at a million miles an hour and was a whirlwind of passion.

She came back for a drink one night to Ivydale when my

dad was out, and we ended up getting it on. Can't say Allan was best pleased but it was obvious she liked me more than him. I told Tracy over the phone the next day.

Andrea was just so hot, and she was very experienced too. On another occasion she took me by the hand and led me to my old bedroom in Ivydale.

'You're gorgeous,' she breathed into my ear, before grabbing my hand and guiding it to places a boy of my age could only dream of. I'd never gone 'all the way', as Tracy and I had still been building up to that. Suddenly, caught up in Andrea's whirlwind, I found myself faced with imminent virginity loss. And I didn't have a clue what to do. Well, within reason. Afterwards, I woke up, my face in her curls, feeling as though I'd died and gone to heaven.

Andrea, though, being a woman of the world, didn't linger too long with anyone and that included me. Within a few months it was over. She dumped me from a payphone on the Ferrier estate in Kidbrooke, where she lived.

'Sorry, Gregg, it's not gonna happen between us,' she said. 'Bye.'

She hung up, but I dialled 1471 and called her back. I let it ring and ring until the pips went. Then I returned the receiver to the cradle and wrote her a letter.

'Andrea, you are one of the most beautiful women I've ever met,' I scrawled with all the poetic licence I could muster. I can't quite remember the rest, but I was sure she'd be in no doubt as to how I felt. I sent it but got no reply. A couple of years later I bumped into Andrea and she told me how she'd walked away guiltily, the phone ringing in her ears. And how she'd shown her best mate my letter at school and her friend had cried. 'She called me a rotten bitch for ditching you like that,' Andrea said, smiling wryly.

Being a bit of a cheeky sod I chanced my arm with Tracy again a few weeks later.

'I'm sorry, babe,' I sobbed. 'It's all been a massive cock-up.'

She took pity and after a very apologetic start, she took me back and that was us for the next five years.

CHAPTER 12

Bubble and Squeak

*N*ow while I had all the diversions of new romances and girls and home life going on, I was still dealing with the tedium of school, albeit not very often.

The most fearsome teacher at school was a nasty piece of work. He was overweight with a face that reminded me of a twisted piece of Spam, his piggy deep-set eyes constantly darting around looking for some lad's minor misdemeanour for him to lose his rag at. He regularly slapped boys around the face and took great pleasure in pulling their hair or ears too, stretching them like pieces of dough.

My fingers often twitched to give him a taste of his own medicine but it was more than my life was worth to do so. Anyway, one time, I was in school and waiting for my lunch, standing in the queue, thinking again how ridiculously unfair this alphabetical system was, when the guy behind me shoved me a bit. I was pushing him back again – 'I'm already a W,' I said, laughing, 'have some sympathy!' – when he spotted me.

He marched over, pushing boys out of his way and making a beeline for the troublemaker: me.

His hard little features were set in stone as he approached, raising his hands to make a grab for me, but something inside me snapped. I wasn't prepared to put up with the sort of humiliation other boys endured. Instantly I raised my fists to his face, inches away from me.

'Come on, then,' I chided. 'Come on, you touch me, and I'll punch you so hard.'

The veins on his fat neck bulged in sync with his eyeballs, as his cheeks flushed a beetroot colour. For a split second I could almost see his thought bubble as he weighed up beating me to a pulp, something I knew he'd take immense pleasure in doing. But he couldn't. He could slap us around but he couldn't fight us.

'Wallace,' he screamed, spittle flying from his nasty gob. 'Get. Out! To the deputy's office *now*.'

I didn't need asking twice, as everyone in the dinner queue parted like the Red Sea.

Once again I found myself standing in the deputy head's office, watching his mouth moving fast as he spewed fire and brimstone at me. By now, I felt so awful that I couldn't bear to hear anything else about myself, so I just switched off, mute, and stood nodding vaguely like a broken Action Man.

It wasn't the first time I'd found myself there and it wasn't the first time we'd had this conversation. In all fairness to him, he did try to talk some sense into me one last time. He asked me to turn out my pockets once and I had condoms, he asked me what I was doing with them and I told him I had a girlfriend. He congratulated me on my common sense and gave them back to me. He was a decent man, fighting a losing battle against an increasingly unruly teenager.

I left, the gist of the conversation having been that I wasn't to stain the solid record of the school with an expulsion to my name, but I wasn't welcome back either.

I grabbed my blazer and slung it over my arm and ran quickly out of the school, fingering the now dull brass jacket buttons on the bus home, thinking how different I'd felt about the jacket when I'd first started the school just three years earlier. I didn't recognise that boy, so excited by it back then. My whole body felt dog-tired by the time I'd got in. I wanted to cry but no tears came. Just a numb emptiness, really. I'd messed up big time and knew of no way back now.

Back home I found Mum canoodling on the sofa with Gerry, looking like love's young dream, and not wanting to burst her bubble I said nothing. Also there seemed to be nothing to say. I mean, had anyone even noticed I'd come in?

I'd started to avoid Gerry too. Our honeymoon period had well and truly worn off. The more I got to know the man the more I thought he was a cold fish. I mean, we were father and son, and of course should have been getting to know each other. He was generous, he was nice, but I didn't feel he made enough effort with me aside from the occasional game of backgammon. He used to love telling me his opinions, though.

Meanwhile my opinion of him had changed. I thought he was a raving snob and Mum, bless her, had quickly turned into one as well, shunning some of the old pals in Peckham and having a slightly superior attitude. Sorry, Mum! I think she has made a lot of mistakes as a parent but now that I am a father, I really appreciate how tough it must've been for her.

Anyway, once Gerry spotted her knickers hanging on the

line, all laddered around the edges. 'Are they designed like that or are they just old?' Gerry asked quizzically. Mum told me afterwards that she felt so embarrassed and started to wonder exactly how the hell she'd been living for the past fifteen years. He had also bought the pair of them matching his and hers Fiats, in yellow and red.

Yep, Mum had moved up in the world and had well and truly turned her back on a life of scrimping in Kincaid Road. But Peckham was a world I still felt part of. She was not only looking down on her old life, but on her son too.

By now Dad had bought out Mum's half of the flat in Nunhead, but because it was his wife who'd held his life together, it was rapidly unravelling at speed now. He became a raving drunk, staying out till all hours, finding himself unable to cook or go to work. He soon took redundancy, and started spending more and more time at Kincaid Road, where I'd see him, sitting there, watching TV like a little boy as Nan cooked him a plate of mince.

The first time I dropped in on Grandad since finding out Gerry was my dad, I found myself deep in thought. Dad had known all along I wasn't his but never mentioned it to anyone. Mum explained he didn't want anyone to know, as it would upset the apple cart – well, his drinking cart. His embarrassment overrode any sense of anger he might've had. And I suppose Mum gave me Dad's name as my middle name to keep the peace. With regards to Grandad, I felt genuine sorrow that I wasn't his blood, but only for a few minutes. He was always Grandad to me, more of a dad even, and I loved him dearly and he did me. No, genes don't matter.

One evening, I was out late, so spent the night at Nunhead. Dad wasn't there, so it was quite peaceful. I made myself a fish finger sandwich – a few frozen boxes were still left over from when Mum had been there – and I settled down in front of *Match of the Day*. I called Mum to tell her where I was – something I didn't bother doing much then.

'You're where?'

'Ivydale Road,' I said.

'Oh. With your dad?'

'No, he's at Grandad's.'

'Oh. Right. Well, we'll see you when we see you, then.'

I put down the phone and carried on eating, swallowing the feeling that Mum seemed a bit too tied up now to worry where I was. She did pop over a few days later, though, with a bag of shopping from Sainsbury's.

'Vesta meals were on offer,' she said, beaming, and put them out on the sideboard. 'Remember not to leave the oven on with them in, though.'

Grandad started coming over more often too. He'd just pop in and do some washing-up or bring me round a few tins of veg or beans, or something to 'fill yer boots with'.

Once he popped in after lunch and I was still in bed with Tracy.

'Whatcha doing in bed at this time for?' he asked, as I emerged, hair ruffled, from my bedroom.

'Oh, um, I am just having half an hour, Grandad. I've, er, got Tracy here.'

He looked a bit startled and then gave a little grin. 'Well, you'd better get yourself back in there for an extra half-hour, then,' he said with a wink.

Now I found myself living alone at 15 and, needing money, I soon turned to my mate Allan for help.

'We can sort out some extra dosh at the Hall,' he said with a grin.

We started working part of the time upstairs in the bars when there was a big show on. The bar area was split into two, alcohol one side, coffee and tea on the other side. We, of course, were under age, so we stuck to the coffees and teas.

We took orders at the bar for intervals, filled up the cups and took the cash. All fine and dandy, except we also had to clear up the cups afterwards, so none of the management knew how many were being sold. So we cheerfully served the customers, pocketing some of the cash for our own self-serve bonus. One pound in every ten. Nobody noticed.

Did I feel bad about this? Not really. I knew it wasn't coming out of the staff's pockets, and I was desperate. It was a case of do it or don't eat much that week.

I saw Frank Sinatra perform live when I was there. What about that? I can't pretend I was his biggest fan, but there was a perceptible buzz around the building on the night. People were all chatting excitedly and every time a side door opened people were peering around it to see if they could catch a glimpse of the great man. During the performance one of the boxes was empty, so Allan and I sneaked in and watched a few numbers. He was an old man by then, sixty-four, quite wizened-looking but still dapper in a blue pinstriped suit and a hat sitting at a jaunty angle. His voice was steely, unwavering, and filled the room, with the orchestra powering below him. Such a powerful presence on stage, and what a performer: even we mods were impressed.

Allan's next trick was even more lucrative. My eyes widened like a couple of saucers when he told me. This was something a little more serious than pinching a few quid.

'This is what we do,' Allan explained, hunched over a coffee at the end of a shift. 'You know how we take out the rubbish at the end of the night on the big wire cages on wheels?'

'Uh-huh.'

'Well, we just need to raid the stock cupboard a little –

y'know, take a few bits like biscuits, tea bags, that sort of thing – and while we take the cages to the compressor bins we can hide the catering packs in the bushes around the South Bank. Then sell 'em on to cafés. Whaddya reckon?'

I stared into my coffee. I thought of Mum and Grandad. What would they think? But at the same time where were they? I thought of my fridge with nothing in it. I thought of the new shoes I needed. The clothes I wanted, to feel as if I fitted in.

'How will we get the gear afterwards?' I asked.

'Easy,' said Allan, leaning back in his chair, his hands folded behind his head. 'We get up dead early, take the bus into town and go get it, then sell it on to cafés in Waterloo. Aw, c'mon, Gregg, you know it's a winner.'

I swallowed hard. My mind was reeling a bit. I mean, what if someone grassed us up? What if an eagle-eyed café owner recognised that the packets of stuff came from the Festival Hall? Unlikely, but still . . .

Allan was giving me a wry smile now, looking at me intently, leaning forward, elbows on the table.

'Lads back to work,' a manager yelled, as Allan raised an eyebrow expectantly.

'Well? Gregg?' he urged, as the other lads scraped their chairs back to get back to finish up for the night. 'You in or what?'

I shook any worries from my mind and just nodded. As Allan punched my arm with approval, I felt slightly shell-shocked. From grammar-school boy to criminal in the blink of an eye. It was as easy and as sad as that.

The first few times we did it, I can't say I felt relaxed. We shuttled the big wire cage, with the rubbish in, chucked out half the wrappers and empty cartons, and then whipped in and out of that stockroom like a pair of, er, whippets. We'd place the large bags of biscuits, tea and whatever else we could lay our hands on, and pile the rubbish on top and down the sides.

Then we pushed the cage past some bushes by the river and with me as the look-out, Allan dumped it in there, theatrically wiping his hands afterwards.

'Job done,' he said, winking, and whistling as we started wheeling the cage back. I didn't show it, but my heart was thumping a bit. Could it really be that easy?

The next day we were up at the crack of dawn and on that number 63 bus going back to Waterloo, with a holdall in which to stow our goods. Allan fished it out of the bush and zipped up it up.

'Now let's go make some money,' he said.

We wandered down the streets, sticking our heads into cafés, all the greasy spoons mainly, and within a few seconds could gauge if the owner's head could be turned by our loot. Most of them were happy, nodding or winking at us to go round the back of the shop area behind the till. They saw us as nothing more than a mobile cash 'n' carry, and were happy to peel off a few tenners for stock they'd have to fork out a whole lot more for otherwise. By the end of the week, our salary had doubled. Not bad going when you're fifteen and supposedly still at school.

While we weren't out working legitimately (and illegitimately) we were still going to gigs all the time, keeping in with the mods we prided ourselves on being. All this excitement and to-ing and fro-ing with girls and dodgy jobs and whatnot did take its toll. I suppose I craved something. Love? Stability? Security? I don't know. I do know Grandad was there, though, throughout all the madness. I'd knock at Kincaid Road, and he'd be standing there with a smile and a nod, telling me to get in quick.

'You need any money, boy?' he'd ask, as he knocked me up something to eat.

Usually he'd crank open a tin of Heinz Big Soup. Lamb was my favourite – I used to drown the soup in mint sauce as well. I was quite partial to the chicken flavour too. He'd also pop a couple of slices of Mother's Pride under the grill. Then, whipping them out quick, he'd slather them with as much butter as was almost decent.

'You like toast with your butter?' Nan'd quip.

Sometimes it would be something easily chopped and fried, like sausages, bacon, tomatoes, bubble and squeak. He used to fry everything all together in one pan, the beans, the toast, the sausages all mixed in one lot, sizzling in the pan. Not something you'd serve up and pay for, but all went down the same hole as far as he was concerned, and the fact it was my grandad frying it made it taste good somehow.

I'd usually scoff the lot within a few minutes, as Grandad watched, his eagle eye telling me he knew something wasn't right, but I knew he'd wait until I told him. Which I never did. After all, I didn't want to worry him. Or worse, make him feel that he'd failed.

So everything was always good. Always grand, always fine. He always offered me the same advice, advice he'd given me since the days I lived with him.

'Money speaks all languages, boy. Told you that before. Don't matter who you are. Gotta pay your bills, get ya card stamped.'

The card, of course, referred to the National Insurance cards that you used to have to get stamped. I tried to explain that they didn't have those now but I got the same advice anyway.

After the soup, he'd pour me a cup of very sweet tea, set the chocolate doings down, or offer me an array of chocolates or toffees or anything he'd picked up from the market and thought I might like. Bless him, I never took him for granted, especially not then, when I needed someone there for me.

CHAPTER 13

Shepherd's Pie

*I*t never really sank in that I'd properly left school, even though that summer while my old classmates would've been doing their O-levels I was just working hard at the Royal Festival Hall, carrying on with outside work with Allan and living in Ivydale on my tod or staying at Tracy's.

I lived off fried egg sandwiches, fried bread and tinned soup. Tracy was a vegetarian – very cutting edge in those days – and lived off tomatoes sliced neatly on toast when she stayed over.

'It's delicious, Gregg,' she'd say between mouthfuls. 'You should try it.'

'You're all right, darlin', might pass on that.' Toast needs butter and lots of it with some tinned sausage and beans on top. Soft food, you don't even need to chew – can't beat it sometimes. I also loved Heinz Toast Toppers: they looked disgusting, like sick really, but I loved the chicken and mushroom or mushroom and bacon ones. Soft, salty, wet, easy.

Tracy's mum used to cook for us both if we turned up at the right time. Decent home-cooked grub like shepherd's pie, with properly beaten fluffy mash and dripping in gravy. I'd clear my plate till you could see my face in it, something about that reminding me of Nan W's.

Aside from that I lived off takeaways: a Big Mac and large fries, a doner kebab, or chicken chop suey, sweet and sour prawn balls and fried rice – the mutt's nuts (a derivative of the dog's bollocks, in case you're wondering). I have to say, it never fails to surprise people that I, a restaurateur, someone who makes a living from food, grew up eating bad, convenience food. I rarely had a decent meal, a proper, home-cooked affair, except from when I was at Nan W's or at a friend's house. But by now, although I loved my grandparents, like most teens I was seeing them less. I was too busy just trying to make money and being with my girl.

Grandad W had fallen ill and had had a couple of heart attacks by now and he'd had a cancerous growth on his lip. I visited him in hospital. He had always been a big man, but now his collarbone was visible above his hospital gown.

'You all right, boy?' he asked, when he woke up. He reminded me of a turtle coming out of his shell, a haunting image.

I nodded. I didn't want to tell him about school. Grandad W had won a scholarship to high school back in the day but couldn't go, as his mum couldn't afford the bus fare in. So he stayed at the village school, helping the teacher, until he joined the navy.

Later on he'd said to Mum: 'I just don't get it. I'd always wanted a good education and never got the chance. Gregg had the opportunity but threw it away. Why?'

For his final few days Grandad went down to Somerset,

where Hazel now lived. I think he knew he was dying and asked to go down so Nan W wouldn't have to deal with it alone. One morning Nan W went downstairs to make him a cup of tea and he had passed away by the time she came back.

When he died Nan gave me his ring, the one from Gregg the farmer in the Falklands. Grandad W had been such a big man that it'd fitted on his little finger but it only fitted on my middle one. It's a lovely smooth pink gold ring, and I've never taken it off since. I wish Grandad W had seen me succeed in the end. He always seemed to know I had it in me, though, bless him. It wasn't until I wrote this book that I realised just how much I loved and admired him.

And so life went on. A young lad, no qualifications, working in a dodgy job, living alone, but with as much energy and drive as a steam train. I wanted to do something, go somewhere, but had no idea how or where.

Then one day, as Allan and I pushed our rubbish cage to the store cupboard, we went to pull the cupboard open and it didn't move.

'Shit, someone has locked it,' cursed Allan, giving it a kick. 'We'll have to come back when it's open.'

I was starting to feel very uncomfortable about what we were doing. Someone was on to us. It wasn't long before our days of pilfering the store cupboard stopped.

Around this time, I found myself in a pub, the Havelock Arms, and bumped into Dad, who bought me a pint. For my birthday that year he came home and gave me a fiver explaining it was all he had. No wonder after spending the whole day in the pub. But, despite everything, I suppose he was still Dad. Probably more so than Gerry, even though neither of them matched up much. I watched him as he downed half a pint of his light ale and bitter in one single gulp. He just opened his throat like a snake swallowing an egg and poured it into his stomach. As if it was less of a drink and more medicinal. Wiping his mouth with the back of his hand, he made a satisfying 'ah' noise.

'So what you up to, then, Gregg?'

'Just still working at Festival Hall,' I grumbled. 'It's not going anywhere, though.'

Dad looked into the middle distance. Actually while I got a bit drunker, I started to enjoy his company a little. He was all right as a drunkard, cheerful, liked to talk about history and politics and could crack a joke. Here I was, aged seventeen now, getting to know my dad for the first time, but we could only do it by propping up a bar half-cut.

'Actually, Gregg, I know someone who knows someone who knows someone who needs a hand in their dry cleaner's. Would that do for you?'

'Yes please.'

The dry cleaner's was on Friary Road, the same road as my old primary school. It was a popular place, with condensation permanently streaming down the front windows.

The man who ran it, Allan, was a slim, trendy-looking chap who drove an Escort van, and wore silk shirts and a gold chain around his neck. He was a nice guy who tried to teach me the finer points of dry cleaning.

'Right,' he said, heaving a pile of trousers into my arms. 'I'll introduce you to the Hoffman pressing machine.'

From then on, I stood there, eight hours a day, pressing whatever simple pieces of clothing, like straight skirts or trousers, he thought I could manage.

Although I was a grafter, he was fighting a losing battle, as I'm pretty hamfisted when it comes to hand–eye coordination, but I did my best and he could see that.

It was sweaty, boring work, but I was allowed the radio on, and so I worked to the songs of any soul music I could lay my hands on. By the end of my first shift I knew all the lyrics to 'Going Underground' by the Jam. I loved the song 'I'm One' by Quadrophenia too. The lyrics just seemed to sum up my life at the time.

I'd switch off, and end up in my own dream world, a fug of steam rising around me, fuelling the fantasy mode I'd started to exist in.

One day, in bed with Tracy, aged seventeen, I woke to face another day of dry cleaning when it all hit me at once. I was totally skint, had no prospects, and had royally messed up my life so far. I had drive, dreams, but also now a lot of frustration and anger. I wanted things, like a nice place to live, a car, clothes and money. Throughout my early years at school I'd been recognised as one of the 'bright boys' but now I was stuck in a dead-end job, doing something I hated. Even failing at the London Nautical School wasn't as bad as this, because then I was earning decent money for a fifteen-year-old.

Around this time Tracy had a chance to go to university. A clever girl, she'd got six O-levels and a couple of A-levels. The world was her lobster, as I told her a few times. But she came home from school one day and shook her head.

'I'm not going, Gregg,' she said. 'I've turned it down.'

'You what?' I asked.

'I don't want to go. I don't want to leave you,' she said.

I didn't argue with her; perhaps I should've done, but she was a clever girl and it was her decision.

I was too busy stewing over my own situation, I suppose. I was desperate to move on in the world. I couldn't go back to school again to get my exams, as I had bills to pay, but I longed to be promoted, get noticed, move up the ladder. How, though? The chance had cropped up earlier to do an apprentice exam to be an electrician but I failed miserably: the maths might as well have been double Dutch and I didn't have a clue. On the way out, though, I saw another geezer in a windcheater jacket, Sta Press trousers and Chelsea boots – the uniform of a mod – and we got talking. His name was Chris and we hung out for a bit; and through Chris I met Miguel.

Now Miguel was a short, very shy, introverted guy, but for one reason or another we clicked. Miguel was doing well as a courier for a fur company. He walked around London, with a suitcase, delivering furs to shops at trade price. It was a business that'd never work today but this was the early 1980s and people wanted to walk round with their money showing on their backs then.

I liked Miguel as well for his spirit, but I also felt inadequate again. I mean, he had more than me, just like everyone else, it seemed.

But being around lads my age getting their life together gave me the incentive to do the same. I decided to try to do something different. So chatting to Andrew Dyne and his mum one day, I decided to give a mobile dry cleaning business a go. The plan was to print off flyers, deliver these through the doors to homes, offering to pick up and deliver people's clothes. Good old Maggie Dyne helped me type up the leaflets, and I dropped them around the Rye Lane estate, the same estate on which Mandela House in *Only Fools and Horses* was based. John Sullivan, who came up with the comedy, was a genius and obviously based Del Boy et al. on the real people of Peckham. Those characters, like Margo's husband Peter, really did exist, God love them. He didn't make any of it up.

I also found another side trade in the clothes people left

behind at the dry cleaner's. A big pile was out the back.

'The way it works,' explained Allan, 'is that if people leave them here, after a year we can sell them but only for the price of the cleaning ticket.' Strange rules, eh! I sold a few and then just bagged the best of the rest, pieces of clothing like new Ben Sherman shirts, and saved myself some money.

So, here I am, earning a bit extra, using it to pay my bills and buy a few records, but that's all it amounted to.

Around this time, I was visiting Mum and Gerry when Gerry's mate rolled up in a brand-new Porsche car. The alloy wheels shone like plates, and it glided almost soundlessly up our road, looking like a four-wheeled goddess.

'Wow!' I said, my eyes nearly rolling out on to the tarmac with it. 'Who is that?'

'My old mate Nick,' Gerry said, with a smirk.

He went outside and the pair shook hands, laughing with the banter of old friends. Nick emerged from his car with a flourish, and I just thought it was amazing what a car like that could do – its aura.

Gerry introduced us, and Nick showed us around this beauty, all smooth and polished with leather inside.

'Take a look at this,' Nick said. Grinning, he reached inside and pulled out a phone handset. 'It's even got its own phone.'

I watched as Gerry's mouth fell open further. This was car porn at its best and it was on our road.

As Nick roared off, opening up the clutch a little as he turned the corner and disappeared, I suddenly had so many questions.

'Gerry,' I asked, 'how do people make that much money? I mean, how – *how* do they do it?' I felt desperate to know. As though it was a secret world I could only look into. It was 1981, and life was changing: people had money and lots of it.

My life was going nowhere, and every now and then I'd see someone doing so well, it bored another hole into my already poor self-esteem.

I managed to persuade Dad in the pub one day to help me buy a Vespa so that I could join in with the lads. He was guarantor for it, thanks to his redundancy. As I say, Dad was a decent bloke if I caught him in the pub with a few drinks inside him. We began quite regularly having a few pints together, as I started to get more of a buzz from drinking too.

The pub would give away free shellfish to encourage people to come in on Sundays, much to my delight. Polystyrene trays of glistening, fresh cockles, whelks, mussels, prawns and crabsticks appeared at midday, and did a roaring trade. I've always loved seafood. Cockles are my favourite: their smell and taste are a gift of Neptune, with malt vinegar for the acidity and enough pepper to make you sneeze. Might have to slip another joke in here: 'A randy lobster went to an underwater disco and pulled a mussel.'

It was over a squeaky polystyrene cup of cockles that Dad opened up his heart about his marriage once. Stabbing a little blue plastic fork in, he pulled a face as the vinegar took hold, or was it thinking of Mum? I don't know. But anyway, once the drink took hold, he couldn't stop talking about her.

'The thing your mum can't take away is the memories,' he said sadly, studying the speared cockle as he spoke. 'I mean, I did have affairs too. Once I was shagging some bird I met in the pub and she took me back to another house one day and before we got down to it, I heard a little cry and saw a baby in the corner in a Moses basket, waking up, and I thought: nah, not with a nipper here, and I legged it. You were only a baby then, Gregg. I realised it weren't right.'

Thanks for that Dad. Nice memories.

I was a bit tipsy by then too, so even though I didn't want to hear such anecdotes, I suppose I didn't see any harm in listening to the man. He obviously needed someone to sound off to. Afterwards I'd sometimes go home with him to see Grandad. Stirring in his tea, one day, after spooning in three sugars, Grandad mulled over my brewing excitement about money and jobs and my ambition.

'But, Grandad, I know I'm working but I just want to work out ways of earning more. It can be possible, can't it?'

He ummed and ahhed, listening to me prattling on as if I was talking a different language.

'Listen, boy,' he said finally, looking me in the eye, 'you're paying your bills. You have food on your table. You have a roof over your head. That, in life, really is enough.'

I stared at him. This was a man I'd looked up to all my life and I suddenly realised it had been enough for him. He had achieved what he needed and was satisfied with that. Grandad was a rich man really; he didn't hanker after anything more. I wished it could be the same for me. Yet it wasn't. I wanted more. I didn't feel bad about it; I just knew a hunger was emerging within me, and I needed to work out what would satiate it.

CHAPTER 14

Sticky Iced Buns

One thing I never ever discussed with Grandad, or indeed my nan or my grandparents in Wimbledon, was the fact that I wasn't Allan's biological son. Nobody needed to tell me not to. Now, it hurts a bit to think I wasn't Grandad Peckham's biological grandson, especially as Mum reckons it would've changed his feelings towards me when I was little. But, you know, it didn't and doesn't matter, as we loved each other deeply anyway. What good would it've done to discuss it? It was the unsaid family secret, a skeleton we'd never dig up.

Grandad'd been unhappily married now for over fifty years. He believed that piece of paper was for life, he'd stuck at it and he could not for the life of him see why Mum hadn't. I mentioned her once at his house and his face changed, so I knew not to do so again. Shame, as they'd really liked one another, but Grandad's loyalty to his son knew no bounds. Plus around this time he had other things

146

on his mind, as Nan's leg had been causing a lot of gyp.

'It aches,' she moaned, rubbing her varicose veins. Now Nan, bless her, always had to moan about something, so we all just told her to sit down and brought her tea, but after a trip to the doctor's, she had to go to hospital and we realised it was serious. Then she had an op to remove her leg because of gangrene.

Poor Nan was now laid up, so that meant poor Grandad was too. He'd be at her beck and call even more now. Still, I bombed round there when I could, on my new Vespa. I had a barney with Mum about that too.

'You need to make sure you've got insurance,' she said.

''S'OK,' I replied. 'I'll be fine.'

'What do you mean?' she cried. 'You need insurance, Gregg. You're no different to anyone else.'

I did what I was told, although I walked away with a flea in my ear from Mum. I think it was less about trying to get away with not having insurance and more about not knowing how things worked, as I didn't have anyone around telling me.

'You think the rules don't apply to you,' she said with a sigh, stating it as fact.

One afternoon, I found myself going round to Nan W's for tea with Gerry and Mum, on a rare visit. Biffo came with us. He made me laugh. He loved his food, did Biff, and eating was definitely his favourite pastime. He had me in hysterics once when he ate a bag of salt 'n' vinegar Golden Wonder crisps so fast that he bit his own fingers and started bawling.

On this particular trip, he started to feel sick in the car.

'Not long now, Biff,' Mum soothed, rapidly winding down her window for fresh air. 'Just hold it in for a few more minutes.'

But it was too late. Biff's face turned a shade of pea soup

and he gagged, throwing up into the foot well.

'Aw, Biff!' Gerry cried.

'It stinks!' I said, shrinking in my seat.

'Sorry,' he said afterwards, grinning. 'I guess I'll have more room for Nan's roast tatties now, won't I? Yum yum!'

I couldn't help but laugh again.

Later Nan W told us how a distant relative had been to visit her after some family bust-up.

'They're looking for their dad,' she said, slicing up the Battenberg.

'Well, here is a good place to start,' I said, laughing and giving Gerry a sideways glance as his face reddened and I muffled a snigger with the sleeve of my jumper. If only she knew. What a pickle our family were in.

The dry cleaning was doing OK, but after I complained yet again to Mum and Gerry about where my life was heading, Gerry decided to step in and help for once.

'You looking for work, Gregg? Well, if you're serious about it I can find you some,' he said, an eyebrow arched.

Mum's new husband, now my stepdad as well as my biological father, was the company secretary of a firm in Bermondsey called Performance Chemicals.

'Why don't you just stop all the dry cleaning nonsense and come and work for us instead?' he said. 'It pays well at least.'

Well, what could I say? I was about to turn my back on the world of dry cleaning, with all its steam, heat and hangers, and embrace the world of grime, filth and stench of chemicals, but it was extra money, so what did I care?

Performance Chemicals, off Verney Road, Bermondsey, was part of a small old industrial estate that made all sorts, from chemicals for floor cleaner to chemicals that made cement set under water. Its offices were in a two-storey brick building; the factory bit was behind, and basically split in half between wet and dry works, wet being the liquid and dry being the powder, for those newbies in the chemical world, one of which I was then. Behind this was a yard full of drums – big oil drums. Behind this was our locker and tea room, and to the right of this a ramshackle 'packing' shed.

Despite the extra dough, the work was very boring and unskilled. My self-worth was on the floor with all the bits of plastic containers I spent all day long filling up. There was a revolving door as far as staff were concerned, the freezing conditions in winter, and general dirt and muck, being enough to put off the most hardened work horse.

Gerry, being the company secretary, had the ear of the owner, Brian, a chap who was a decent sort, and sported a moustache, which he smoothed down while he was deep in thought, overseeing how things were ticking over. He was actually all right as they go, but Peter Scully, the foreman, was a bitch to work for, always nagging us about timekeeping. You'd think we'd threatened a strike if we took so much as a few minutes longer over lunch.

'You're here to work, not to eat/slurp tea/stand around,' he'd snap.

Not that I did much standing around, eager-to-please pup that I was.

Maybe more eager to please than my work colleagues, who included a chemist, a hippy sort who I'm sure wasn't immune to making up his own chemical 'concoctions'; Gary, a tall young lad who had less fat on him than a chip; and his brother Doug, who was the receptionist, and who was blind.

Doug only had to answer the phone, though, which he could do, as long as nobody moved it out of reach. And he could hear footsteps when people walked in right enough. I liked him the best; he had a good sense of humour.

One morning I was a little late and asked if Gary had already arrived.

'Which Gary?' asked Doug.

'Tall Gary,' I said.

'That's not a lot of good to me, Gregg,' he said, laughing. 'How would I know what size he is?'

Like automatons we clocked in and out, with a mid-morning tea break, lunch break and afternoon tea. The tea breaks were so welcome: when you're cold and your work is so tedious, the idea of a steaming mug of sweet tea, and a toasted cheese and pickle sarnie eaten while you are sunk in a bashed-up armchair in a paraffin-heated shed, was Shangri-La.

Can't remember the old dear who helped us with lunch, but she constantly had an Embassy hanging from the corner of her lips, something we turned a blind eye to as she toasted our sandwiches, dropping ash everywhere.

Often I'd nip to the local bakery and bring back the same thing every time. A Cornish pasty, with some sort of peppery, potato-y meaty filling and soggy flaky pastry, or a steak and kidney pie, or a cheese and onion sandwich, a bag of salt 'n' vinegar or prawn cocktail crisps (why they messed with the colours, changing blue to cheese and onion and green to salt 'n' vinegar, I'll never know – that still gets me today), all washed down with a can of Pepsi. And it always had to be Pepsi, as it has a more rounded flavour, though apparently Pepsi puts more sugar in than Coca-Cola, so that had something to do with it.

We'd sit, knackered even after just a couple of hours of shovelling, and chat. Gary and Peter were always competing for telling 'tall stories' and they just got laughable. I suppose in a job like that, hard graft with little reward, it was human nature to beef up elements of your life.

Gary stated his friend had a Rottweiler that weighed two tonnes.

'Get out of here,' cried Peter, laughing. I couldn't believe that some of the guys took this stuff seriously. Another claimed he possessed an original antique colour TV. My favourite story was from a fella who swore black and blue it was true.

'I was just driving around minding my own business in my Cortina when the police started tailing me,' he said, taking a bite from his sarnie. 'And, I thought: sod this for a game of soldiers. So I put me foot down. The next thing I know I am hitting an icy canal bridge, at speed, and am takin' off in the air.'

'Whoa, really!' cried Peter.

Again I couldn't believe the other lads were swallowing this rubbish, but I listened and laughed anyway.

'And then I landed on top of a stack of cars in a south-east London scrapyard . . .'

Peter's eyes widened further. 'No way!'

'And as I sat there, stunned, still in my driver's seat, I saw the owner of the scrapyard step out of his caravan. He looked up at me, and said: "Sorry, mate, we're closed."'

And on that note, our tea room dissolved into laughter. Not all the lads were as mental as this. One guy, Paul Bradley, was a friendly, happy-looking boy about a year older than me, with black and orange dyed hair that came down in a floppy fringe over one eye. He was a 'New Romantic' and always singing songs from bands I'd never heard of at the time – Adam and the Ants and Culture Club. We got chatting and went drinking. As we grew closer, Paul started confiding in me about his life and the darker side.

Over a pint one day, he started telling me about his amazing record collection and I couldn't contain my envy.

'How can you afford all that?' I asked. 'On the wages we're on?' £18 a week seriously didn't go far.

Beckoning me with his hand to come closer, he lowered his voice. 'I ain't proud of this,' he said, 'but occasionally myself and my mates go and stay in a caravan park near one of the more expensive villages in Kent or thereabouts. Thing is, Gregg, you never ever walk down the street looking like a burglar; you put on your smartest suit and shoes and walk with your head held high. Then on a nice day you look for the idiots who leave their windows open. It takes five minutes: in, upstairs to the bedroom to the drawers for the jewellery, and the kitchen for the handbag . . .'

I sipped some more beer, taking it all in. Of course I'd grown up in Peckham, where people got 'a bit of bunce' for things that weren't being used by anyone else. Margo's brother and brother-in-law had done time inside for counterfeiting ... But this – well, this was off the scale.

'Oh, right,' I said, not wanting to sound green. 'That's how you do it.'

'Yep,' said Paul. But his face had fallen. He wasn't boasting, and he didn't look proud.

'Thing is, Gregg, once you do it, it's hard to stop. I mean, I need the cash. It pays better than any job and money soon gets spent. So you do it again and again and ... You know, my brothers have done time a few times now.'

'Right,' I said, staring into the bottom of my beer glass. 'Poor fellas.'

'Yeah, well, see the thing is, if you tell the judge you did it on impulse, they're always lenient towards you. You admit it was premeditated and you go down for it.'

And then I saw it for what it was. Paul was a petty thief but he was trapped doing it. His options were so limited, as mine were. He was as trapped as I was in many ways.

Overtime was to be had at weekends, particularly in the summer, as I remember. Brian, the owner, had teenage kids, who were much posher than me. They turned up with a gang of their mates to earn 'pocket money'. It was all a bit of a giggle for them, a dirty, relatively well-paid part-time job to earn extra money to go travelling or whatever. They were lovely, friendly and fun, but walked around with an air of knowing who they were and exactly where they were going. Something you notice profoundly when you don't yourself.

'After a quick whizz over to our chateau in France it's Durham uni for me and then we'll see what happens. I might continue with law or go into the arts – I am keeping my options open,' said one as he held open a bag for me to shovel caustic soda into.

The word 'options' hung in the stinking chemically smelling and tasting air. To have options, and for them to be open … wow!

On the days they came, we didn't just get sarnies for lunch: Brian would send someone out with some fivers to buy pies, pasties and cakes, long sticky iced buns and strawberry tartlets with glazed tops. What a feast! And he shared them around as well. I got on with these fellas too, but they were just here for a few days a month, whereas this was my full-time job. My sense of low self-esteem and isolation increased. No one's fault, nobody was nasty to me, but I was just very skint and felt quite worthless.

Most of the time my work was on the dry side of the factory floor. I worked on a big machine. There were metal steps up to a platform, about 10 or 12 feet high, to the mouth of the

153

machine. This was a trough about 7 feet long and 3 feet deep, with a kind of turning screw or multi-bladed propeller that turned and mixed and blended whatever you poured into it. First I would assist in making up the formula, and eventually I was trusted to make it myself.

Just to explain how this worked – bear with me. The chemicals to be mixed would be lifted on to the platform with a forklift and then we would open the bags into the trough and set the big screw in motion. I'd then leave the platform and nip downstairs to the bottom of the machine, where I'd hold a bag around the pipe and, using the electric buttons, with a bag on the scale, fill the bags until I'd got the correct weight. The bags were about knee high and weighed about 10 kilos. Then I had to twist the bag to give it a neck and fasten it with thin wire, using a strange hook-like gadget.

I'm sure there are proper names for this process, but I was never taught them. It was a case of 'do this and do that', so I did. No questions asked – I just did what the man told me to and got paid.

This went on all day, every day, the only difference to the routine being the formula that was poured in the trough. Hour after hour, day after day – thank God there was a radio playing.

Now of all the chemicals I was mixing, caustic soda was the worst. Of course you got given protective clothing: a mask over your mouth, a boiler suit, boots and gloves. But the nasty corrosive stuff was in huge quantities and somehow it would work its way into your boots or under your gloves, any opening. It was of course all over your gloves too, so if any part of your head or face itched or if you sweated you couldn't wipe yourself with your hand.

On the odd occasion, I'd forget, and a quick harmless wipe turned into a dash to the toilet to strip, usually hopping one-legged, out of your clothing, squinting while you went, in desperation, to wash your face with water. It wasn't an immediate thing to notice either; it was nasty stuff, and it would start as an itch and then it'd turn more intense and start to burn, badly.

I still have scars on my hands and feet from that awful job. Looking back I'm certain health and safety would have had a field day with a job like that. I should've quizzed the foreman more about the issues, about the burns, but I just shut up and got on with it. In those days, that was me, always eager to please. I wanted to be seen as a hard worker; I didn't want to make a fuss. I should've left and looked for something else, but part of me was waiting for somebody to come up with a plan for me. A plan B, because plan A wasn't working.

Walking out and finding something better would've been the sensible option, except for the minor detail that I had no qualifications, no money and nowhere proper to live. But considering what was to happen next, it would probably still have been a better option.

CHAPTER 15

Lucozade

*O*K, so we're still in the chemical factory and there in the yard were large tanks, big things, 15 feet long, 8 feet high and full of liquid.

'You need to empty out the last remaining drops of dirty liquid from one tank as the new delivery comes,' said a guy called Gavin, who was standing in for the foreman, Scully, on this particular day, which happened to be my first day working in there. 'You release a valve at the bottom, see? Easy peasy.'

And so I took up a squeegee on a pole, and as I released the valve let the strong-smelling liquid out. The tank unhelpfully wasn't sloped, so there was an inch or so of liquid left at the bottom.

'Damn,' I muttered, as I peered over the top of the tank.

How was I supposed to get that out? As usual, eager to get a good job done, I climbed to the top to get a good look.

Hmmm, the only way, I thought, is to climb in and sweep that stuff out . . .

I never gave it a second thought. I didn't want to look stupid and check with someone. I was just using common sense as far as I was concerned. A quick sweep round inside and then job done.

In a flash I was through the manhole and had dropped into the tank. And that was the last thing I remember.

When my eyes flickered open I felt tubes sticking out of my nose, mouth and top of my hand.

'Urrrrrrrmm.' I tried to speak, and Mum's face loomed into view, all out of focus, and I drifted off again. Finally I woke, this time with Tracy by my bed, stroking my arm.

'You're OK, Gregg. You've just had a terrible accident at work,' she said, soothingly.

'You've been out of it for four days,' continued Mum.

Four days? I was still bleary-eyed, but very slowly all the faces came into focus. Mum, Grandad, Nan and Tracy were all there, standing over me, their faces full of worry and sympathy.

I felt bad for making them worry.

Tubes were taken from my mouth and I was able to mutter very hoarsely. I had so many questions, the first one being: what the hell happened to me? The picture slowly emerged. The tank I'd climbed into had in it a spirit called methylene chloride, better known to you and me as the base of paint stripper. You dilute it many times to make a very strong paint stripper. And as soon as I landed in that tank, the fumes overcame me and I collapsed.

Mum, who was then eight months pregnant with her third son, had come home from work that day to find Gerry and his boss sitting at her dining-room table, their heads in their hands.

When they said I was in hospital, she just started running from the house. 'Take me to him,' she screamed. They called Tracy and when she arrived she started screeching like a caged animal and they had to gently take her home.

For the first time since the divorce Grandad saw Mum. They sat in uncomfortable silence the whole time, Grandad glowering at Mum over the bed.

For four days I was on life support in an induced coma. On the third day they tried to bring me round, but I went straight into cardiac arrest in front of Mum. That didn't kill me, but it almost killed her, having to stand by and watch it.

Afterwards a doctor told Mum, 'We just don't know what we're dealing with. There's a chance he's got internal damage. He might be brain damaged for life.'

Nan W cried as she asked over and over again, 'What are we wishing for, though, Mary?' as they prayed I'd wake up.

When the nurses first peeled back the bandage covering my right foot, they all gasped. It was so badly blistered it looked like something out of a horror film, and there were fears that the rest of my body was the same. All this makes me want to cry, to think what my family went through.

Mum wasn't allowed to stay in overnight, so she went home every day, but she couldn't sleep with her bedside light off. 'If I turn it off, I feel like I am turning Gregg off,' she said to Gerry. The tension was unbearable and Gerry came into his own, as my biological father, for the first time then. He was devastated. Mum was sobbing at the kitchen table after telling how she'd watch me convulse with a heart attack earlier and Gerry lost the plot.

'I am not losing one son,' he said, firmly banging his fist on the table, 'and then just having another one. It's not right. Gregg has to survive this, he has to.'

Then on day five, they brought me around one morning, before Mum arrived, and this time I woke up. They called her and she broke down.

'Thank God, thank God,' she just said, sobbing.

Back at my bedside within minutes, she saw me sitting up, my eyes rolling around like marbles in my head.

'Is he all right?' she asked a nurse.

'It's just the drugs,' one explained. 'The first person he asked for was Mary. It was confusing, as his girlfriend is called Tracy!'

Mum gently told me I was going to be fine. In the end I'd woken with a serious burn on my left arm and the backs of both legs and my right foot. It was bad, but not that bad, and it could've been a whole lot worse. I'd survived the wars, as Grandad said.

After a few days in intensive care, I was taken into the ward, where a nurse came to visit me.

'I am doing a study of people who've had near-death experiences,' she explained. 'Do you mind telling me if you remember anything?'

I've no idea what the study was for or if she was just being curious, but I was happy to tell her.

I knew I had had an experience, but I hadn't realised it until she asked me this specifically. I had a very clear memory of two things. One of them seemed a bit dream-like and the other definitely felt like a real memory. I don't know what it was. It felt like something very deep, though, ephemeral and weird, and I reckon it could've been a near-death experience and that I was sent back.

The first one was having a vision of waking up from a dream to find doctors and nurses all around me and I felt shock, pain and fear, but I couldn't work out where. Then the doctor said: 'Put him out again.'

The next one was far more frightening and real. I was in the hallway of Kincaid Road, playing football one minute, and then the next I was floating up to the ceiling. It was fun at first. 'Wooo, hooo, I can fly,' I cried. Until I went higher and higher and Grandad started trying to jump to reach me, but he couldn't.

'Come down, boy,' he was mouthing, panic in his eyes. 'Come down!'

I carried on weightlessly floating, my head and back skimming the peeling paint on the ceiling, and I was moving fast, as if being sucked outside towards the front door by an unknowable force, taking me from Grandad, my home, everything I knew ... I could see a big sky outside, a horizon, and I was heading straight for it; suddenly as fast as it'd been fun it'd become very frightening. I was going to God knows where, and I was by myself and I didn't want to. I needed someone to save me before I floated away for ever. Gone for good. No, no please, someone catch me, make an effort, I thought, panic rising. Then, just as suddenly, things changed again. I wasn't going after all; I was just hanging. I'd seen I could've disappeared into that sky but something was holding me back and, wow, was I grateful. Still sends a shiver down my spine.

Miguel wasn't allowed into the intensive care ward while I was unconscious but he waited outside for news every day for hours, bless the lad. Our friendship had grown through a will to get on in life and also Millwall.

When he approached my bed I could tell he was shocked at how I looked, tubes still poking everywhere.

'Millwall lost,' he said simply.

'Cheers, Mick,' I replied. 'I'll die now then, shall I?'

Good old Mick. He hadn't got a clue what to say to me.

I was on really strong painkillers, which gave me vivid and terrifying nightmares. Once I was a werewolf crawling on all fours, biting people. Work that one out, Freud.

Sometimes I'd wake in a sweat to find Grandad next to me, stroking my hairline, over and over again. 'Just try and drop off again, my boy,' he would mutter. And I'd drift off again, feeling safe.

When I was out of intensive care and away from the more hardcore drugs, that was when the pain kicked in. One doctor standing over me kept doing a double take to his notes, as he looked me over.

'It really is a miracle you didn't have any internal damage,' he kept saying. Apparently they even wrote up my case in some medical journal. One afternoon Mum overheard two doctors chatting about me in the lift.

'Did you hear about that Wallace chap?' said one doctor to another. 'Bloody amazing,' said the other.

But I was burned. Methylene chloride is paint stripper, as I've said, so you can just imagine what it does to human skin. If it had just landed on my skin it would have evaporated and that would have been that, but my clothes held it on to me, and so it took layers off.

The bandages came off and my elbow scabbed over, but at the back of my legs in the knee joints the skin turned to mush. Painful mush. I was laid on a sheepskin cover, which was soft, but my legs stuck to it, and then the bits that were stuck on sheepskin became hardened and crispy, and dug painfully into my wounds like shards of glass. Skin grows back very quickly, but it couldn't grow back when my legs were bent, so every morning the nurses would have to straighten my legs, splitting the scabs as they formed. All quite horrible. The only thing I

161

had to look forward to then was warm salt baths. I felt free in there as I almost floated, and my legs stopped hurting for a few wonderful minutes.

I was stuck on the ward for six weeks, but my bed was near a window, so I could look out at the skies of London, usually the colour of a badger on a hot wash, and see people scurrying to and fro to the nearest Tube or bus stops.

One morning, I was gazing out, when I saw a man crossing the road, at the traffic lights, his shoulders hunched and his chin pressed to his chest, the features on his face all balled up against a fine spray of drizzle. He doesn't look very happy, I thought; he really doesn't want to be walking to work in the cold at this time of the morning. Then I realised that, in spite of the rain and the grey and the cold, I'd do anything to be up and about and out there working.

Later that day more doctors arrived to talk about the possibility of plastic surgery. I wasn't up for a skin graft, though, but I did try to see the funny side.

'A plastic doctor?' I joked. 'Bloody NHS cuts. I want a real one.'

I turned any more ops down. I'd had enough. I wanted to get out and get on with my life.

While I was laid up, Grandad and Dad redecorated the bedroom at the flat in Ivydale Road. They painted it Millwall blue and white, bless them, and put a new wooden flatpack wardrobe in there. But the doctors explained I'd need some serious looking after, so Mum told me I was going back with her to share a room with Biffo again. I wasn't in a position to argue and was grateful just to get the hell out of the hospital and back in front of things like telly and normal food.

Nan W had made me some stripy nightshirts because I couldn't bear the pain of pyjama bottoms, and I had a few by the time I went home. Still rather like them now, though I've never found a partner who approves!

And so I found myself back in Sydenham, with Mum running my baths, the highlight of my day for a while, as I hobbled painfully up the stairs.

Things slowly improved and it was nice to spend some time with Biffo during my convalescence. Once I decided to take him to the video shop up the road to get a film with which to while away the day. We picked some title I can't quite remember, which was a 15 certificate, a bit old for him but nothing too serious.

'Listen, Biff,' I said. 'It's got a little bit of sex and violence in it, nothing much, but if Mum catches us she'll go mad, so let's not tell her. Let's just stick it on in the living room and watch it quietly, OK?'

He looked at me all wide-eyed as he always did. 'OK, Gregg,' he said.

We went home and as soon as we got through the front door, Biff saw Mum. 'We're back!' he cried. 'Gregg just got a film with a little bit of sex and violence in it but don't worry it will be fine!'

Predictably Mum wasn't. She went mad and ordered me to take it back. 'Biff, what on earth were you thinking?' I said afterwards. Sometimes my mental little brother just didn't get it but he did make me laugh.

Another time soon afterwards, Mum and Gerry wanted to sell up the place in Sydenham and move somewhere in Kent. They had lots of potential buyers coming to see the house and one man asked Gerry, 'Do you get much noise from the traffic outside?' and completely truthfully he said no. But then Biff piped up: 'Yeah, but I can't sleep in my room thanks to the lorries going to the Continent . . .' Mum and Gerry looked at him as if he was mad, which he was. His bedroom backed on to the garden and no lorries were anywhere to be seen!

Mum insisted to Gerry we took my accident to lawyers to seek compensation.

'If that had happened at a big firm like ICI they'd be sitting at his bedside every day, worrying for the company, as they'd have been worried about being sued. And they should be sued so this never happens to anyone else again,' she argued.

Gerry agreed. He was the company secretary and it was his mate, the director, who was responsible, but the company had insurance, and it was the insurance company I had to battle against, not the actual company.

I read health and safety reports on the substance I'd been dealing with, the methylene chloride, and they said any container needed to be clearly marked with a skull and cross-bones and danger signs. No tank was to be left unlocked, no person was to be allowed to work with it alone, breathing apparatus was to be worn at all times and workers should work in a relay of no more than fifteen minutes at a time. I was a teenager in jeans, clambering into an unmarked tank full of deadly chemicals and armed with a squeegee.

After three months off work, I returned to see my old mates there. I was painfully thin and hobbling with a walking stick – not quite the Jack the lad who was eager to please any more.

While meeting the old crew, including Paul and Gary, I bumped into my replacement, a guy called Tony. He was my age and quite short, with thick glasses and bad skin, but he seemed chirpy and confident, and we always found ourselves having a cup of tea if I popped my head in.

'Do you like this line of work?' I asked him one day.

'Ha ha! What do you think?' he said. 'What's your next plan, anyway?'

I didn't know what I wanted to do with my life, but thanks to being on full pay and being stuck indoors, I'd inadvertently saved up a bit of money. And I had compensation on the way too. Happy days.

But with regard to Tony's question, I'd no idea.

I was still chatting a lot to Andrew Dyne, and one day he told me about his mate.

'You know Phil,' he said, one day over a beer. 'Well, Phil's doing really well with his window cleaning business.'

'Phil?' I said, thinking of a guy I'd met once or twice, pretty quiet and unassuming, but then it wasn't rocket science, climbing up a ladder and mopping the muck off windows, was it?

'Yep,' said Andrew. 'You should see the car he's bought recently. Must be a roaring trade.'

Roaring trade. Cleaning windows. I wouldn't have put those words in the same sentence but Andrew was a friend I trusted. And if Phil could do it, why couldn't I? I'd also heard from my mate Paul Bradley how his dad had a nice little business doing windows. It was definitely something do-able.

The next time I popped into work, to see Tony, I mentioned my business proposition.

'All we need to arm ourselves with is a sponge and a ladder,' I said. 'What d'you reckon?'

Tony laughed a few times, snorted, and slurped his tea in thought. But I could see he was coming round to the idea.

The next time I saw him, he'd obviously had a think. 'You know, there's an area I know, south of Catford in south-east London, called Bellingham, and it's literally street after street of Edwardian brick houses, people with extra cash, the types who're not going to have much time to clean all their windows. Imagine the bay ones as well as the upstairs? No, it's not gonna happen . . .'

'But at the same time,' I chipped in, 'they're the types who want to keep up with the Joneses and would notice smears on their glass.'

Tony jabbed the air with his index finger. 'Precisely!'

We did it. Tony handed in his notice, he had the car and I'd saved up the capital for tools. What a dream team!

I asked Paul if I could chat to his dad about any tips. We weren't covering his patch of London, so I didn't see any problem. Tony and I turned up at Paul's dad's.

'So you lads think you can clean windows?' Mickey said, eyeballing us as though we wouldn't know a sponger from a squeegee (actually we didn't).

We nodded.

'Well, you need all the proper tools and techniques of the trade,' Mickey said, sucking his teeth.

I'd no idea what techniques were used to clean windows, but I was definitely glad Paul's dad was kind enough to show us. It wasn't a case of turning up with a bucket and sponge and hoping for the best, as I'd first thought.

He pulled out a fluffy soap applicator gadget, a squeegee and a chamois leather. As for the bucket, we needed a soap applicator one, over a foot long, shaped as an oblong. Who would have known? Then he brandished a grey cloth.

'A scrim,' he announced to our puzzled faces.

Then with his dab hand he showed us how to clean and polish a window without leaving a trace of a smear within a few seconds. It looked like magic and was a case of knowing how.

'Ha ha,' Mickey said, laughing, when I commended him on the sparkling window he'd just cleaned. 'It's a bit of an art, lads. Most people don't have a clue.'

And you might think a ladder is a ladder, but window

cleaners need one that is not metal but wooden, and comes to a point at the top. The two sides of the ladder bend inwards and are held there with a big rubber stopper. This enables the ladder to be placed at almost any angle, which a standard ladder wouldn't be able to.

After thanking Paul's dad for his crash course in the tricks of the window cleaning trade, we took a trip to Wacs cleaning supplies, just south of Blackheath. After shelling out a small fortune on tools, we set off to make a fortune of our own.

CHAPTER 16

Toast

'Well, there is one thing for it,' I said. 'Let's test your theory and make our heady way to Bellingham, my friend . . .'

We targeted some streets that evening, as I'd pointed out more people would be in then. Tony took one side of the street and I did the other, armed with a pad and pen to look that extra bit professional about what we were attempting to do. We didn't have a pattern and would just knock on their doors to see if they were interested in having their windows cleaned.

Now very quickly I realised I shouldn't just use the tired lines of a salesman. I used the gift of the ear, not the gab. If you're talking talking talking, who knows who's listening to you or not. So I learned the art of getting people started into conversation. I'd talk about something they were wearing, something in their garden – anything to get their attention.

Being a good salesman doesn't mean rehearsing the same lines; we've all had these guys on the phone to us, trying to sell us stuff, and it's infuriating. Being a good salesman means treating everybody as if they are fresh and new and you are talking to them individually. Even something like: 'Listen, I don't get time to clean my own windows at home. I don't know about you . . .' Soon I discovered that when people like you they will want to get their windows cleaned by you.

To our amazement, our patter worked, and we filled up five days a week for three weeks. We simply kept going up and down, lifting door knockers and pinging door bells, until we had enough orders.

On our first day we strapped the ladders to the roof rack on Tony's Cortina and put two buckets of soapy water through the gaps in the ladders, giving it a rock to see if it was stable enough to take off.

'That'll do,' I said, pushing it. 'Let's hit the road!'

We hurtled off through the streets of Sydenham on the way to Bellingham. All was going well till Tony had to pull up fast at a set of pedestrian lights.

'Whoa!' I cried, as I put my hands out to the dashboard to stop myself. Jimmy Saville's 'clunk click' campaign was everywhere but the seat belt law hadn't come in yet!

I'd avoided being splattered over the windscreen but the hot soapy water hadn't and it doused the front of the car. Tony pulled up, laughing his head off.

'Free car wash anyone?' he sniggered.

The punters weren't always in when we cleaned their gaff, so we'd go back later for the money, which everyone was always happy to part with. Suddenly we were earning a living, and a very decent one at that.

We charged £1.50 for the front of the house, which you could get done in five, say ten minutes flat, if you worked up some elbow grease. That's £9 per hour. None of this seemed particularly courageous at the time, but actually we were pretty enterprising. The practice of speaking to strangers and selling my wares, even something as simple as cleaning windows, stood me in good stead. Almost by accident I became a cracking salesman.

It was a summer of fun, let me tell you that. Hot days, up and down a ladder, chatting to Tony, in our little shorts, with girls stopping to admire us in the streets.

I was tanned, slim, confident and cheeky, and there were girls, quite a few of them, starting to gravitate towards me. We even caught the housewives' eye, giving them a wink as we soaped up their windows and another one as we squeegeed the soap off again.

As well as setting up my new business, I'd also recovered enough to live independently again and was grateful to go back to Ivydale to have my own space.

My skin peeled and the pain subsided. It felt as though I wanted a new chapter to start along with this. But aside from doing the window cleaning, I didn't know what. Things were changing, though: people were settling down, and my friends started to leave the days of desert shoes and Ben Sherman shirts behind, as we started to move on from our mod days. Things weren't quite the same: we'd been to all the gigs (including all three Q-Tips' farewell tours) and well and truly got the T-shirt.

It was time for us to grow up, I suppose.

Having a proper job and business of my own boosted my confidence. The work included meeting new people and having new experiences. Once I got chatting to a guy who had cancer. He spotted me with my B&H hanging from the side of my gob as I doused his windowsill.

'You smoke all you like when you're young but you don't realise what it's doing to your body,' he said sadly.

I promptly dropped the fag and stubbed it out. He was a nice fella and I'd stop with him for tea and chat. Every three weeks we cleaned his gaff, but one week I turned up and he wasn't there. He'd died.

With a nine o'clock start, we'd stop at the baker's for a pasty and Pepsi and then carry on till three or four, putting all the money in the bag and divvying it up at the end of the day. On a good day one in six houses we knocked on wanted their windows done. On a bad day it was one in twenty. As we got chatting to stay-at-home mums we'd ask them if they needed anything else doing. Soon we were making money for taking people's rubbish away to the local tip.

'Eh, Tony,' I said one day, as we heaved a pile of bric-a-brac to the car for dumping for a few quid, 'why don't people just do it themselves?'

'Same reason, I suppose, they don't clean their own windows,' he replied.

With extra money in my shorts, I went and bought myself some driving lessons. Getting my own car was a turning point. Tony was no longer in the driving seat. I started to think maybe, just maybe, I could do this on my own. I'd grown in confidence with my smiley salesman patter. I could persuade the tightest housewife to part with a few pounds to get her windows sparkling.

Then I started to persuade myself I could do better on my own. After all, I was probably getting most of the customers myself and I wouldn't have to split the money.

I ran my idea past Tony. At the end of the day, I thought to myself, a partnership has to be about having something you can both bring to it. To start with he had the car and I had the money for the materials. Now we were just working together for the sake of it.

'What do you think?' I said.

To my surprise he agreed wholeheartedly. So we set about splitting up our tools. There were three ladders so we had one each and then split the third one in half. Horizontally obviously.

So we split the kit and split the rounds, and split our friendship. Looking back, I can see this became a bit of a pattern of mine: set up with someone and then become a lone wolf again. What's that about? A control issue? A need to prove myself alone? Who knows? I could sense I was getting to the point of being almost in competition with my business partner.

Doing it on my tod wasn't all it seemed to be cracked up to be, though. I found it hard to motivate myself alone.

I'd find myself snuggled up to Tracy on those howling cold winter mornings, knowing I faced another day with frozen hands, trying to make the best of what seemed like a boring job again. No banter in the van to look forward to, and summer seemed long ago. So I'd put off getting up for another couple of hours, and before I knew it, it was getting too dark in the afternoons to clean anything.

Then a letter came through the door that threw me a lifeline again.

'How much did you say?' Tracy asked, as I shouted at her to get up and look.

Bleary-eyed, she squinted at the letter from the insurance people.

'Oh my God, Gregg, what are you going to do with that?'

Seventeen thousand pounds in today's money is a lot, but back then, it was a small fortune.

'I don't know,' I whispered, dumbstruck.

Tracy had a brother-in-law then, called Jim, little Jim, as we knew him. He was a painter and decorator, and when the weather got warmer, I had a brainwave for another little money-making scheme.

I was still doing my old window cleaning rounds and I started to ask punters if they needed any decorating doing. I had hundreds of customers, and I reckoned the chances were many would, which they did. So I asked little Jim if he fancied going in with me and he said yes. And we were off. I'd stay at Tracy's house on the Friday night – she lived in Hackney in east London. Her brother-in-law Jim lived in Stepney and I'd pick him up early Saturday morning and then a mate of his who'd help. We charged £500 for a house in a weekend, pay the mate and split the rest. Every weekend through summer and spring we'd do this, while I stuck to window cleaning during the week. I was rolling in it for a while. Happy days.

But the old competitive streak kicked in, and it messed up our growing business.

'I'm getting the punters,' I said to Jim as we sat with our pasties over lunch.

He stopped mid-bite and looked at me. 'What you sayin'?' he said.

'I just think I should be earning more of the money,' I said bravely, knowing this wasn't going to go down well. 'I get them in, so I should get more dosh.'

'Well, if that's what you think of me just put me on a day rate, but don't ask me to help you,' he said, clearly annoyed. But of course this didn't work at all. I needed his skills as much as he did mine. We'd actually complimented each other perfectly but I ruined it. It was a stupid thing to do, as we'd had a really lucrative thing going. But I was too arrogant to see this. Sorry, Jim.

I just wanted to move on up. Although I was still, after all this time, looking for where 'up' was.

This next era feels as if it happened to someone else, not me. Lost now, I was trying jobs as often as I now try on shoes, but never ever finding the right fit.

All around me, though, Thatcher's Britain had well and truly kicked in. Mum and Gerry seemed happy enough and moved out of London, as part of their own decision to 'move up in the world'.

They went to Millfield Road, in a Kentish backwater called West Kingsdown, just past Brands Hatch motor-racing track, yet another light year away from the life Mum knew in Peckham. They bought a modern, brick house, three beds with a garden. Mum kitted out the house really nicely actually, very minimalist, neutral colours – she did Terence Conran proud. There were lots of clear surfaces, wide armchairs in pale blue with no arms, and long black sideboards and cupboards with no handles.

Once I popped in for a cuppa, and was sitting chatting to Mum, with Gerry swigging a glass of whisky in the chair opposite. Ever a portly chap, Gerry heftily swung one leg over the other and the momentum took him off the edge of the armless chair, so he did a kind of half pike turn in mid-air, landing on the floor sitting up, and he didn't spill a drop of the whisky either!

Mum and I watched, rather in awe of this nifty manoeuvre, and then burst into laughter.

It was funny, as Mum had a lovely kitchen now, but she still didn't have much time for cooking. Though she'd even less need now, thanks to the microwave she'd bought. With a brown glass front, it was enormous and took up half a sideboard, looking like a dysfunctional TV. Once I marvelled to see her line up some raw sausage, bacon, beans and mushrooms all on one plate for breakfast, and sizzle the lot in the microwave on high power.

Shortly after my accident Mum had a little boy, called Adam. So now there were three boys: two Wallaces and a Press, middle brother Biffo and me with different dads but the same surname, baby Adam and me with the same dad but different surnames. As I was so much older than Adam we were never close and I was more like an uncle to him. Biffo adored him, though. I watched one day from across the living room, the pair lost in their own worlds, playing cars together. Such brotherly love. Then Biffo spilt a drop of his Coke on Mum's new neutral grey carpet and covertly sat Adam on it to hide the stain. I couldn't help but laugh. Biffo did confide in me, though, that he now felt left out. He was our half-brother and it upset him to think we were not all the same and that he was the odd one out with a different dad.

Nan W sold her place in Wimbledon and moved to live near Mum. She must've been the wealthiest woman in the area, with two pensions – Grandad's naval one and a Civil Service one. Moneybags Lil.

My own problem was that I still didn't really have a home. I always felt like a lodger at Mum and Gerry's. Sometimes I stopped in the empty flat in Nunhead, sometimes in Kent, sometimes at Tracy's. I was just a nomad really. I splashed out a lump of my claim money on a convertible Suzuki jeep. Brand new, white, with a red strip. It was so cool! I also put a big rack for ladders on the top and worked again all summer cleaning windows, after my decorating venture predictably failed. As hamfisted as ever, I was useless at doing even the basics like putting up shelves.

Aside from that, life seemed to be on the up because of my compensation windfall. With some great friends and parties along the way. I met people all the time. Once I offered to repaint Mum's woodwork on the outside of her house, and listening to Capital's top 100 most requested songs blaring out, just as the chap across the road was, we got talking. His name was Spike and we started belting out 'Bohemian Rhapsody' in unison, laughing as we heard each other, and became mates.

Bermondsey became alive with smart bars, like Sampson's and Willows, two-floor affairs, with guys tapping their sovereign rings on their glasses of champagne in time to the music. Bus drivers pretended to be gangsters at the weekends, while dustmen with shirts from Moda 3 or Le Pel claimed they were going to have someone 'blown away'.

Sade was laconically singing in every bar and restaurant. Women and men alike waltzed round in ripped jeans, shoulder pads and big leather jackets. Convertible Golfs skidded at every traffic light.

There was a pub just off the Old Kent Road where guys would meet for a Sunday drink, and they'd hire really expensive cars just for the weekend. There were Jags and Porsches outside this pub, driven by scaffolders who lived in rented accommodation.

Miguel was still around and doing even better for himself now. He had bagged a smart blue MG and in it we used to cross Tower Bridge and go to pubs along the Hackney Road and Victoria Park.

I met Errol, too, another mod who was in a separate group

and who lived in Nunhead, although we dressed less like mods these days. With a name like Errol, everyone assumed he was a black man, but actually his mum had just loved Errol Flynn. I hit it off with his brothers and friends, and we all hung around in a big group of lads, looking for girls and parties and basically living the high life. I started window cleaning less and less and lived off the claim money more and more.

Errol was in the building trade and despite the fact that I wasn't very good at it, he asked me to join in.

'It'll be a laugh and it's so easy to make some dough,' he said.

I had my doubts but Errol wasn't wrong. We were constantly busy. Once while we were all working on a house, we were sitting on the kerb having a break, drinking some Pepsi, when a man in a very smart BMW pulled up.

'You lads,' he said, 'here's my card. Call me Monday for some work,' and he skidded off, leaving us in a cloud of dust.

Errol rang the number and for the next few weeks we found ourselves working on British Rail sites earning a good whack by doing some basic building bits. It was that easy. Yes, summer was sorted, though what did I do in winter? Not a lot except go into hibernation.

One thing I did still do regularly, though, was to keep up with the Millwall games with Dad and Grandad. We'd troop down together when Grandad got the season tickets, all feeling the same heartbeat of the game and shouting at the top of our voices to help the lads on.

A few times we were joined by Graham Breen, my old buddy who'd taught me how to catamaran on my skateboard. Our first attempt at being good mates hadn't really worked out, I suppose, but now we were both good listeners – well, after a couple of pints at the Waverley Arms anyway.

I lived for these games. The atmosphere never failed to lift my spirits; as we walked on to the stands, you could almost taste the roar in the back of your throat. If I didn't belong anywhere else, I belonged here.

'We are Millwall, sup-er Mill-waaalll, and noooooo one liiiiikes us . . .' they sang to the tune of Rod Stewart's 'We Are Sailing'. This became the anthem of Millwall fans in response to all the press attacks we got. Sad how Millwall attracted such bad press. It was the start of demonising the white working-class lads, really, I think – something that still goes on today. I mean, why is it OK to call someone a chav?

It'd been a good game against Brighton, but there was a definte tension clinging to the voices of the crowds after each goal was scored.

The language was getting more and more aggressive and the atmosphere was getting more and more charged. There was a dividing fence between the two sets of fans, and as the Brighton fans goaded the Millwall fans, they started getting angrier and angrier. I knew that sound, the noise, the smell, the sense of our partisan position. The moods of the fans were changing and you could sense they were fuming. The game ended with a tangible bad feeling in the air. Brighton had won and we could sense there would be trouble.

We decided to stay behind in the ground for an extra fifteen minutes, to wait as it emptied, to let the crowds disperse, and avoid any trouble. Once they'd gone, we decided to leave too, expecting the streets to be empty.

As we walked out of the ground, there was a raised section, with stone steps leading up to the car park. We walked past the dog track end, where there is a narrow lane that bears off to the right; we needed to go left on to Illerton Road, so we turned up towards the car park. As we came up the stairs, expecting them to be empty, we found ourselves slap bang in the middle of a huge mob of Millwall supporters, trying to get at Brighton fans, with a wall of coppers and vicious-looking Alsatians stopping them.

'Oh God,' I said to Graham, as a policeman came flying over, along with bottles thrown by fans. 'Miiiiiiiiilwaaaaaaaaaall', the crowds were chanting. As far as the policeman was concerned I was one of the crowd, not someone who'd just wandered in.

He shoved me in the chest and I put my arms up to remonstrate.

'Oi, oi! What have I done . . .' I began, as a snarling dog leaped up into the air and started tearing at my jacket. I felt a sharp pain in my arm as his teeth sliced through the material like a hot knife through butter.

'Argh! Gerroff!' I yelled, shaking the dog's jaw as he tore at me as though I was early dinner.

The fabric on my windcheater split and tore right off, the dog was barking like a maniac and the copper was now looming over me, baton at the ready. What a palaver!

'What you doin'?' I gasped as the policeman grappled with me.

I twisted my head to look at him. I felt furious. Why were they picking on us?

He shoved me a few times, to try to get my hands behind my back.

'Oi!' I cried, incensed. 'What you doing? I want your number. I'm going to make a complaint.'

Now lesson number one, if you have any gripe with any policeman at any time, is: don't threaten to take their number.

Because then they will arrest you and then it looks like that's the reason for the complaint.

'You're nicked,' came the response.

CHAPTER 17

Sweet Tea

I sat in silence, handcuffed, feeling every bounce and jolt in the police van, while sirens blared as if I were a proper dangerous criminal. I was supposed to be in the pub by now with Graham. How'd this happened?

Next stop was a police cell, where I sat, staring at the bloody teethmarks on my arm and glad Grandad hadn't come along to this game. A doctor came in and doused my wound none too gently with an antiseptic wash; then another copper came in and had a chat with me.

'Honestly, officer,' I said. 'We just walked right into the trouble but were only looking for a way out. I am sorry.'

He nodded, taking a few lines down, and then snapped his notebook shut.

'OK, lad,' he said. 'You've been co-operative, you've been apologetic.'

He let me go, but before I went I had to sign a few forms,

181

and instead of just getting a ticking off, my case still had to go to court. I was gutted. It was yet another example of the wrong direction my life seemed to be going in. My mum was distinctly unimpressed.

I went round to Grandad's.

'They nicked me,' I said. 'They arrested me, the dog got me, but I didn't do anything, Grandad, I swear!'

He said absolutely nothing. He just slid his arm around my shoulders and patted my back.

A few weeks later, I told him when my court date was, and again he said nothing, just handing me a cup of sweet tea.

The courtroom that Monday morning was packed full of Millwall fans. I was nervous, I'd never been to court before and I didn't feel I deserved to be there like the others. I knew I wasn't a hooligan.

Then I heard a familiar voice clearing his throat. I looked up, and Grandad was sitting bolt upright where families can go, smartly dressed, twisting his flat cap in his hands, his blue and white tie neatly pressed against his dickie dirt. He gave me an almost imperceptible wink as the judge bashed his wooden hammer and it started. Good old Grandad.

Of course I'd done something wrong without realising. I'd been apologetic and the court's argument was: 'If you hadn't done anything wrong, why did you apologise?' That's lesson number two: never apologise, as it makes you look as if you really have done something wrong.

As we left, Grandad enquired how to pay the fine and peeled off a few notes then and there. Then he slid his arm across my shoulder and we walked out. We never said another word about it.

This was the 1980s. This was when the government was putting police under pressure to clamp down on hooliganism. I was a Millwall supporter in the wrong place at the wrong time.

Christmas should be magic. I want to be Santa when I'm a granddad.

Love this picture: me and the two most precious things in my life, Tom and Libby.

Three Wallaces, all indulging our sweet tooth.

My old mate, Charlie Hicks. He's the poshest greengrocer you'll ever meet!

Fruit and veg have always been good friends of mine. I've continuously made a living out of it and probably always will!

Believe it or not, some puddings don't work!

You can take the boy out of Peckham . . .

John has been buying veg from me for over 20 years, ever since he was a sous chef at a very small restaurant and I was going door-to-door selling veg.

Two of my favourite things: food and rugby. From left: Charlie Sharples, Nick Easter and Riki Flutey.

Sir Terry Wogan, arguably one of *MasterChef*'s biggest fans.

My good friends over at *MasterChef*: Michel Roux Jr, John Torode and Monica Galetti.
A wealth of broadcasting talent!

Watch out, a taste of things to come! Who'd have believed it, Peckham boy having lunch with the PM.

Without a leg to stand on. Later on, though, I regained my faith in the British justice system. Gosh, writing all this down makes me sound terrible – brushes with the law. But once again I was a young lad, doing something stupid. I was very green in so many ways, despite living on my own, despite my swagger.

As I've said, we were all running around on scooters, feeling like the bee's knees, and while I was having a few lads round to Ivydale Road, a friend of a friend called Simon spotted my old scooter, which I'd left in the tiny back garden.

'Can I have your old number plate, Gregg?' he asked.

'Yeah, OK,' I said, not thinking anything more about it, and certainly not knowing it was illegal.

I think it was a couple of weeks later, after the Millwall incident was well forgotten, that the police knocked on the door.

'Gregg Wallace?' he said.

'Yes,' I replied.

'Where was your scooter on 5th August? We're arresting you for allowing an unroadworthy scooter to be driven away. We have your details from the number plate,' an officer said.

'Sorry, officer,' I said, trying to keep calm. My brain took a second or two to catch up. Then I thought of Simon walking out with my scooter number plate tucked under his arm and suddenly it made sense. He probably put it on his old busted-up scooter. At last I explained 'Oh, right!' I said, my face flooding with relief. 'I gave my number plate away. It's not my scooter.'

The copper looked distinctly unimpressed and started reading me my rights.

This then went to Mum.

'It all sounds very complicated, Gregg,' she said, sighing. 'Very complicated indeed.'

'It isn't, Mum,' I cried. 'I told you it was just a big mistake giving my number plate away.'

I went to court, determined to clear my name. I was innocent.

So there I am: court appearance number two and I know right is on my side – I'm determined to clear my name.

Before things kicked off, the copper who nicked me came over.

'Have you got any witnesses?' he asked.

'No,' I said. None of my mates wanted to take sides between me and Simon.

'So it's just your word against ours, then,' the copper said, smirking.

'So much for British justice, eh,' I shot back.

I couldn't afford a lawyer, so I stood there on my tod.

'Are you representing yourself, Mr Wallace?' asked the magistrate, an old fella, myopically looking down through his glasses held up by a beak nose.

'Yes, sir,' I said.

'Would you like a pen and paper?' he asked.

'Yes, please,' I said. That alone filled me with confidence. I was going to be allowed to say something here. Brilliant.

An usher handed me a pen and notepad, and I clicked the pen open, taking a deep breath. The copper came on the stand, spouting a load of claptrap to cover his own back. He said I'd lied about the scooter and that I didn't have it.

Then it was my turn to question him, as part of my defence. I cleared my throat and stood to my full height, referring to my notepad.

'Do you not remember me telling you it wasn't my scooter at all?' I asked.

'No,' he replied.

'And if it was supposed to be my scooter you'd found, why was I not given it back?'

'Um,' he said, suddenly flicking through his notepad.

'Why does my mate Simon still have it? Was it because it was his scooter and not mine?'

'Um,' the copper's face reddened.

'And why did I bring a logbook for a Vespa to the police station,' I said, going for the jugular, 'when the scooter in question is a Lambretta?'

I could see the magistrate's eyebrows shooting up, as he scribbled furiously. He whispered to an usher. My turn was over and I flopped down on the hard court bench, feeling exhausted.

'Well,' said the magistrate after a short pause, 'I'm absolutely convinced, Mr Wallace, what you are saying is the truth.'

I resisted an overwhelming urge to punch the air.

'And,' he said, glancing at the policeman, 'can I suggest honesty is always the best policy?'

Afterwards I longed to go and knock Simon's lights out, but he was a much bigger lad than me, and I knew it was best just to leave it. My faith in the British justice system had been restored and I was really proud of how I defended myself.

Living day to day all the time wasn't working. The claim money was running out, I still didn't have a proper job and then Tracy dumped me.

Talk about out of the blue. I'd been at a party, of a friend of mine, and Tracy just turned up, looking a bit annoyed. We ended up having a barney and then she said, 'Gregg, this isn't working for me. I can't do this any more.'

I looked at this girl, the one I'd loved for six years and fancied so much I wanted to jump her even if I saw her just brushing her hair, and I was speechless.

Her life was going in the right direction. She'd got a good job, working for the GLC as a clerk, and was earning good money. I was going from one dead-end job to the next.

'OK,' I said, brazenly, trying to hide the dam of tears threatening behind my eyes. 'Is that what you really want?'

'I think so,' she said, sighing. 'It's just not the same any more, is it?'

I nodded now, mute, and turned my back to go to the kitchen to crack open another lager.

Everyone around me was laughing, joking, but I couldn't hear anything, not in my bubble of pain. I went back to the flat in Ivydale. The heating was off, it was cold and dark, and I'd never felt so alone.

I looked around me, feeling as if my heart was trailing behind me as I walked from living room to kitchen to open the fridge, to find it empty. I flicked on the radio.

The Commodores was playing. I flicked it off again and sank to my knees, crying. I couldn't bear it. What had happened to my life? What?

I walked to the local off-licence and bought the biggest bottle of vodka I could afford. I slumped back on the sofa. Drinking was the only way to make the evening more bearable. Somehow the warmth of it took the edge off.

I woke up the next day, my mouth like dried sawdust, the imprint of a sofa cushion marking my face, and then I remembered. No girlfriend, no family, no money, no career … with a hangover to top it off. Of course I've had down times since, but I've always had a clear plan for how I would fight back. Back then, I had no idea. I'd no idea how to get happier. I was twenty-two and little did I know lots was going to happen. Luckily, before I could crack open yet another tin of lager before breakfast, a knock came at the door. It was Miguel and Graham Breen, standing there with their familiar cheeky grins on their faces, despite my circumstances.

'You not topped yourself yet?' Miguel half laughed. It wasn't funny, except it was, because Miguel had said it. If I had nothing else now, I had my mates.

'Come over to mine,' Graham said.

Graham's dad was a builder and he'd always had this idea of converting his house into two separate flats and selling them, but it was their family home. I don't really think he wanted to sell it, what he did do was create a little studio apartment for Graham at the back of the house. Graham had a living room, with a sofa bed, beyond that a little kitchen and beyond that a shower and a toilet. He was a very popular man, was Graham, and there were people coming and going all the time, but we spent a lot of time together. He had a big TV, an outrageously expensive deck and speakers, and a huge collection of records, mostly rock. We'd drink beer, listen to music and chat a lot. He was making good money of his own now, and had a good deal going, working as a courier for a bank.

At first he was working for an agency, but then was offered the chance to undercut them, and he was earning what seemed to us lads a small fortune. He bought a new Kawazaki 1100, and would often take me for rides on his bike, on the open road, giving a sense of never-ending possibilities. Actually as a young lad I didn't realise this, but I do now: Graham really helped me out through a hard time. Cheers, Graham!

Being Graham's mate didn't stop me from feeling so low, though. Not only did I feel lonely, but I had a strong feeling of having less than and being less than everyone else. I suppose you could say this feeling scarred me or spurred me on to greater efforts. To be honest, I am never sure. Maybe it's left me with the will to achieve and the need to accumulate and save. I think that bit's fine, but it's also left me with an insatiable need for approval. Being successful or decent or nice is still my top priority; what people think matters – too much, probably.

I was nursing a pint, probably one Graham bought me, in the Waverley one day, when a guy known as Bendix Steve sidled up to me.

He was a bit older, a slight man with greasy hair and a raspy voice who smoked as if his life depended on it. I took him out a few times on my window-cleaning round, which was slowly coming to a grinding halt. What Bendix didn't know about washing machines, the Queen didn't know about corgis.

'How 'bout you and me start a little venture then, Gregg?' he suggested over his light ale.

Always up for trying something new – anything, really – I said yes. We put a small advert in the south-east London press, offering to repair washing machines, and got an answerphone with a professional-sounding message on it, and to my amazement quickly customers from all over rang up.

It never ceased to make me laugh when someone said, 'My machine is leaking . . .' and I'd ask, 'Where is it leaking?' and they always replied, without missing a beat, 'The floor.' Really! Not up the wall, then, eh?

To begin with, we worked well together. I was the driver, the one who chatted to customers, while Steve worked his magic on the machines.

But one day, as with most of my jobs, I didn't see it going anywhere. It didn't help that I was still heartbroken. I spoke to Tracy on the phone occasionally and one evening I managed to persuade her to come to a party with me. I was thrilled when she said yes.

As she walked in, with her honey-blonde hair, sexy wiggle and looking as amazing as ever, it was as though this angel had walked in, a Ready Brek glow all around her with a choir singing in the background.

Tracy. The Woman I Still Loved.

'Hello, Gregg,' she said, trying to be friendly.

This time, I decided I'd just have to style it out so tried chatting to her normally. A proper conversation – our first since we'd split. No need to show her how much she'd hurt me.

188

'All right, darling,' I said, in my most chipper voice. 'How you doing?'

Perhaps because I'd behaved more like old Gregg or perhaps because she genuinely missed me, she seemed chuffed to see me. One thing led to another and we found ourselves on the bed alone, with all the coats from the party-goers. My head felt as if it was about to explode with stars and sparks as we started to get it on again. Oh Tracy! We went back to Ivydale Road, hand in hand, and I wasn't walking on the grey pavements of Nunhead, I was walking on air. She stayed the night; I held her close, back where I belonged. Perhaps everything would be OK after all.

My reprieve lasted just twenty-four hours. The phone rang and it was Tracy, her voice sounding small and hoarse as she said those dreaded words: 'Sorry, this doesn't feel right any more.'

I didn't try to argue this time. I croaked a few lines of 'Take care' and put the phone down, sliding down the wall afterwards.

CHAPTER 18

Sticky Toffee Pudding

*B*y then the washing-machine fixing, along with the window cleaning, had pretty much petered out. I shouldn't have let it go: I could've made a decent living out of that for ever – in fact anybody could. Get yourself a van and a ladder and just knock on doors – simple! Most people in the world appreciate clean windows and won't turn you down if you offer to do them for a couple of quid.

I tried several more jobs, including cab driving, Artexing and even window cleaning for a big company. I think this was actually my lowest ebb. I wasn't eating properly, I didn't have much money, and one day as I sat on the Tube on the way home, how low I'd fallen became apparent to me. The train was almost empty except for a guy opposite, maybe a couple of years older than me, wearing a smart suit, cufflinks and a silk tie. I was dirty with a rash on my face, and one of my training shoes was split open at the toe. I felt ashamed of my appearance, especially when he noticed my shoes. The contrast between us was quite striking. It makes me really sad now, thinking about it.

So when I heard there was a job coming up at Performance Chemicals as a van driver, I decided to go for it. Go back to where I started. I'd nothing to lose.

It's not a bad job, you know, driving a van all day. There's no real pressure, you are on your own, and you can do a lot of thinking and singing! I covered the Home Counties, making a few stops in town but mostly going to rural areas. I learned a little bit about the country that way. It didn't pay brilliantly well but I was content at first. I didn't mind being on my own, discovering new areas, finding sights, ticking off the workload; there was definitely a spirit of exploration and a certain amount of freedom.

If I ever had a coastal run, say to Brighton, I'd pick up Grandad en route.

'You fancy a spin, Grandad?' I'd ask. He'd grab his coat and cloth cap and we'd be off.

I loved sitting in that cab with Grandad, turning the heating up and having a chat. We'd talk football, jobs, girls. Or I did and Grandad listened, sucking his teeth, winding down his window to take in some sea air when we hit the promenade.

At our stops I'd leap out the van and start taking out the boxes. Once there were a few very heavy pieces that needed carrying into an office. Huffing and puffing, Grandad got out of the cab. He looked at me as I pulled up the shutter.

'Right. I've just gotta get this lot out, Grandad, next,' I said.

Grandad's brow furrowed as he shook his head at me. 'Sorry, son, I can't help ya, you know. I'd like to but I can't.' He glanced down at his brogues with a slightly pained expression.

'Nah, don't be silly, Grandad!' I cried. 'I don't expect you to. That's all right. Course it is.' I marched off, carrying the box, watching him as he stood by the cab, not knowing where to put himself. His shoulders and back were more arched than usual, as if he was carrying a load. He looks so old now, I thought sadly. Afterwards, I slammed the door shut and jangled my keys. 'Let's go and get some fish and chips, then,' I said.

We'd always find a café, a greasy spoon or chip shop in which to enjoy flavours I was brought up with. Meat pies, fried fish, piles of chips soaked to a soggy mush in vinegar, frosty with lashings of salt. Then we'd get back in the van and go home.

We both had a surprise when Dad turned up one day to say he'd got a new girlfriend. Considering Dad was still as hopeless a drunk as ever, I suppose it wasn't so much of a surprise he'd met her while propping up the bar in his local.

Rachel was the mother of three young kids and had just got divorced. She'd been touring the locals looking for another husband, I reckon, and Dad fell for her or got carried away by her, whatever way you look at it.

I nipped round one day, to have a cuppa, and the house had two little girls in there, Dad's new stepkids to be. They were screaming, chasing each other with My Little Ponies or whatever, and Grandad struggled as he stood up to greet me from the sofa.

'All right, Gregg, in ya come,' he said, shaking a little. 'What you want to eat then, boy?'

One of the little girls bumped into his knees with peals of laughter.

I looked at Grandad as he tried to laugh. He doesn't need this, I thought. He's too old for all this now.

'You sit down, Grandad,' I said. 'I'll put the kettle on myself.'

In late 1986, I popped round to see Grandad, and Nan answered the door. Her face was pinched and drawn.

'Where is he, then?' I said, smiling and looking behind her shoulder at the stairs to see Grandad's brogues appear.

'In hospital,' she said, her eyes not meeting mine.

'You what?' I replied.

'Intensive care, Guy's,' she continued. I backed away as if I'd been shot, to jump back in the van and get to hospital.

Grandad was flat on his back, the bed sheet neatly pulled up to his chest, wires poking out of him. I just stood there, stunned. I'd never ever seen him without his shirt on before. He looked extremely pale, lily white and vulnerable. I worried he'd get cold with a bare chest like that.

I pulled up a hard moulded plastic chair and sat next to him, resting my forehead on the cool starched white sheet next to his hand. I slipped my palm into his. It was so warm, as always, as I curled my fingers around his.

The sound of his breathing, calm, deep and even, exactly as he sounded when he was having forty winks on the sofa, was the one thing that comforted me. It was a sound I knew, had grown up with. I hoped this proved he'd be all right.

'Hello, Grandad,' I tried to say, my voice sounding raspy.

A nurse passed by. 'He can hear you,' she whispered. 'Keep talking.'

I sat for hours, telling him how much I cared. I'd never said anything like that before. Actually maybe I didn't need to.

Just before I left that day, the nurse handed me Grandad's belongings in a clear plastic bag. His winceyette striped pyjamas were crimson with blood.

I sat with them on the van seat next to me, folded my arms on the steering wheel and cried my eyes out.

Two days later, I was getting up early to go and see Grandad again. I'd been in the day before and couldn't sleep. I'd just flicked the kettle on when the phone went.

'It's ya dad. Sorry, Gregg, Grandad's gone.'

I couldn't get any words out. Just managed to squeak a 'Thanks' and put the phone down. I knew he was ill, I knew he had to go some time, but it felt like a hammer blow in the guts. Grandad. Gone. How could this even be possible? Why had nobody told me he was ill? How could it happen so fast?

Later, I found out he'd died of a perforated ulcer. Maybe those Rennies hadn't done him any good after all. I didn't even know how old he was – nobody did. At a guess he was in his eighties. As I drove over to Kincaid Road, I spotted a huge billboard past the Old Kent Road flyover. 'If you see Sid, tell him . . .' It was the start of the British Gas privatization campaign. For the next few months it was everywhere. 'Have you seen Sid?' A constant reminder, just when I'd have done anything to see my own Sid Wallace again. One day, I want to be a grandad too, one as good as he was to me.

Losing Grandad was one of the biggest blows of my life, after losing Tracy. I didn't see how things could get worse. I'd not bumped into Tracy for a while, thank goodness, which had given my poor old heart at least a little time to heal. Until one day I was in the King's on the Rye, a posh boozer, one of many that cropped up around that time. A tired old spit-and-sawdust boozer, it'd been painted in pastel colours, all greens, blues and pinks, had a nice fitted carpet with 'King's' written on it and had a 'happening' disco on till 2.00 a.m. upstairs. I'd quite a large group of local friends by now, Graham Breen being one of them. It felt good: everyone had the same accent, the same aspirations, the same background. Virtually all were manual labourers, scaffolders, drivers, with the odd tea leaf thrown in for good measure, hanging out either there or in the Kentish Drovers, another local on the Old Kent Road. Both pubs were owned by the same man, who drove a Rolls-Royce with the number plate 'IFLY'. Rumour had it he'd bought it from Kerry Packer after

Skytrain had collapsed, although in pub landlord being friends with a millionaire airline owner seemed slightly improbable.

I'd go down to the King's on the Rye every Friday and Saturday night with my mates, to have a dance. I always had a few good moves – well, I thought I did. Anyhow, one night I was in there, the beat of the music pounding in my chest, sucking on a Pernod and lemonade, when I spotted the familiar blonde hair which triggered a familiar lurch in my guts. Tracy.

'What's she doing here?' I groaned to my mate. 'She doesn't even live anywhere near here!'

As usual she looked incredible, in a tight mini skirt and shoulder-padded leather jacket, long hair flowing – you get the picture. I felt unbearable. Didn't know where to put myself. So when a girl twirling on the dance floor, who'd been giving me a bit of the eye earlier, started spinning around closer, I grabbed her hand and gave her a twirl.

'Hello, honey,' I said, grinning. This was the way to take my mind off Tracy. She told me her name was Christine and I'd no idea I'd just pulled my first wife.

Christine was a skinny girl with masses of mousy curly hair, beautiful eyes and a winning smile, and she was a proper Peckham girl with a temper to match. The perfect person to take my mind off Tracy, or so I thought.

I will tell you my favourite Christine story. We were at the home of her big sister, a lovely girl who was doing well for herself in Essex and had some aspirations, and we were sitting around the kitchen table, Christine regaling the family with some kind of story and she said, 'That's where we was.'

Her sister corrected, 'No, Christine, it's were.'

Christine replied adamantly: 'That's not right! It's *where* we was, not *were* we was.'

Neither I nor Christine had any money, my compensation being long frittered away by now, but it didn't matter. She was always happy to humour me in my own aspirations, though. I'd be lying in bed at the weekend, staring at the ceiling and coming up with my latest business idea. Or suddenly having a brainwave while up to my arms in soapsuds washing up, throwing ideas into the air of how I could make money. Proper money.

Christine came up with one once. The government had just announced the end of free eye tests.

'I know,' she said, turning to me, her eyes wide, gob open. 'Why don't you open a shop running free eye tests? There's a gap in the market, after all!'

'Yep,' I said, laughing. 'But it probably wouldn't do as well as a shop selling free cars or free fish 'n' chips.'

I pointed out the obvious and we both fell about laughing.

It didn't take us long to fall in love, or at least for me to think that I was in love. I'd lived on my own now in Ivydale for six years or so. To have someone in my life again, serious about me, felt amazing. I felt wanted.

And so Christine moved in pretty much straight away. I loved having her around, someone to come home to. Someone to cook for me. And she did her best, bless her. She'd buy up half of the frozen food counter and shove it in the oven. That was her speciality.

Then, just as we settled down, Dad announced he was marrying his girlfriend and was selling up.

'Oh right,' I said. 'But that's my house. That's where I live!'

Dad frowned. 'Can't you just be happy for me?'

'Sure, congrats, Dad, but where am I gonna live?' I cried.

Under much pressure from Mum, Dad gave me a small deposit for us to buy a studio flat. I nearly said 'bedsit', which it was really. While we waited to move in there, we went to live with Christine's sister, Rita, in Bermondsey.

It was all a bit of a squash but it was good of her to take us on. I loved being there, being around people again. I'd not realised how lonely I'd felt in Ivydale Road.

Christine left her job in a Peckham bank and Gerry gave her job as a secretary in accounts at Performance Chemicals, which meant we were both living and working together.

While we were all squashed in at Rita's place, I had an overwhelming urge to move on. I was fed up with being stuck in my rut, driving around, not getting any promotion, never moving on with my life. Now I had Christine it felt as though things were changing a little. I just needed something else to happen.

I was flicking through a local paper when I saw an advert: 'Warehouse men needed, New Covent Garden Market, apply today.'

'Whoa,' I said to Christine. 'Am I gonna go for this.'

She glanced over my shoulder. 'Why's that, Gregg?'

'Because it will be much more money than I am on now. What better reason?'

What I knew about fruit and veg you could write on a stamp, but this was good pay, proper man's wages of £100 a week, and it was working at the UK's leading wholesale market, so a step up from Performance Chemicals, in my eyes at least.

CHAPTER 19

Physalis

I rang the number and spoke to a man called Alfie.

'Come in tomorrow,' he said.

'Er, sorry, I can't,' I replied. 'I am working tomorrow and can't just take a day off like that. I am sure you'll understand.' I hoped he understood anyway.

'Right,' he said.

'I just mean,' I blathered, 'if I was working for you, governor, you'd not like me to be taking random days off either.'

'I like it,' he said, finally, sounding a little impressed. 'Come in at the weekend for a chat, then.'

I turned up at New Covent Garden Market warehouse, a huge sprawling affair based at Nine Elms, just south of Vauxhall Bridge, that Saturday, keen to make a good impression. Two things hit me when I walked in. First of all the smell, a beautiful fresh mixture of apples, strawberries and greenery. And second the noise: trucks parping horns, forklift trucks whirring past, men shouting and yelling at each other – it was mental.

'Nah, Jack, I said three pallets of apples not four . . .'

'Lemme have them tangerines . . .'

'Gotcha, sunshine . . .'

The market is split into two types of companies: wholesalers and catering suppliers. The catering suppliers bought from wholesalers, wholesalers bought from importers and growers. Turnell's, the company I was going to see, was a catering supplier. Keeping up?

The market provided most of the fruit and veg eaten outside the home outside London – places like restaurants, factories, shops, bars, cafés, schools, hospitals and local fruit and veg stalls, all over the south-east mainly. It was the depot where fruit and veg arrived from around the world, from Holland to America, from Kenya to Australia: every single type of fruit or vegetable you can imagine and some you couldn't.

Straight away I was intrigued.

A man with a bushy beard, wearing tartan trousers and a trilby, came marching over, holding out his hand to shake.

'Gregg?' he said, pulling a slip of paper out of his pocket. In biro was scrawled 'Gregg Wallace'. 'Alfie Rogers,' he said, pumping my hand up and down with a grip I tried to match.

He sat me on a pallet, as trucks and people ran up and down in front of us, his eyes roving around, never still, as if he was keeping up with what was going on as he fired off a string of questions. Was I fit? Was I healthy? Was I a grafter? Could I lift boxes all day? Could I add up?

'I'd want you in charge of the pot,' he said. 'That's the fridge where we keep all the stock. You'll also need to load vans. They come to the warehouse and drive off quick all across the country. It's hard, noisy, heavy work, but if you make the best of it, you'll love it. It's a 2.00 a.m. start. What do you think?'

At that precise moment my senses were so overwhelmed with the noise, commotion, smells and energy of the place that my head was reeling, but something inside me told me I wasn't just going to like this place, I was going to love it.

'When can I start?'

My first day working at Turnell's catering suppliers in New Covent Garden Market was something else. It really was a breathtaking baptism of fire in the world of wholesale fruit and veg. Something inside me also told me it was going to be life-changing, but I had no idea just how much.

The layout of the market was baffling at first, but easy once you understood it. The warehouse was split into two big identical buildings, with very high ceilings and very wide. A road ran between them for the vans, lorries and scooters to fly up and down, the lorries and vans stopping and opening their doors to be filled at the apron. Beyond the apron was the warehouse with the stock, empty pallets and pallets filled. As fast as we loaded them up, more lorries arrived to refill the pallets. The place opened around 10.00 p.m. at night for the first new stock arrivals and went on all day to around 12 noon. It was mayhem, with men running round like flies, sweaty and shouting, but organised mayhem.

Alfie quickly rattled through the instructions for my job.

'Look at this list,' he barked, jabbing his finger at a scrap of paper. 'If there is a cross next to what we need it means it's a whole boxful. If there's no cross it's just a single item. So "2x tomatoes" means two boxes of tomatoes, "2 tomatoes" means just two of 'em. Got that?'

'Yes, boss,' I agreed.

'Good lad,' he said, slapping me on the back so hard I felt my chest rattle. 'Now get going.'

I found myself running back and forth, up and down,

heaving the boxes, following the lead of the other boys, who knew exactly how to stack them in, as if we were in a mass game of *Krypton Factor*, packing a lorry to the roof until you couldn't see a chink of daylight between the boxes.

As fast as we packed and the fruit and veg flew out of the fridge, it was stocked again. The van was packed according to the chef who ordered the fruit and veg. Orders came in two types: either part of a box or sack or a whole box or sack. The fruit and expensive items were put together on trays. The bulky stuff – the carrots, onions, potatoes, stuff that didn't have to be handled with care – were then tossed in.

The big boss of Turnell's was a ferocious geezer called John Reeves, known as JR. A tall, broad-shouldered guy, with a menacing grimace, he was as hard as nails. He'd arrive like an angry tornado, shouting a few orders before setting up at his own metal table in front of a van. He'd have all the tickets of the orders and start barking for drivers and men to load up the vans. This went on from 3.00 a.m. to 9.00 a.m.

'Go and get the fruit for the Dorchester Hotel!' the manager would yell. And I'd rush off to find fruit on racks on wheels, labelled 'Dorchester', to put on the back of the van. Then I'd run off to get the extra as the manager shouted it at the top of his lungs. 'Ten pounds of onions, three boxes of melons . . .'

'Melons are down today!' a young man with a 'tache would shout, as I turned to hear a whole pallet fall over.

'Heard they're on the floor,' an older geezer would laugh.

The amount of fruit and veg I saw boggled my mind, especially all the exotic stuff. I'd never seen physalis before, their shiny firm orange balls and beige crunchy leaves looking like something from *Star Trek*. I saw crates of papaya, prickly pear, passion fruit, lychee, star fruit – stuff I'd never heard of.

I wasn't sure if we were allowed to, but one of the guys

noticed me looking in wonder at some of the fruit, picking it up, turning it over in my hands, and he suggested I take a bite.

'Go on!' he chided. 'Nobody minds!' He was right: eating the odd piece of fruit in this place was like nicking a bucket of water out of the ocean.

I nipped one of the physalis and pulled off the scrunchy leaves.

'What . . .' I asked, tentatively. 'Do I eat it like this?'

'Just pop it in ya gob,' someone else shouted. 'It won't bite.'

It was crunchy, sweet, fleshy and slightly bitter. I'd never tasted anything quite like it before.

Depending on supply and demand, prices could go up, and a good buyer would realise this before it happened, but this was something I was to learn much later. Then the doors were slammed shut, a shout went up to the driver and off he roared into the night, to make sure that the fruit and veg reached the hotel – or restaurant, café, caterer, school – with plenty of time to spare.

By the end of the first day, my forehead was shiny with sweat, my biceps were bulging and I felt as though I'd run a marathon. But I couldn't have been happier. There was a real spirit, a sense of teamwork, and the men were decent, solid, hard-working family men. And for the first time in my life I was earning a decent wage too: it was treble what I had been on at Performance Chemicals. Hallelujah!

By 8.00 a.m. most of the vans had disappeared and so we stopped for lunch. The market had its own café, and even its own bank and pub for workers: it was like a little microcosm of bustle. Some of us retired to the café for a big plate of steak and kidney pie, washed down with tea and cake for afters. As we ate the lads chatted to me, eager to explain how this brave new world worked, and I found myself fascinated by it. I'd noticed many of the boxes had 'Holland' stamped on the sides of them, whereas other countries tended to put the area of their origin. Holland grew peppers, aubergines, tomatoes, all that Mediterranean stuff too – things you wouldn't expect. In fact they were the largest growers of Mediterranean fare, because they grew things hydroponically, using specialist micronutrients instead of soil. It amazed me. I also saw grapes from South Africa, avocados from Israel, mangoes from India. I also learned that mangetouts and French beans came from Kenya, which is the biggest producer there is of flowers and French beans, but that can cause problems, apparently.

'When it's Valentine's or Mother's Day there is always a shortage of French beans, because the planes are stuffed to the rafters with flowers for your mum or girlfriend,' explained a guy.

For the first time in a long time, I was looking forward to going to work the next day. But first I had to go home and sleep it off.

Finally we got keys to our new place in Honor Oak. It was tiny. A bedroom/sitting room and a kitchenette. You couldn't swing a cat in it. Not that we wanted one: we were too busy with each other. And Christine kept me busy, feisty as they come. We rowed non-stop, but somehow we still liked each other enough to stay.

We didn't even bother with a sofa bed and just slept on the floor on a duvet. I bought a sofa from World of Leather, a new CD player, and got spotlights and new carpets fitted. It was so groovy – well, at least I thought so, and it was mine! We struggled to pay the mortgage on our wages but we managed.

That Christmas, Mum asked what Christine would like and I suggested a microwave. She screamed when she opened it.

'Oh my God!' she cried. 'It's amazing, innit!' We felt like proper yuppies now.

This was 1987 and there was a property boom. Just eight months later we sold the flat for a massive profit – well, a good few thousand, a big sum for me – and bought a little one-bed house in Bermondsey on Abbey Gardens, built by Abbey National. Yes, that's how well life was going back then: banks were actually building people houses.

Now Bermondsey I loved. I felt at home, just walking down the street. It was one step up from Peckham but it was full of good solid working-class families, some of whom had lived there for five or six generations – my kind of people, I felt. All the young guys dressed the same – jeans, trainers, windcheaters, polo shirts – and they all had short but not cropped hair. Family people who worked hard for a living. I found my perfect boozer, the Queen Vic, in Bermondsey and it was just forty-two steps from my front door to the bar. It quickly became our local.

In there I met an old fella called Tommy. A Welsh guy, he was always coming out with pearls of wisdom, or what appeared to be so after a few pints. He actually got me back into rugby, a sport I'd not forgotten enjoying at school. The year 1987 was also the year of the first ever rugby World Cup, and the Six Nations was on the pub telly: we'd meet and watch it together, enthralled. Although I'd never been any good at rugby at school, I enjoyed the complexities of the game, and that summer, Tommy and I were right on it.

And what a tournament it was, with England reaching the final. I clearly remember the semi-final against France. A ferocious game! I'll never forget the moment Brian Moore bared his teeth in the pack scuffle or the England winger was knocked out.

Tommy liked to talk about the match afterwards and I found myself getting animated about it again. At the same time I started playing for the pool team in the pub, and one day the captain, Laurie, came in with some other bloke and they spotted me and Tommy chatting about rugby.

'Not many people in Bermondsey like rugby,' said Laurie's mate, laughing. Anyway we got chatting too and it turned out he was the scrum half at Eton Manor in Leyton. So that set us off again.

'You're really into this, aren't you?' he said. 'Why not come down to our training session on a Wednesday night and have a game?'

'I dunno,' I said. 'I'm not very good.'

'Don't matter,' he said. 'Just come and join in.'

So that Saturday I did. I went down and I was a far cry from the first team, but I was a decent enough hooker. Now in my mid-twenties, I found myself playing for a season or two. It was fantastic. I loved the way it was so physically demanding and you had to be really tough for eighty minutes, and fight for the ball without being intimidated. I loved the way people were knocking each other around one minute and then at the end were patting each other on the back, bruises all forgotten, and having a drink like gentlemen. Rugby players are some of the politest people I've ever met. After that, I got right into watching it, going to matches and watching it on TV, even in slow motion. I became an unashamed rugby fanatic.

Things were going well at the market too. JR had spotted me as a hard grafter and always picked me to sort out loading the van. A tough man and uncompromising, he knew what he did and didn't like. He'd arrive at 3.00 a.m., bright and breezy, ready to go, and somehow he took a shine to me.

'You never stop, Gregg,' he said. 'And I like that.'

205

He was right. While some of the other blokes milled around a bit, waiting for orders, I just kept going or organised the fridge a bit to keep on top of things – there was always something to do. And I enjoyed that. I wanted to impress, as I wanted to move up the ladder in this place. For the first time I could see it was somewhere worth going to. It was hard work, though, and took a while to get the hang of. All the lads would go off at once to follow the orders but often arrive back at different times, and it was up to the manager at the desk to work out which box went where. We were always fending off problems too. If the night was cold there was a bunfight to get the salads in. If they freeze outside they turn to mash when they thaw, and nobody wants that. If you buy them and they're frozen you can send them back to the supplier, and if it's the company's fault it loses the money. And avocados…Don't get me started on them! They're a nightmare, as everyone wants them ripe, but once they are ripe they are turning. Greengrocers throw away as many avocados as they sell.

Of course with these huge piles of fruit and veg everywhere, people nicked some of it, as nobody noticed. We got a box of *cotchell* (a Hebrew word meaning 'a box of various products'), too, after work every week. We were allowed that – well, the directors didn't know but the managers did and turned a blind eye, and indeed were doing it themselves. But with nobody looking at what anyone was actually taking, the place lent itself to a bit of a culture of pilfering and stealing. The van drivers were the worst; it was so easy to make off with several extra boxes for markets on the street. The managers would call out the orders and the van drivers would put more on the van than they needed. For example, they'd put four boxes of tomatoes on the van when they only needed two: nobody would notice, nobody could keep track. They'd then sell it on to other lads or to other restaurants on the way home after doing their rounds. It was so easy for them.

I just stuck to a bit of extra here and there. There was no way I could see myself pilfering thousands of pounds' worth, although the culture of taking what you wanted when you wanted it was so normal that it seemed stranger not to take something. Once I asked a manager if I could take an extra box of veg and he looked at me as if I was stupid. I was a young man and learning from those around me, and I can honestly say it really didn't seem as if I was doing anything wrong.

It was around this time I bumped into Charlie Hicks. He was the French buyer for Turnell's who, at the time, was the only catering supplier sending out someone to markets in Paris. By far and away Charlie was not your average worker in the warehouse. A public school boy, he sounded like a City lawyer and was completely different to everybody else working there, the most unlikely greengrocer you could ever meet in your life. But we got on, we chatted about films and music, and we became friends. I was very proud he saw something in me, a warehouseman from Peckham. He was a cut above me, but he still liked me. He came over for dinner in Bermondsey and I went to his. Brilliant.

Charlie completely stood out. Once George, an old porter on the market, asked Charlie what he was doing over the weekend.

'Actually, George,' he said, 'I am getting married.'

George couldn't hide the look of surprise on his face.

'Why do you look so surprised?' asked Charlie.

George shrugged and looked shifty.

Then Charlie started chuckling. 'Oh, you thought I was gay, didn't you,' he said.

'Well, I thought it was obvious,' replied George. 'You don't like football and you take home fresh herbs.'

And on the market that was enough to question a man's sexuality!

Even though I was making more money than ever, I also had more outgoings than ever. We'd overstretched ourselves a little on the mortgage and money was a worry.

After a hard day sweating over pallets and boxes and running round like a Labrador, I longed for that first cold, long beer in the afternoon.

Once I turned up in the pub and found only £2 in my pocket, and I had that to last me the rest of the week. That afternoon I went home like a bear with a sore head, even more annoyed when I realised that the last beer in the fridge had been drunk. Getting in and having a row was the last thing I wanted, although that was happening more frequently. I was so tired, especially at weekends, as I was used to getting up to start work at 2.00 a.m. and then falling asleep in the afternoon, and Christine didn't like it.

'We never go out, we never do anything together,' she cried. 'You're just tired all the time!' She was right: it wasn't fair on her. But then again, I needed to work.

And so it went on. Christine and me, love's young dream, except our love was more beer and cactus than hearts and flowers.

The pattern of our day, our life, was set. Me working all night, sleeping all day, grouching around on the sofa, worrying about money before I set off, and my girlfriend's ship passing in the morning, she as grouchy as me sometimes. My urge to move on was so strong, though. I felt life slipping away and I'd not done anything yet. I had so much energy and was happy enough at work, but I worried non-stop about how we'd pay the mortgage, and Christine, bless her, wasn't the best with money. We were broke.

My job was my saving grace: it was fun, it was all consuming, and even though I was now struggling a bit on the wages, it looked as if the extra produce we were 'allowed' could help me out.

Nick, who always looked as if he could do with a few extra hours in bed, was the one to tell me what the lads were doing.

'You need a bit of topping up? Bit extra? Go for the cheese. We all do it now and then. It's nothing. They won't notice. Put it in your box and sell it on with the fruit and veg. I make about a tenner a week this way.'

I just nodded and shrugged it off, but actually, what with things kicking off with Christine, and realising everyone else was doing it, I started to wonder if I was the mug for not giving it a go myself. It was a very short hop from taking other stuff.

A few days later, Nick ushered me over to where the cheese was in the fridge: giant slabs of Cheddar, red Leicester and Edam.

Without thinking, I half closed the door behind him and helped myself to a good 4-kilo 'slice', wrapped it in cling film and then popped it into the boot of my car, thinking, well, it is a bit of bunce . . .

I didn't think anything more of it. We knew we were hardly touching the sides when it came to swiping a few bits. We just all turned a blind eye. We had to: nobody wanted to be a grass, nobody wanted to lose their own job. We were all grafters.

Not all the drivers were dodgy, though. I grew fond of a few, like Terry Bailey, a thickset man who was actually very clever when you got to know him. A strong character with big ideas. He lived in Stepney, so there was only the Rotherhithe tunnel between us and we'd give each other lifts sometimes. I hit it off with Andrew Baxter too, the son of Mark Baxter, Turnell's owner. Mark struggled to cope with his company at times: he'd become a bit of a laughing stock, as he spent a lot of time in the pub. He was from Covent Garden proper, when it was not up by Nine Elms but down in Covent Garden, so not far from Fleet Street and all the pubs there. The *Daily Express* cartoonist drank with him, and often drew vans with Turnell's on them if he ever drew a London street scene, as a nod to his drinking pal's business. I found Mark was either drunk or seriously hung over and often thought his behaviour was completely irrational – you never knew where you stood with him.

Once he snaked his arm around me as I was off looking for stock.

'Gregg, lad,' he said, 'if you ever need any help whatsoever, you just say the word. Just ask, fella, and I'll tell ya. I'm always happy to help.'

The next day, I was desperately searching for a pallet of golden raspberries when I saw him passing. ''S'cuse me, Mark, can you point me in the right direction of the—' The words had barely escaped my lips when he turned to me, snarling.

'What the *hell* are you asking me for?' he screamed in my face, spittle flying from his lips.

Sometimes he'd clear a floor with his temper, his rages making people shrink and suddenly become busy elsewhere. One of his pet hates was the weighing scales area being messy. This was one of the busiest areas, with about four vans loading at any one time, and the last thing on anyone's mind was the mess of veg and empty boxes strewn round the scales, but for Mark in his madness it had to be spotless. Often when he was about I'd find myself spending too much time chucking out old boxes rather than concentrating on getting the fruit and veg together.

On the whole I kept myself to myself. I mean, I was there to graft. New blokes were always coming and going, and one day this short, slightly weasely looking guy turned up called Mike. He was keen from the start, wiry, and quickly worked out the packing system. A bright lad, he didn't need telling twice.

One afternoon, he winked at me, pointing to a box. 'Gregg,' he said, 'is it a free for all?'

'Pretty much, mate,' I said, shrugging. I guessed it was such common knowledge it was just one of the unofficial perks now.

Mike winked back. 'Gotcha!'

I was actually mainly eating most of the stuff I took, as we were still strapped at home. But I did sell the odd piece of cheese or frozen gâteau in the local pub after work, for a fiver or so, after occasionally a manager would chuck me the keys to the freezer.

'Pick me up two strawberry tarts for the Molcombe Hotel,' he'd ask.

So I would, but I'd also pick up an extra one for me. Now that is stealing, but again, it seemed like a small addition.

It often made its way to my local. The landlord of the Waverley Arms always had an eye for a bargain and didn't mind. He'd take it behind the bar, covered in a bar cloth, and slip me a note or two. It helped ease life at home, with every bill that came in. At this point my bit of bunce was helping us out, or at least providing a bit of light relief with beer money.

A few weeks later, I came into work as usual at 2.00 a.m. and we set up the pallets and started running round like flies – a normal day. By 4.00 a.m., things were as manic as ever, a whirlwind of men, boxes, vans and shouting. The lads always made me chuckle. 'That's shallot,' yelled one as the last bag arrived on the van, while the new word for 'melons' was 'Mel 'n' Kim', and when poor Mel became ill it switched to 'Not Well 'n' Kim'. The cheeky lads' sense of humour was never far off.

Anyway, we were all working like the clappers as usual, having a laugh where we could, when we heard some shouting from outside.

Then, amid us workers, came a whole crowd of other men, dressed in very smart suits and ties, looking completely different to us, and Mike, the short guy, appeared to know them.

One of them tapped me on the shoulder. 'Gregg,' he said, 'come with me.'

As if I'd been playing a game of musical statues, I froze.

CHAPTER 20

Truffles

I dropped the box of tomatoes I was carrying and watched them roll over the floor as people walked on them, squishing them into pippy mush.

'We've been working under cover for weeks investigating theft on a giant scale in this joint and you're all nicked,' said the man. 'We've got all the evidence.'

He frogmarched me to my car and asked me to open the boot. I did so, to reveal a big slab of Cheddar.

'I was taking it for personal use,' I protested. I had to say something.

'All 4 kilos?' said the copper with a laugh. 'That's a effing big fondue!'

I knew the same thing was probably happening to all the other lads. Eight of us were taken in different cars to Battersea police station.

And for the second time in my life I found myself in a police cell. I was allowed one phone call and rang Christine.

'Aw, you're bloody joking, Gregg!' she cried.

Sitting in that cell, I had plenty of time to think and it didn't take long to work out what had happened. JR wanted to take over the firm over from Mark and he was baying for blood. He wanted all the old management gone and of course they were aware there was a bit of looting going on. So what a perfect solution: round up and sack a whole swathe of the workforce in one quick go. We were small fry. In comparison to some of the stealing going on what we were doing was nothing – not that any stealing is acceptable, but that kind of culture is hard to resist. I was nicked for a couple of lumps of Cheddar, yet some were getting away with thousands of pounds' worth.

I was kept in and hours later, I woke to a plate of eggs, bacon and sausage on a plastic plate. The copper who handed it to me was surprised how grateful I looked for it, but I was starving and had a lot on my mind. I'd no job again. No job and a mortgage to pay. That was all I could think of. When the copper came in and opened the cell door, I was offered a call to a solicitor, but I didn't bother with legal representation – a lawyer couldn't get me out of this. So a few weeks later, I just turned up in court, pleaded guilty and accepted the £50 fine.

As soon as I was turfed out of the station I didn't take long to find work. I answered an advert for a driver in Battersea to deliver magazines and newspapers all over London and quickly started a new job. I didn't tell them of my recent conviction; they never asked anyway. It was boring and dead end again, but I needed the money. I only lasted a few weeks, kicking myself the whole time for being so daft as to get dumped from a job I had loved, just for a bit of bunce. As I drove round, my mind was driving me crazy thinking, always thinking, of ways of sorting this situation out. And I came to just one conclusion: I'd have to try the market again. Even if I'd been sacked for stealing.

There are over 100 companies working in New Covent Garden Market. I spoke to Alfie and he suggested trying Associated Catering Supplies, a company a few doors down from Turnell's.

A Greek man, Andrew Savolis, short and resplendent in a tailored shirt and Rolex, ran ACS. He'd bowl down the corridors like a bullet, barking orders and leaving people almost reeling in his wake, trying to keep up with both his energy and his poor command of English. I turned up early one morning and steamed up to him, trying to keep up with him as he marched down the corridor.

'Mr Savolis,' I said, 'can I have a talk with you, please?'

He stopped, and turned and looked at me. I wondered if he'd heard I'd been done for stealing. I longed to be honest but dared not mention it.

'I'd like to come and work with you. I'm a good hard grafter,' I blurted out as he rocked on his heels. 'And I won't let you down.'

He gave the briefest of nods and that was that: I started working for him as a driver the very next day.

After about two months of delivering veg for Mr Savolis, he started asking about my knowledge of French produce.

'You worked at Turnell's?' he said thoughtfully. 'You know about French food?'

I nodded. I was handling and packing the produce so knew what herbs and types of lettuce they bought out there.

'Right, well, I want you to go out to the French markets and start bringing stuff back,' he said.

I could've hugged him, but I knew this was the last thing Mr Savolis would appreciate.

The next day I turned up and he handed me a piece of paper with some instructions on it. He wanted a buyer to go to France to the Paris markets overnight and bring back as much produce as a van could manage, to sell on direct to restaurants.

'Things like rocket, bunches of fresh herbs, lollo lettuce . . .' he raved.

I just nodded, taking in his rapid-fire instructions and wondering how the hell I'd manage to drive on the left-hand side of the road.

The next day at about 3a.m., I worked my shift doing deliveries, the other job Mr S had taken me on for, went home to change and then he sent me off on my new challenge. 'Here's the bag of change,' he said, handing over a bag that looked as if it should have 'swag' written on it. It had thousands of pounds of cash in it and weighed plenty. This proved to me how much he must trust me.

'Change it into francs on the ferry,' he ordered. I'd never been to France before but, armed with a map, money and a van to get me there and back, I was now going, on the way to my first French market to discover Europe's undisputed masters of the culinary arts for myself.

I set off at midday for Dover, caught the ferry to Calais and then drove off to find Paris. I was aiming for the Marché des Enfants Ronges, Paris's largest market. I say 'aiming', as coming off that first roundabout from the ferry baffled me (in fact however many times I tried to remember, I always hit the wrong side of the road when coming off that roundabout) and I had to negotiate what was a mini M25, le Périphérique. I had to keep my wits about me, but it appeared all very straightforward, and I arrived in the Parisian market at around 9.00 p.m. It opened at 3.00 a.m., so I had time for a quick kip on the roadside. That first night I lay down on the front seats, under a quilt I'd grabbed before I left, putting the gear stick into first so that it didn't dig in my back, and dropped off. I slept very well, having done a full day's work and then driven to France in another eight-hour day. It was absolutely exhausting.

Actually, some of the best sleeps I've ever had were in that van. Even today, when I can't sleep when I've too much on my mind, I imagine myself in that van, under that quilt, listening to rain drumming on the roof and windscreen, and I find it very relaxing!

Anyway, I opened my eyes before my alarm went off, with the sound of Frenchmen yelling to one another and the clanking of metal and pallets on the ground. I leaped up and couldn't wait to get my first glimpse of a real Parisian market.

This one was based on the layout of our English ones, with a big walkway for buyers down the middle and two enormous warehouses on either side, except these were ten times the size of ours. The frenetic bustle was the same, but everywhere I looked seemed like a lesson in food: it was a wonderland of colours and senses I wasn't used to. I felt like a child in a sweet shop, except the wares I was looking at were a whole galaxy away from Peckham grub. How did I end up here? I asked myself, laughing. I am a French buyer. This is amazing! How has this happened to me? It was quite an incredible thing.

Most of the French spoke English – fortunately, as all I knew was '*bonjour*' and '*oui*', and even my pronunciation of these words seemed to make them snigger. So I just dealt with those who understood me.

I picked up trayfuls of rocket, *champignons*, the lollo, and a few tinned truffles – everything Mr S had asked for. I'd no idea what truffles were then. I went back and forth to the van, loading and stacking as best I could. My new job was exhilarating. I was getting stuff the restaurants would snatch off us and Mr S would be pleased. Few wholesalers or catering suppliers were making such continental trips at the time. The pallets of salad in New Covent Garden were full of things like iceberg lettuce. None of this continental salad stuff had come through yet and reached the plates and palates of the UK, but some of the big paying restaurants were looking for it.

Once all the money had gone, I walked into the big bustling café in the market, smelling the unmistakable smells of Paris – grilled meats, fresh coffee, beer and brandy – as I grabbed a steak sandwich for breakfast. Then it was time to hit the road again. I made it back to London at around 7 or 8.00 p.m., and I was back lifting pallets a few hours later. Mr S was made up: I'd achieved my main goal, keeping him happy.

'You've done well there, lad,' he said, fingering the leaves of the rocket and pushing his nose in the herbs. And so this became my new position: official buyer, or dealer, or whatever you wanted to call me. I didn't care what I was: I was learning new skills and learning fast.

I met Charlie Hicks over there too, my old mate from Turnell's. He'd been a buyer for a couple of years now and could speak the lingo fluently, putting me to shame. He'd learned to speak French working in the markets so the French he'd learned was blue collar French. One afternoon, a bilingual German, who'd been listening to Charlie haggling over some herbs, laughed his head off.

'Are you aware you speak French with the most appalling working-class Parisian accent?' he said. I found this hilarious too. In England Charlie is really posh but in Paris he was more of an oik than I am.

Back in New Covent Garden, Mr Savolis never failed to make me laugh as well. He was always getting his sayings mixed up. Once he asked me to train up a new lad.

''E doesn't know the ropes, Grick,' he said. 'So can you keep him under your clothes?'

'Er, you mean under my wing, Mr S?' I said, grinning.

Another time he overheard me say, 'Give him enough rope and he'll hang himself' about a rival buyer and later on he tried to use the saying himself: 'You see they were climbing up the string, and I cut it and leave them hanging,' he said to a puzzled face.

When we weren't laughing, his poor English could sometimes be a liability. 'Our salads are good because we use a German machine that gases everything,' he explained to one buyer, describing how the nitrogen in the salad bags kept them fresh. Not exactly what a buyer wanted to hear. Another time I heard him on the phone to a customer, giving directions to Nine Elms, where the market was based.

'You know the way to the market? You come past Battersea Dog's Houses,' he was shouting on the poor phone line.

'Psst, Mr Savolis, it's "home",' I said.

Mr S nodded and went back to the phone. 'Oh, you're coming from home still?' he asked a van driver who was understandably losing his rag now, to groans from everyone listening.

His management style was completely bonkers sometimes too. He fell out with a van driver over something or other and was so annoyed that he decided to weld up his sliding door, so the poor lad had to clamber in and out of the back of the van, which caused him to take even longer with deliveries.

But to Mr S I owe an enormous debt of gratitude. If you're a working-class boy with no qualifications it's easy to get stuck making a living by moving things around – manual work: lifting or delivering or driving. If you want to get on in life, the hardest bit is making the leap from working manually to using your brain. And when I became a buyer, the seal was broken: I was out of the bottle. I'd escaped from the straitjacket of being paid to move things. The possibilities became endless. I was talking to clients, buying produce, and all of a sudden I was something.

I once got pulled over by the police on our way back from Paris. They looked inside and huffed and harrumphed at the boxes. I knew we couldn't import meat and dairy, but fruit and veg was OK, although they viewed me as suspicious. I used to smoke roll-ups, and as I was tearing off the Rizla cardboard to use as a filter, a French *garde* clocked it.

'Drugs?' he cried, pointing to the packet.

'Nah, mate!' I shot back. 'It's a filter for a fag!' I quickly demonstrated, making the roll-up and taking a pull from it.

The other copper arched his eyebrow, peering further into the back of the van.

'*Champignons?*' he said slowly, pointing to a box.

'Yeah, go on then,' I said with a sigh, twisting around and grabbing it. I threw it at him and he nodded a quick '*Merci*' and let me go on my merry way. Guess that's the border police's own way of having their 'bit of bunce'.

Later that night I took home some of the veg, a sample to try out. I handed Christine a paper bag of wild mushrooms.

She looked at me as if I was mad.

'What do I do with this, then?' she said, eyeing the strange shapes and textures, and sniffing it as if it was something found on the bottom of your shoe.

'Er, I dunno,' I said, laughing. Christine did all the cooking in our house, usually, as I've said, something frozen chucked in the oven. She filled up a saucepan with water and brought it to boil, and then chucked these specialities in, hoping for the best. Ten minutes later she pulled one slimy, sad, boiled-to-death mushroom out of the pan. 'Do you want beans on toast instead?' she said, wrinkling her nose as the mushroom slid off the fork on to the cork lino.

CHAPTER 21

Pie & Mash

*A*fter a month working at ACS, I really longed to come clean and confess to Mr S that I'd been sacked for stealing at Turnell's. I feared he'd find out anyway and then sack me again.

'Can I have a word?' I asked him. He stopped checking over pallets and looked at me.

Before I had a moment to think twice, I launched into my big confession. 'I was sacked from Turnell's for stealing, but it will never happen again and I am looking for a second chance,' I said in one breath without stopping.

His eyes narrowed and he drew nearer to me. 'Thank you for telling me, Grick,' he replied. 'I been working in this market for thirty years. You think I don't know? But it OK. You perform.'

'Th-thank you,' I said. I wasn't expecting that. I mean, I don't know what I was expecting, but not that.

'This is how I see it,' he continued, warming to this theme.

222

'If a man kills someone and he goes to prison, don't mean he's gonna get out and kill the whole world. I will take you on.'

So I carried on. And I was so proud to do it too. Delivering in the van all day and then once a week off over to France. When people asked me what I did for a living now I said it with pride, real pride. 'I'm a buyer in Paris.' What a step up!

Although the market stint was going well, I felt more ambitious than ever and I wanted a chance to move up, so I decided to take a chance on Mr S again and see if he'd consider letting me do something else.

Mr S was riffling through orders, looking intently at the paperwork, and didn't even glance up to see who he'd allowed into his office.

'Yep,' he said impatiently.

'I'd like to try out as salesman,' I said, quickly, knowing he was a busy man. 'I mean, I'll work all day as always and do the salesman's job for free at first … and then you can decide if you want to take me on.'

I took a breath to continue but Mr S was showing me the palm of his hand already.

'Grick, go for it,' he said.

You can measure the productivity of a person in sales very quickly. There is no room to hide. Sales is about skill, but also about hard slog. What you need to be doing is hitting as many new prospective customers, in this case prospective buyers, as you can, and if you are successful they will become clients. Your conversion rate should always be low; if your conversion rate is high, it means you're only going after surefire bets. Ideally you should have a conversion rate of about 20 per cent, which means you are doing lots of work. If you have a low conversion rate, ultimately you will end up with more customers. But if you only go after ten clients you'll only get one or two extra. To be a salesman you've got to have the skin of a rhino and hit everybody. I will always, always be able to make a living – I'd even go back to window cleaning – because I know if I hit every single street in London I'll have a big company. That's all it is: the law of averages. Got to get out there and pound the streets.

I've always said, though, that if you can't make money in London, where it's hanging off the buildings, hanging off people as they walk down the street, then you can't make it anywhere. I've always been able to talk to people, always been persuasive, always liked a laugh. It's something that is natural to me and I needed it now as Mr S gave me another chance to use my brain. In fact I have lots to thank Mr S for.

As I set off round the restaurants, I'd no idea what was what, where the good ones were or what they sold, and I needed to make it my business now to find out. I walked into any joint, big or small. Someone once said to me if you become friends, real friends with people, they stay with you. That is to say, you can always tell a faceless company you don't want to buy their stock any more, but you rarely tell someone who's your friend you don't want to buy their stock any more. At first I turned up wearing my smartest suit, bought by Mr S of course, because I couldn't afford one. But I soon realised that I was seen as a 'suit', not one of them. The chefs didn't want to speak to someone with a corporate image. Chefs come from all walks of life: for example, Alistair Little used to be an archaeologist. I needed just to be casual, dressed as they were.

I'd go and find the entrance around the back of the restaurant – sometimes it was concealed but there had to be one! And I'd just wander in. There was no need to be nervous. The chefs were always more nervous of you than you were of them. Many must've thought: who is this lunatic rolling in?

The best time to go was between 5.00 p.m. and 6.30 p.m., as just after lunchtime they wanted a break and to leave the building, and during dinner they were too busy.

I think I am quite an insecure person and people like me make the best sales people, as we want people to like us. People don't always buy the best products: they buy where they like shopping. They may carry on using the same barber or car cleaning place not because it's the best but because they like people in it. They use restaurants not always for the quality of the food but for the environment. People say selling is about the gift of the gab. I'd say it's about listening. If someone's talking to you they like you; if they don't like you, they won't buy from you.

It's also about being able to balance and accurately sum up where you are with a prospective client. If you think you won't get a client, then walk away and come back later. Say to him: 'Look, I am actually a bit busy right now. Tell you what I'll do, I'll come back and chat again,' or 'I'll tell you what, I'll come back in a week with some of those Italian tomatoes I was telling you about,' and then he might go for it later. If he says, 'No way, no thank you,' get him talking. If a chef is talking to you about problems with his girlfriend or football, he's gonna buy veg from you. This is what I mean by the gift of the ear not gift of the gab. Joe Gormley, the miners' leader, once said, 'Get them by the balls and their hearts and minds will follow,' and I agree.

So I carried on night packing and then walking around Covent Garden and Soho during the day, finding new customers. I just used to walk in, explain to them I was a rep for a veg firm and that I would look after them and they would sometimes begin buying from us. I had no idea who was trendy and who wasn't. If they were selling food, I was walking in.

'Is there anything you need?' I'd ask. Then I'd rattle off a list of places I was already supplying, however small. I started to pick up loads of new customers. I was learning and earning and I couldn't have been happier. I walked past Alfie one day and he looked me up and down. 'All right, Alfie,' I said, grinning like old times. But he barely gave me a nod. That hurt. To him I seemed to be going up in the world and I realised he probably didn't like it.

Someone else who didn't seem to like me any more either was my girlfriend. Christine was losing her rag every night now, and as I had a spiky temper myself we clashed like the Titans. One evening, after another furious row, I can't remember what over, we both slumped on our sofa like two boxers after several rounds in the ring, spent.

'I can't do this any more, darlin',' I said.

'Me neither,' she agreed. For the first time in months we had a calm, civilised chat, and we decided I'd move out and she'd stay and pay the mortgage. I didn't need any persuading. I went straight out, found a paper and looked for somewhere to rent. Very quickly I spotted a place in the Isle of Dogs, an area that used to be an actual island but is now surrounded on three sides by bits of the River Thames. It was near enough to work, so I went and had a look. The area had recently been redeveloped by the London Docklands Development Corporation and had become really cool.

The house was shared by two Canadian girls, Stacey and Jayne, a social worker and a teacher. The pair were total nutters, immense fun, and I agreed to move in the next day. It was one of the best eight months of my life. So many parties and all-nighters! The place was a den of booze and music for most of the neighbours. One night we had a Mexican-themed party and I found myself outside, with a big sombrero, a holster, a round of caps for my gun, downing tequila slammers till sunrise. I invited Andrew Dyne along and he loved it. Within a few weeks I'd gone from being man of the house to being sixteen again and it was brilliant. Working hard, playing hard – that was the way I liked it.

Christine was on the blower one day, though, sounding stressed.

'Aw, Gregg, you gotta help me,' she said. 'I'm behind with the mortgage.'

I sighed. Good old Christine. But my name was on it too, so I knew I had to help her out, which to be fair I would've done anyway.

'Let's go for a drink,' I suggested.

We met for a beer in the Queen Vic. Christine was her usual giggly, fun, feisty self, and as I stared at her across the table, my guts told me I missed her. By the end of the night we were smooching like a pair of teenagers again. Christine, never one to stand still, had already got a new man in tow, a bald flower seller from New Covent Garden Market, but she assured me he was in for the heave-ho and we'd get back together.

I'd also had a big idea.

I'd decided I was a good enough salesman now to see if I could open a business myself. After all, how hard could it be? I had the contacts, I knew how it worked and what the customers needed: I could keep everyone happy easily, or so I hoped. All I needed was the capital. I knew the restaurants took at least thirty days to pay, and while you were buying in more stock, you need to keep cashflow going. For small businesses cash flow, and problems with it, is often their biggest stumbling block. I needed credit and a good overdraft. And who did I know with cash? Well, I knew the wealthiest family in Peckham way, the Dynes. So I took Andrew, who lived nearby on the other side of Brands Hatch, out for a drink and he listened intently.

'I'll have a chat with my dad. This could work,' he said.

A day later I was sitting in front of Allan Dyne and repeating my plan. He was just as impressed.

'I can sell a person their own pen back to them,' I said. 'I can do this. I just need the capital. Andrew can help me. We can be partners.'

Allan Dyne stumped up several thousand, by asking his dad for a loan as well, and around my nan's dining-room table, my first business was born. We plumped for the name George Allan, using both our middle names, as this was to be a joint partnership. I was twenty-four, it was October 1989, and I felt as if I'd arrived.

We divvied up the work, so I'd deal with the customers, telling them all I'd started a new business, Andrew would do the invoices and we'd split the rounds. With the money lent we hired two vans from Dynes', an answer machine for orders, and a load of business cards and paper. We used the money left to buy the stock and off we went.

I'd leave for the market by 1.00 a.m., buy what we needed, pack up orders and put them in the van. Then we'd drive off in different directions to deliver to the restaurants who would order from us. At first we used the Dynes' backyard to stock our produce, but then one day I bumped into Jim, from Turnell's, while I was buying stuff in New Covent Garden Market. 'Do you need an office here?' he asked. 'I am looking for someone to share the arch in a space in the market.' I didn't need asking twice. We were real market traders now, oh yes!

I moved out of the girls' house and in with Nan W for a few months near Mum's in West Kingsdown, so that I could be living near Andrew while we got George Allan going. Things were going great guns with Christine too. We were getting on better than ever and I decided that now life was moving apace our relationship should do so as well, so I decided to move back to Bermondsey. For as long as I could remember I'd craved some stability, and I was willing to take the next big step.

'How 'bout we get married?' I asked her, over a kebab that night. Her mouth fell open and she laughed out loud. It was not exactly the response I was looking for, but she did say yes. She was down that dress shop faster than you can say, 'Now you may kiss the bride.'

Our wedding day on one windy Saturday was a small affair, just as we wanted it: Camberwell register office, with just fifty people as guests. I vividly remember putting my suit on that morning, my last morning as a single man, and looking in the mirror, a tight knot growing like wild weed in my guts. Just nerves, I told myself. Natural. But even after a nerve-steadying quick shot of brandy, the feeling wouldn't go away. And it was at that point I knew it wasn't right. I was getting married, yet it didn't feel right.

After we had whizzed through the twenty-minute ceremony, I took Christine and our best man and witness, Andrew Dyne, off to Manze's for pie and mash, much to the amusement of the ladies behind the counter.

'You know 'ow to treat your lady, doncha?' one ruddy-faced server said, laughing, as she plonked our plates in front of us. Christine just giggled, but chucked me a look afterwards.

'Shame we can't afford a honeymoon, though, innit?' she said, through a mouthful of pie.

My forkful of mash needed a few swallows to get it down. I kept smiling but for some reason I wasn't hungry. The champagne we had stored in buckets of ice by the back door for later went down a treat, though, and took the edge off the day and any misgivings I'd had. To be honest, I was glad it was over. Christine was now my wife and that was that, and now I could focus on my new business.

Andrew and I worked hard, all hours, and at first well together. But as the company grew, Andrew was reluctant to take on more work, always 'concentrating' on the invoices, until I found myself doing them, the rounds, the deliveries, the whole shebang. Credit became an issue too, as in we quickly had none. He was supposed to be the one telling us how much we were earning, but he didn't have a clue.

I needed someone else on board and I decided there was only one person I could think of who would be good enough. That was Terry Bailey, the van driver I used to know from Turnell's. I'd always liked Terry. He was bright and fun, and I knew he would work hard. I needed someone with some business acumen as well as extra financial clout, and he had just sold some flats he'd had built. So over a drink in the Queen Vic I asked him if he wanted to come in with us.

'Listen, Tel,' I said, 'I know you only knew me as a warehouse man but I really am a demon red-hot salesman. I've got this business going. I want you to be part of it.'

Tel sat quietly, sipping his pint. He didn't look impressed.

'Yeah, but you need customers, Gregg,' he said. 'Lots of them.'

'Don't worry about that, mate. I can do that,' I assured him. 'I already have.'

After ten minutes' more thought, Terry joined us too.

I spent so much time in restaurants chatting to chefs that I started to get to know them more. A young brash Aussie called John Torode was one. Wearing a tartan baseball cap and baggy white chef's get-up, he looked a bit like Wham meets Superchef.

He was only a sous chef at a small restaurant in Sidney Street, but seeing the way he stormed the kitchen I knew he wouldn't stay there for long. The first job I did for him was to find him some coriander root, a spice that tastes very different from real coriander: it smells more like bubble gum than anything else. It was incredibly hard to get hold of. If you cut a herb it will regrow, but if you pull out its root it's gone, so not many people wanted to supply it. But John needed it to make coriander paste for the Thai dishes he was cooking. Lots of the Aussie chefs did Thai food. You'd expect them to do European, as obviously they look European, but actually they're closer to Asia and Thai cuisine was popular in Australia, and they knew better what to do with a bean sprout than a chestnut, long before it was here.

I'd no idea where to get coriander root, or even what the hell it was, but I went to the herb specialists in the market and said I'd pay them double for it. I knew Torode was a man to please. The next day I had it in my hand and his eyebrows shot up.

'Good man,' he said, impressed.

A little while later Torode joined Le Pont de la Tour, a Conran restaurant at Butler's Wharf, but before he arrived, I decided to try my luck at the Blueprint Café, another Conran venture. I wandered in off the street and, with my usual patter, spoke to the chefs there, Rod and Lucy.

It was a posh place, right above the Design Museum, where diners could enjoy panoramic views of London while they dined on fantastic food. For me, it was a case of the right place at the right time. A veg firm had just let them down, I promised to deliver the goods, whatever they needed, and they took a punt. I personally hand delivered them too, and the next day. What a coup:, to have a Conran place on our books! Things were definitely looking up.

From then on I was always bumping into John. The Conran offices were above Le Pont de la Tour, and I'd have to go in there to discuss invoices sometimes. Plus the kitchens were glass and you could see into them from Butler's Wharf, so I'd wave to John. I was desperate to supply Le Pont de la Tour as well but the head chef already used another veg company called Lays. I couldn't get in there, although it didn't stop me trying.

CHAPTER 22

Pavlova

When customers bought fish or meat they tended to buy only one or two types, so they would look at where they could grab a bargain. But with fruit and veg they were usually buying thirty different types of veg and herbs, so nobody looked as much for a competitive price. No one would look to see if a bunch of basil, for instance, was 20p pricier than another one. So when I popped into restaurants, we did talk about the food I was delivering but we also had time to chat about life. Becoming good friends with the chefs, as I've said, was key. One of them, Timmy Payne, was a big fat lad with an appetite for life as big as it was for food. He was also a Blackburn Rovers supporter, and when they were playing Millwall at home, I invited him to come and watch.

I knew another lad who was in charge of security, and he kindly sorted us with access to the director's lounge after the game. It was brilliant: the pints flowed non-stop as we mingled with the game's sponsors. Timmy was dead chuffed to be there too. After the game, in high spirits, he whipped off his jumper and jacket, bundled them up and put them down as goalposts. Clapping his hands together, he rounded up the director's kids.

'Right, who fancies a game?' he said. They were all up for it, and within seconds, all the kids were kicking footballs at Timmy while he was doing pantomime dives for the goal, with me egging him on. It only took about ten minutes for things to get completely out of control, footballs flying in all directions. All the while loads of sponsors were sitting round in suits drinking G&Ts. We quickly decided it was time to head back to mine for more beers and to relive the game.

Back in Bermondsey, I was patting my pockets for my keys as we were staggering on the doorway, Timmy still making me laugh about something or another, when the door flew open. Christine was standing there, hands on hips, her face screwed into a familiar expression, like thunder. She shoved me on the shoulder to give further indication of her mood.

'We were *supposed* to be having a dinner party tonight,' she screamed. 'And look at the state of ya! What's going on, Gregg? What?'

I managed to get past her into the hallway. Smelling the food cooking, I caught sight of some bottles of Prosecco on the side, and our little dining-room table opened out and set with cutlery.

'Aw gawd, sorry, Christine . . .' I started, slurring badly. I really had completely forgotten. She'd invited some of her mates round for her first dinner party. She'd said she'd wanted to do more grown-up stuff like that, now we were married. Genuine mistake. I held my hands up, but that wasn't always good enough for my new wife – I knew that much.

She pushed past me, stalked around the house for a bit and then grabbed her white handbag off the side and slammed the door so hard that I waited for a sec for the glass to tinkle and shatter.

'I'd better go home,' said Timmy, sobering up quickly.

The next day I had the biggest hangover, coupled with the worry of not knowing where Christine was. She'd completely disappeared. I tried her sister, Rita, who lived down the road from us, and everyone else she knew, but nobody knew where she was.

Eventually she called. 'I've got back with Shane,' she said.

'OK,' I replied. And put the phone down. Wow! I couldn't believe it, but at the same time couldn't say I was devastated. Not really. Things in my life were looking up for the first time in many years. I'd got a good job and my own business; I could afford the mortgage on my own. If Christine wanted to go, I sort of just wanted to let her.

Anyway, a few weeks later I popped in on Rita and her boyfriend, Frank, as we were still friendly and I fancied a cuppa. She'd already heard that Christine had done a runner.

She invited me in. 'Oh, Gregg, I dunno,' she said, getting out the PG Tips. 'Shame if you two can't sort it out.' We didn't have long to muse on the possibility, for Christine waltzed in, with a bald bloke on her arm, looking like love's young dream again.

'All right, Gregg,' she said, airily, as if nothing had happened. And as if we'd never made the most solemn commitment a man and a woman can make just six weeks earlier. 'You putting the kettle on, Rita?'

I stood up, took a little breath and held out my hand to shake Christine's bloke's. He looked at her briefly, a bit confused, but grasped it and I gave him a firm shake.

'See ya later,' I said, and went straight to the pub. Rita's boyfriend, Frank, came in to find me a few minutes later.

'Sorry about that, Gregg,' he said. 'That was awful. I can't believe she hooked up with him again so soon.'

I took a slug of beer, but shrugged. I wasn't even putting it on. 'It's OK,' I said to him. 'Really. I think it's OK.'

And it was. I knew from the start our marriage had been one big mistake. Our marriage lasted six weeks, but actually we split amicably in the end and Christine doesn't have any hard feelings.

So I was back being a single man. I felt it was time to grow up a bit, now I was alone again in our place in Bermondsey. I started doing proper things, like learning to iron. I'd stick on a video, one I'd seen many times, like the *Godfather* or *Bladerunner*, set up the board, and I'd be away, ironing, but not worrying if I missed a bit of the film, as I'd already seen it. The halycon days of being a bachelor again, eh! I had some money and what looked at the time to be a decent future, nice clothes: things looked great. Within two weeks I was happy Christine was gone. Happy days. This was what I wanted. I was a pro, keeping the place tidy, eating properly. I wanted to change for the better and I was proud of that.

Because I was now supplying to restaurants, I was able to expense my dinners out through the company. And not just in the local kebab shop. I wanted to learn how these restaurants worked, what they needed and to get to know the chefs better. Up to this point, I'd lived off fast food and frozen food, and the only interest I'd had in good food was flogging it as fast as possible for as much money as possible. Now I was single again, I was always going on dates, and I fancied doing something different. One afternoon I was standing in NatWest in Peckham waiting to cash a cheque when I saw a very pretty, dark-haired, dark-eyed girl at one of the windows. I ambled up to her and paid her a compliment, and we got chatting. By the time I was finished cashing my cheque we were going on a date the next evening. I decided I didn't want to take her to the local boozer or nightclub: I wanted to try one of the restaurants I was selling to. I plumped for the Soho Brasserie.

My date arrived, impressed by my choice of venue, and as I pulled out her chair for her to sit down, I tried to look as if I did this all the time. The menu was amazing. Lots on there, and I just couldn't decide what to have, so I went for the chicken breast with a side salad.

We were chatting amiably, as she was a nice girl, but when the food arrived, I was dumbstruck. The chicken looked so succulent, with sauce drizzled on it and around the edge of the plate. It looked like something out of a photograph. The salad was neatly piled with some sort of herby dressing over the top. It was a chicken dinner like I'd never seen before. The colours were so vivid, it looked so elegant, and to me it was a revelation. This was art on a plate, not just food that you bolt down to satiate your hunger. This was good food served to appetise and impress. And I was very impressed. I'd been seeing good food in restaurants for a while now but hadn't eaten any of it. It was everything I'd thought it would be.

I turned my plate around, admiring it. 'Wow, this looks so good,' I said, grinning, before getting stuck in.

Afterwards we went for a walk down to the Covent Garden piazza and made our way into a wine bar. I'd no idea what to order. Everyone around me was ordering with gusto, so I just closed my eyes and pointed.

The waiter brought it out with a flourish. 'Would you like to taste it, sir?' he asked.

I nodded, my date looking on. I bet she'd not been expecting this boy from Peckham to look so confident. I sipped it and nodded, as I'd seen them do on telly. As we watched Londoners ambling across the square and tourists milling around, and sipped our wine, I felt truly happy.

'What a lovely evening,' I murmured. I'd never ever thought to do this before – have a delicious, lovely looking meal and then sit and enjoy some wine. I'd only ever been to nightclubs before this. After our date I wanted to see this girl again; moreover, I wanted to experience good food again, and soon.

I must admit, though, it took me a long time to wean myself off my lager tops and get into wine. In fact it took a chef giving me some advice there. A while later amazing Jerry Lee, who now runs Quo Vadis, spotted me taking sips of wine over a meal. 'Gregg, you're not enjoying it,' he said in his Glaswegian accent. 'Give yourself a great big mouthful and enjoy it,' he said. 'Quaff it!' Now I give people the same advice: 'Take a big mouthful, keep it in your mouth, feel it, enjoy it, love it.' That's the only way to drink wine.

I started to try to experiment with food a bit. The next day I came home with some Alpine strawberries and laid them on the plate, admiring them. I'd no idea what I was doing, but I got some fresh cream and drizzled it carefully over the top, and put a sprig of fresh mint on top to finish it off. It looked lovely, something different. Around this time I popped in to see Mum to tell her how I was getting on. Things had thawed between us by now.

'Sounds ideal to me, Gregg,' she said, laughing. 'You'd make a natural salesman.' She was making a roast at the time and I was chatting to her in the kitchen, watching her.

'You know what potatoes they are, Mum?' I asked. 'You know, King Edwards make lovely roasties, I've heard. What herbs are in that stuffing?'

Mum gave me a funny look and laughed. 'Blimey, Gregg,

what's happened to you?' she said. 'Dunno about the food, but you can help with the washing-up if you like.'

With Christine gone, I felt a sense of relief, tinged with sadness because it hadn't worked of course, but at this point I didn't have too much time to dwell on it. Just surviving in the market was sapping most of my energy. Try as I might, things were not working out with Andrew, and very suddenly we'd run out of money even to buy enough stock now. I was faced with letting the clients we did have down. Cash flow problem: it's a classic cause of failure for most small businesses. I suppose we needed help, we needed advice, but we didn't seem to be getting any from anywhere. Slowly Andrew was being pushed out, as Tel and I did most of the grafting, so I decided to call it quits. I didn't beat around the bush, I told Andrew straight.

'I'm splitting the company,' I said. 'In fact, I'm going to take it over.'

'No, you're not,' Andrew said. 'I will run it alone.'

'Do that and I will set up on my own and take all your customers,' I said. 'I've got the relationship with the customers.'

I had wanted the partnership with Andrew to work, but this wasn't one for me. I still wanted to be in business with Terry, though, as he proved himself a good man to work with. And, as if history was repeating itself, Andrew and I fell out. But the partnership wasn't working and that wasn't good for business. I made sure I paid the Dyne family back every penny and we went our separate ways.

Our credit was stretched and we couldn't even afford to buy any more stock. But actually it was Tel who came up with a way. 'I'll ring Johnny Fowler. I bet he could get us some stuff for a fee.' He said, going on to explain what he meant.

Johnny Fowler was a catering supplier like us, but an

impressive, successful one, who I'd got friendly with. I explained to him how I had all the set-up but no cash flow with which to buy in the produce. So I asked him to buy it for us, and then we'd buy it off him for a mark-up and sell it on. He thought for about thirty seconds and then grinned. So there I was, in business again.

Terry said he thought it would be a mistake to make this company big, though, which I found annoying at the time, to be honest.

'You're joking! We want to be big!' I said, expanding my arms, thinking of the money. 'The bigger the better!'

'No, we don't,' said Terry. 'We want to be manageable. We want to find the best customers, and squeeze as much profit as we can from them. Be careful. Do things small and build on what we have.'

I started laughing. 'Nah, Tel. You just lack ambition,' I said, only half joking.

It was his turn to laugh. 'Lack ambition! I'm more ambitious than you. That's why I think we should keep it small and profitable.'

But I didn't listen. At the end of the day Terry had a great gut instinct for business at the time, but neither of us knew just how good it really was. I was very happy to be working with him. Tel was bright, a grafter, and for once I felt that I had someone working with me on my side. Although this company was gonna get big, whatever he said. And didn't his words come back to haunt me . . .

Terry did stump up money to buy his way into the company though after he sold the flats he built. He trusted it that much. Andrew took the money and I put mine back into the business.

So, finally, now aged twenty-five, I'd started to become interested in food – really, really interested. I didn't see crates of fruit and veg just as a commodity to sell: for the first time I knew how enjoyable it could be to eat them too. And I'll tell you what, learning how to cook and what tastes good from chefs directly is one amazing way to learn about food. Then someone else came into my life to really show me how this could be done, not just in a posh restaurant but at home.

Denise Lovall was a very pretty, petite blonde, with high cheekbones and a sunny smile, and she worked as a chef at the Sanctuary, where I was delivering vegetables. Over a bit of a cheeky banter, I chatted her up and walked away with her number for a date. She was so well spoken, so pretty, I fell for her, bang, just like that. She was the daughter of a postman from Jersey but had grown accustomed to the high life after working as a personal chef for a businessman and his family, who treated her like a daughter, giving her a Range Rover Vogue to run around with. Every day she made them business lunches and it was a job she loved. She had originally trained as a pastry chef, but had given it up to move in with her boyfriend near Chelsea, but she wasn't happy; hence she was out on a date with me. After our date, which lasted all weekend, she moved in with me at my place in Bermondsey the following weekend.

I remember our first meal out. It was Stringfellows, which was famous at the time not for being a lap dancing place but as a restaurant and nightclub. They had a decent grill and served good classic French cuisine – caviar, oysters, excellent steak. And once I'd discovered it, I wanted more and more of this.

Denise appreciated good food, more than anyone I knew, and suddenly I was eating like a king at home. It was amazing. I'd come home, usually a bit drunk after a boozy night with clients, to find a roasted joint of meat on the kitchen sideboard with a tea towel over the top, with pickled veg and crusty bread. Wow! She'd make roast beef, properly seasoned and served with home-made horseradish. She taught me that simple food could be delicious. She taught me it was worth making the extra effort. Suddenly every single thing I ate was presented to me in style: a sandwich was perfectly cut with a side salad, a cup of tea came with a slice of cake. Making it appear effortless, Denise'd knock up a batch of home-made scones as easily as someone else would open a packet of cereal.

For the first time I was ready to learn as well. 'Can you teach me how to cook?' I asked one day. And she nodded. She pulled out her professional knives and started to peel a potato, talking me through.

'You have to get the eyes out too,' she explained. 'Just poke and twist at them.'

'Nah,' I said. 'I want to learn how to flambé and that sort of thing, like the chefs do, not this.'

'No,' said Denise firmly. 'If you really want to learn you have to learn the basics first. That means prepping the veg properly.'

And so my first lesson was how to handle a knife. How to chop carrots, cabbage – simple stuff. It was fascinating and I enjoyed it. Taking a little time over a meal was worth the effort, and it didn't have to be complicated either.

The first meal I cooked was Delia Smith's recipe for a Lancashire hotpot – brown wet food, of course, my favourite. It's beautiful and I still love it. The crispy potatoes on top, with the soft fluffy layers underneath, with the really nice juicy fatty lamb all melted down in the sauce below it with slices of kidney … for this hotpot has kidneys in it and with plenty of pepper the slices of kidney with slightly deeper, stronger notes really finish it off. And served with mint sauce – wow, it's more than this boy can bear! I could seriously paddle in it.

Just as unforgettably the first dessert I made was a pavlova. It's still a favourite now and Denise taught me how to make it step by step, including the coulis, where you take a few of the raspberries or strawberries and heat them gently in a pan with caster sugar until they start to weep, and then press them through a fine sieve. So simple. Once you've made your meringue, you leave it to cool in the oven, making sure it's thick enough, as meringue breaks so easily. Then you smooth over the whipped cream, touching around the edge with a kitchen knife to make a wave-like ripple effect, and set against the vivid red fruit it looks amazing. A dessert to impress but actually pretty simple to make.

CHAPTER 23

Lemons

*O*ur company, still called George Allan, was cooking up a storm as well. Tel kept saying, 'Let's not make it too big again, Gregg,' but of course I didn't listen. I always think knowledge is the most expensive commodity, so you either make costly mistakes or you pay a consultant for advice. We worked like Trojans, Tel doing the admin and deliveries and me waltzing into as many new restaurant kitchens as I could manage, always talking to the chefs, never the managers, who didn't have a clue. We worked our nuts off, until finally, finally, we started to make a profit. We had a van each, we packed up the orders through the early hours, we were on the road at 6.00 a.m. Gerry came along as well: I took him on as our bookkeeper. He never said he was proud of me, but I suppose one reason I did it was to try to impress him. That was to come, though.

One practice that went on, but I never approved of, was the

art of giving a bung. A bung is when you gave a customer 10 per cent on top of the order in cash. Around this time, I met a Jewish printer who told me how you could keep customers happy without actually stooping to an illegal bung. 'You do it by going out, socialising with them, having a meal, getting a bit drunk and then making a stupid bet you know they'll win. I always make sure I have the cash on me, and then say something like: "Oi, I bet you £300 the next man who walks through that door will be a bloke with a ginger beard" and when the next bloke is actually a woman, you say, "Aw, hell! You've won!" and pull out the wad of cash. Your client will then leave, having had a good meal and a good drink, and with £300 extra in their pocket, but nobody's mentioned a bribe or done anything illegal – it was just a silly bet. Genius.'

Tel and I didn't take long to get stuck in. It was around that time that the young brash Aussie I was so impressed with, John Torode, went to work at Terence Conran's Le Pont de la Tour, overlooking Tower Bridge, which served the finest classic French food. Then he became the sous chef for a new opening, Quaglino's. Funnily enough John was far too clever to make drunken friends with me. He was always purely professional.

Quaglino's was a totally different venture for designer-turned-restaurateur Conran. It was the early nineties, we had supermodels, superpowers and now super restaurants, and this was one of them, off the scale. First built by Giovanni Quaglino in 1929, Conran reinvented it as a colourfully designed classic bistro to host everyone from royalty to rock stars. It was tucked away in Bury Street, and you came into a small entrance to find yourself on a sweeping staircase going down into a massive dining hall, which was always in full swing, always packed, and served hundreds a day for lunch and dinner. And Torode was now running it.

He suggested to the head chef, Martin Webb, that they take a punt on us to provide their fruit and veg.

'But George Allan's is so small,' the manager quite understandably protested. 'I mean, how the hell will they keep up?'

'Trust Gregg,' said John. 'This man will bust his balls to get you anything you need, whenever you need it. It's better to take on a smaller firm who will specialise in what we need. He'll bend over backwards.' And he was right: I would.

Tel and I had to pay the market every month for our produce and we struggled to get credit there. We gave restaurants more credit than we had and they sometimes took longer than six weeks to pay. I explained this to John. 'There's no way we can get credit for a place as huge as Quaglino's,' I said, so he went to Conran's head office and they agreed to pay us fortnightly on all Conran restaurants. This meant instant cash flow, and actually funded our expansion.

I went to Quaglino's opening night on Valentine's Day and the place was buzzing. I'd helped provide some of the food for the big do. And as I stood on their staircase gazing down at the opulence of the place, I spotted two pyramids of lemons, stacked high and firm, all shiny and beautifully yellowy down the sides of the central crustacean altar. I just couldn't believe it. They were my lemons, I'd packed them myself, and delivered crate after crate, and there they were. So perfect they were decorations for their big night. I was beaming.

At this point we were making a profit and able to pay back everyone on the market. As things really started to take off, Tel and I were literally dropping with exhaustion at the end of each day. Now I had a really lucky stroke as Johnny Fowler had a falling-out with Charlie Hicks. He was a good salesman but a bit lazy, and after trying his own business, which had flopped, he was looking for work.

Although we were from opposite ends of the spectrum background-wise, I loved Charlie. Once someone said to me, 'Don't worry about public school boys: as long as they have enough money to pay their mortgage and buy a decent bottle of wine that's their only ambition,' and when I repeated that to Charlie he laughed and said it was absolutely true. Charlie's biggest ambition when he left his front door in the morning was to get back to it as soon as he could. But he made me laugh so much and had such a passion for food, so eighteen months after Andrew left, I wanted him on board, as I also knew he was good at marketing.

We decided to change the company's name too. We decided we didn't need a fancy name for it. Instead of describing ourselves as 'High-class Purveyors to Quality Catering Trade' as many companies called themselves, we went by the name of our real trade, 'Greengrocers'. That was something that let everyone know instantly what the company was about. I suppose in a way we were being fashionable by using an old-fashioned name. Around this time we also moved into a bigger warehouse and took on more staff.

And our rep was growing, massively. The interest in Quaglino's was phenomenal. People wanted to know who the chefs, managers and suppliers were. It gave us great kudos to become part of it. And of course lots and lots of fabulous chefs were going through their kitchens, and they would move on elsewhere and want to keep us on.

Keeping up with deliveries to this super restaurant was a job in itself. After dropping off the rest of the deliveries I'd go back and take a whole van there. Business with Quaglino's quickly became half our turnover. But by now I had a fabulous team behind me. We'd brought in Paul, a skinny lad I knew from my Turnell's days, and he was the fastest packer I'd ever seen. Plus he had a phenomenal head for figures, so we made him our manager, and we needed him to keep up.

John Torode was right when he said I'd go that extra mile. I always did. Once Quaglino's wanted thirty to forty boxes (2.5 kilos a box!) of French beans, topped and tailed. Now beans come with a knobbly bit at one end and a stringy bit at the other, and the only way of sorting this out was to cut them by hand. I ended up taking home the boxes, and Denise and I sat in our tiny living room, cutting for hours. In the end there was too much to do, so I knocked on the door of our neighbours.

'Would you please top and tail some French beans for me?' I asked, giving them my best smile. 'I'll pay you for it.'

That evening half our street in Bermondsey sat in front of their tellies, with veg knives, cutting beans like the clappers.

As our rep grew, Charlie had the idea of starting a newsletter. Primarily this was to let chefs know what was in season, what we had in stock and what we could get in. But at first it seemed dry and dull, so Charlie decided to litter it with jokes to get people reading and make them laugh.

After Charlie arrived, he told me about another salesman, Rushton Scranage, who worked for John Fowler. Not only did he have a brilliant name, but he was also brilliant at his job. 'He's got loads of trendy restaurants on his lists too – the River Café, Joe Allen's, Orso, Alistair Little. Shall we ask him to come over?' Charlie said with a twinkle in his eye. He didn't need to ask twice.

Much to the wrath of Johnny Fowler, Rushton came. A six-footer, with blond hair that was slowly turning ginger (something we found out he was quite sensitive about – cue much ribbing), Rushton was old school, with old-fashioned values of honesty. His handshake was a good as a contract. He was massively influenced by his mum (aren't we all?) and once I was talking about how if you weren't royalty then you were a subject of the monarch and a commoner, so that made all of us commoners, and he announced: 'My mum isn't.' I just laughed my head off and this affected his sensibilities. Oh yes, Rushton thought he was better than that: he was a comprehensive boy who aspired to be a country gent, bless him. And with his charm and impeccable manners he brought with him an amazing customer base. With my Conran lot, we had everything, every single quality restaurant in London. We were smashing it. By joining forces we became unstoppable. Charlie even started a new cartoon character for the magazine.

'Here, look at this, Gregg,' he said, chuckling. 'Meet George Allan, the multimillionaire greengrocer . . .'

I looked at a picture of an old man superimposed on a cartoon body and laughed. Charlie had found a picture of the Krays' grandfather, with his unshaven sticking-out jaw, flat cap and cravat, and decided this is what our 'George Allan' character would look like if he existed. He had superimposed it on a cartoon-character body.

'You've got some wild imagination,' I said, grinning. 'Can't see a celebrity greengrocer working, somehow.' How little did I know!

Charlie's jokes brought light relief, as we worked our socks off. The demand for the produce was phenomenal. From 9.00 p.m. to 3.00 a.m., after they'd served dinner and cleared up, chefs were phoning in their orders for produce for the next day. We had up to 500 calling in any night. I got eight answering machines and two numbers, and got BT to set up a system so that they were hardly ever engaged; as soon as one answerphone was full, the next one would click into action.

Then I'd put in new tapes as they filled up. All in our little prefab office in New Covent Garden Market.

Some of the chefs drove us mad, though, when their demands were ridiculous. I mean, kitchens are not always efficient businesses, as they operate at 100mph. It's hard for them to know what's going to happen in their day, who is going to walk through their door, and this has a knock-on effect. Once a chef has forgotten something, all hell can break loose. Chefs are half dead at the end of the night and sometimes they swore blind they'd ordered something (although they never had) just because they'd scribbled it down on their list.

I always just agreed with them, though. 'OK, mate, let me know what you want and we'll get it across.' I could argue with them but I'd win the battle and lose the war. Sometimes they called up two or three times a day, and we were not charging for deliveries, but we still kept up with the demand. We had more vehicles flying around than a cab company.

We had a computer that logged every single item we ordered. Every piece of fruit and veg had its own code, which sounds complicated, but when you've taken 500 orders in a day you soon remember herbs start with a '30' or whatever it was. And if you didn't remember you could type in the name and the computer would recognise this too – very clever.

We'd have loads of stock already delivered from the night before and Rushton would hotfoot down to the market to order in the latest stuff. Then around midnight the vans would start loading, organised and run by me and Terry. It was always chaos. It was a fine balancing act: you wanted to make sure you had enough of something, but not too much or it would spoil.

You'd get the bulk items on, the iceberg lettuces, the peppers, the potatoes, the cucumbers, and then the driver would be waiting for the buyer to sort out the last item, like a bottle of orange flower water for Sally Clarke who ran Clarke's in Kensington, or for the fraise du bois or the golden raspberries. Often we'd find ourselves in situations where the size of the tomato ordered by the Ivy that day would hold up a whole vanload. It was madness.

The speed the van could pull away also depended on our packing team. And what a team we'd acquired by now. We'd found a fantastic African guy to head the packers, Jamie, and he had a constant supply of fit young men working from 7.00 p.m. to get the boxes packed with speed. He trained people up all the time; a job like that had a high staff turnover, and as soon as a job was available he'd slot someone in. As I say, we all pitched in, and finally, finally, we'd send the vans off. At one point we had a stream of fourteen vans.

In any one day I'd be running backwards and forwards several times to various restaurants. I'd get whatever they wanted, and if I couldn't find a wholesaler who had it, I'd even make a mad dash to a supermarket myself. Once I found myself emptying the shelves of Sainsbury's of their vanilla pods and running full pelt back to John Torode on Sunday morning just so they could get their ice cream finished in time. Another time he rang and said he urgently needed slices of white bread, so I ran around with two trolleys full.

Keeping up with the more diva-ish demands of some chefs was something else. Once one rang me on a Saturday and asked me to help start his car and when I refused he cancelled his order with us. Another chef told me he'd cancelled his order with his last delivery company because they'd not sent him a Christmas card that year. Crazy!

Sometimes the chefs' demands for food quality reached ridiculously stupid levels. Once we delivered six punnets of fresh raspberries to a well-known chef and he picked one punnet up and dropped it on his workbench, and then opened it to look for any juice running through it. If it did, he'd send them back for not being fresh enough.

Another asked for flat parsley leaves, all the same size. I mean, what?! One chef would even send individual fruit and veg back if he didn't like them. We invoiced twice for the same thing after changing it but it was still an extra trip.

Often we bit our tongues and nodded, trying to meet demands where we could. Occasionally it was impossible to prevent yourself from losing your rag.

'Right,' yelled Charlie down the phone once. 'I am taking you to France.'

I did a double take as I listened.

'Well,' he continued, 'you've shouted at the van driver, and you've shouted at me, so now I am going to drive you to France so you can shout at the field your turnips grew in.' Then he put the phone down and we both laughed.

Nonsensical rows could be rather funny. Once I had a manager on the blower telling me to take back my salad as it was dirty and had insects in it.

'Well, I am afraid salad grows in the ground,' I said, patiently, 'where insects also live, so you have to wash it beforehand.'

'Yes, but my chef has already done so,' insisted the manager.

'Well, I hate to argue with Chef,' I said, laughing, 'but he obviously hasn't.'

'How would you know?'

'Because it's got insects in it.'

We had fashions and whims to keep up with too. At one point a few places were boycotting South African produce because of the political situation, with apartheid going on. Now don't get me wrong, I wouldn't agree with anything like that either, but at the same time you try to get the grapes and melons they wanted from anywhere but Cape Town and you're stuffed.

Another time French products were scrapped off the menus because the French had done some nuclear test in the South Pacific and this time I just laughed. I mean, no way could we provide good produce for restaurants and not touch anything from France. It was like asking a barman to run a bar without ice.

With our range of restaurants expanding, we were desperate to get our hands on produce other suppliers didn't have. We wanted to give these modern restaurants everything they wanted so that they wouldn't go to any other veg firms.

Every week we had a lorryload of stuff from Italy coming over, stuffed with rocket, artichokes, bell peppers, Violetta aubergines, proper misshapen bell peppers – all superior to the standard stuff from Holland. We'd also cornered the Thai market for things like snake beans and winged beans. These went to Mezzo's in Wardour Street, another Conran joint of which John ended up becoming head chef. One place we didn't get, though, was Le Pont de la Tour, as they were still wrapped up with the Lays company and their relationship was so solid I couldn't find a way in there.

I loved seeing what went on behind the scenes. For instance, I marvelled at how John ran his team at Quaglino's. He'd set up a huge soup tureen filled with strong milky coffee and greet all his staff as they arrived. 'You doing OK, sweetie?' he asked the girls, handing them a cup of coffee. 'How was your night, lads?' he'd say to his juniors. They'd come in, heads bowed, tired, and within minutes were buoyed by both his enthusiasm and the caffeine, ready for work, ready to have fun under John. Once John likened his job to working a big game of Pac-Man for eighteen hours non-stop. It was horrifically hard work, but he was passionate about his job, as I was about mine.

However hard I tried sometimes, however much effort I put in, sometimes things didn't quite go to plan. Once Sally Clarke asked for some truffles from Milan. But they somehow missed the lorry. I knew I needed to get them, come what may, so I rang our buyer over there and arranged for them to be sent via DHL, the worldwide delivery company. Four days later they'd still not turned up.

'Oh, effing hell,' I cursed as I put down the phone to Sally herself. Understandably she wasn't happy. Customer service was everything to me and when I promised something, I tried never to fail to deliver.

'Right,' I said to Terry. 'Today I will find that package!'

I rang DHL and spoke to a customer service jobsworth.

'Please don't worry, sir. It's not a problem. We've located your package now. It's at our central London distribution centre as I speak, waiting to be dispatched directly to you.'

'Brilliant!' I cheered. 'Well, your distribution centre is in the Oval, isn't it, and I am in the market in Vauxhall, so I'll come straight down and get it.'

'Er, sorry, sir, you can't,' he replied.

'What? Why? Don't worry, it's only down the road.'

'No, sir, you can't, I am afraid.'

'But it will be faster,' I pressed. 'It'll take me five minutes. What's the problem?'

'I'm afraid we don't have anyone trained to speak to the public in our distribution centre,' he went on.

I couldn't believe what I was hearing and started laughing. What on earth did that mean? I'd no choice but to wait after that.

Anyway, around this time, I decided to look into trying to

buy from the growers direct. I was always seeking out new suppliers and because I was around chefs all the time, I could sense where new trends were heading. And one of them was for home-grown British produce, local and seasonal.

When I first started supplying fruit and veg, it was all about the French produce and the French style of cooking: complex. But places like the River Café were revolutionising food. Opened in 1987, the River Café started as a staff canteen for Ruth Rogers's architect husband, Richard Rogers. Rose Gray, a fabulous chef, ran it with Ruth and then it opened to the public, specialising in Italian food. Now if you follow Italian or Spanish food, or Provençal for that matter, to its purest form it's all about local produce. If we wanted a food culture like theirs we'd have to look to local produce too. I had this debate with Rushton once. He loved the River Café.

'Customers just want Italian, Italian, Italian,' he said. 'That's all they're interested in.'

'No, you're wrong, Rushton,' I argued. 'They want to cook like Italians, and that means getting good-quality local stuff nearby.'

He didn't agree, but it turned out I was right.

Following the River Café came an explosion of brasserie and café-style eating. This brought eating out into the price range of many more people and brought about the decline of the pubs really. That café-style eating was less reliant on highly trained chefs creating complicated dishes, and placed more emphasis on the quality of the produce. So after seeing what the River Café was doing, I thought to myself: if this continues we'll be looking at sourcing produce locally now. And I have to take my hat off to myself for this, as I was banging on about it twenty years ago and was right.

Actually I'd like to say that sometimes I feel slightly sensitive when people say to me about being a judge on *MasterChef*: 'But you're not a chef, you're just a greengrocer, so how can you judge food?' Often people's idea of a greengrocer is someone in a beanie hat standing at a stall. The reason I was chosen for *MasterChef* is that I ate out five nights a week for twenty years and few people have done that! Michel Roux has said: 'Gregg has the most extraordinary palate of everyone I know. Gregg is the punter and if you can't please him, we can't be in business.' John Torode says, 'If you want to know what's happening in London restaurants talk to Gregg Wallace. I don't know anyone else who eats out like he does.'

And, as I say, I saw trends changing, and I wanted my business to change with them. So I bought Henrietta Green's *Food Lover's Guide to Britain* and flicked through it, looking out for farmers in the area who could help us out. And I came across Charles Secrett. He was a third-generation farmer, whose grandfather started a place in 1908 down in Hurst Farm in Milford, Surrey, with a £1,000 loan. They grew all kinds and ran 'pick your own' days and a farm shop. I had rung every single farm in the Home Counties and Charles was the only farmer, a real gentleman farmer, who was open to experimenting, and willing to meet me. I went down there and we had a chat.

'I sell to top London restaurants,' I said. 'And I really want to get my hands on British products. There's so much coming in from France, Italy and Spain, and I want British stuff.'

It was so simple. Charles was a romantic and wanted to be involved. Even if it didn't make a huge amount of money for him, he loved the idea of his family name being synonymous with quality food. It made sense and he said yes.

We'd cracked the market in the trade and we'd become famous as a business; now we became famous as a direct seller from growers. We really took pride in the restaurants we supplied. We ate in them and took a real interest in what they did. A lot of fruit and veg was supplied just as a commodity but we were as passionate about food as chefs were. I started to get invites to every restaurant you could think of. I started to become known. The boy from Peckham who was brought up on Vesta meals and hated his mum sneaking vegetables on to his plate now dined in the finest joints in the land and was known as Gregg the Veg. Now that was some turnaround.

CHAPTER 24

Foie Gras

*N*ow we'd reached the top of our game, we seemed unstoppable, thanks to Charlie Hicks and his PR machine too. I mean, he was a genius and coming up with more and more original ideas. For example, in their wisdom, the EC had recently banned lime leaves. In Asia these carry bugs which could annihilate citrus crops in Europe, so they didn't want any coming over. But this is England: we don't have any citrus crops. I am not suggesting that any of you have ever bought drugs, but if you had you'd know that they come in what is unmistakably a wrap. We sent a wrap out to every food editor with lime leaves inside, with a covering letter saying, 'Gregg Wallace and Charlie Hicks from George Allan's are sending you an illegal substance,' and explaining what the EC had done. It was a gimmick that worked, and they came to Charlie for quotes. Our company started to be mentioned in *Private Eye* and the *New Statesman*. It was inspired publicity, thanks to Charlie.

Earlier, just after Versace was murdered, we couldn't get rocket because of weather issues. Charlie put a picture of a naked man with a wheelbarrow on the newsletter, with the caption 'Modern harvesting techniques are not helping the Italian, many of them haven't worn a stitch since Versace copped it.' He printed a free 'cut out and keep' mask of the *Evening Standard* restaurant critic Fay Maschler, with the words: 'Let the power of Fay work for you. No more sloppy service, no more dodgy tables by the gents!' He also ran a campaign to see the real Fay, as the photo used on her column had been taken in the 1970s and he wanted to see an updated picture, and the *Standard* obliged. Charlie was brilliant.

Our unstoppable machine just kept growing. Now I had the contracts of the trendy restaurants, I got a call from a catering company who provided food for the big banks, the boardrooms of the City. Suddenly things exploded even further. We were talking of providing sumptuous ingredients for lunches for 2,000 staff now. It was insane. Suddenly, too, Charlie's funny multimillionaire greengrocer character George Allan didn't seem quite so silly after all. We had started to do very, very well.

Now we'd exploded to such an extent, money was rolling in faster than I could spend it. And spend it I did. Terry once came up to me, while I was in the Bank bar quaffing my third bottle of Cristal, and warned, 'Easy, Gregg, you're spending money like you've never had it before!' I just looked at him as if he was mad.

'What you on about, Terry?' I said, laughing and clinking his pint glass with my champagne flute. 'I never have had money like this before!' Vintage champagne, Cristal or Krug, £170 a bottle – that was all I drank. Even then it was a lot of money and it seems a bit obscene now. But going out and drinking and eating, especially eating, had become my life. It seemed impossible not to. Now I had the money and the contacts, I was enjoying fine dining at its absolute best in London, the world. I'd worked bloody hard, so I didn't see why I shouldn't.

With things on the up, my thoughts turned more to my family life and I'd become broody as they come. Denise also wanted kids, so that was the next step. We'd become more like best friends living together, not a recipe for an ideal relationship, but that didn't stop me from suggesting having a baby. For ages now Mum had been on at me: when would I give her a grandchild? I'd always wanted kids, even from a young age. I dreamed one day of being a grandad, and being as mine had been to me, and I knew Denise would be a fantastic mother. So I suggested it to her and she agreed.

She fell pregnant quite fast and gave up work quickly, to be a full-time mum. I was working all hours anyway and as long as I could provide for her, with a nice car and gym membership (she loved to swim), then we seemed to rub along well. And we both couldn't wait to meet our baby.

She went into labour on 5 March 1994. I drove her to Guy's Hospital, the same place where I'd lost Grandad eight years earlier. I really got a sense of life coming full circle there. If only he'd been here to see it.

The birth was horrendous. It was an emergency C-section and as doctors filled our little room wearing blue scrubs, ordering Denise to be prepped for surgery, we both cried with fear.

'It's going to be OK,' I kept saying, stroking her hair. 'I promise.' I trembled all over as I watched her being wheeled off to theatre, making a mad dash to keep up behind.

'I'm here,' I managed to shout as she disappeared through some double doors.

I stayed up the head end as the anaesthetic took hold. As I held her hand, tears dripping off my chin, I couldn't stand it. I'd never felt such fear before, for Denise, for our baby, for myself. Then almost as soon as the operation had started, I heard a strange cry and the midwife's face was exploding with delight. 'Congratulations, you have a baby boy!'

A boy! I almost dropped on to my knees to thank whoever had helped us. Oh my God, I was so happy. I'd always wanted a son. Before I'd even had a chance to look, a tiny bundle was pushed into my arms and I was holding our baby. I looked down at this little thing, all warm, bony, blue and bloody. He looked like the dinosaur that hatched from the egg in *Jurassic Park*. 'Waa, waaa,' he cried, his face all screwed up, sounding like a reptile too! But my God, he was so, so beautiful. We called him Tom, as we both loved the name. And you should've seen the face of Tommy, the old boy in the Queen Vic, when I told him our choice.

That evening, we were high up on the hospital ward overlooking the city and it was a grey day with steely skies. But I just gazed out and thought: this is a stunningly beautiful, brilliant day.

I rushed out and bought Denise a huge bouquet and vintage champagne, and all the ladies on the ward shared it, toasting us and them and the wonder of what we'd all done.

Denise was out in a few days, and back home, learning the tricks of being a new mum, and I went back to work. I never felt that I could leave the business for long. It needed so much overseeing; so much was happening. We'd taken on many more staff and our numbers were rapidly rising all the time – and we needed them. I had an in-house bookkeeper now, after getting rid of Gerry. To be honest, I got some pleasure from that. I harboured resentment from the way I'd been treated as a kid. I felt that he'd looked down his nose at me and finally, finally, I'd done better than he had. I was nice, all the same, and although he was disappointed he knew he couldn't keep up. I'd also employed a new office manager called Lorna. Now Lorna was a lovely girl I'd met in East Sheen's branch of Lunn Poly. She was so helpful and efficient, and I always wanted to deal with her. When I needed a new credit controller for my company, I offered her a job and she took it. Within months she was running the office, always on top of the invoices and making sure everyone was chasing them in our new offices.

I needed someone I could trust, as the invoices were a nightmare. There were around 600 to 700 a day. Because the margins on what we sold were so small – we were lucky to get a 10 or 15 per cent return – we had to always stay on top of selling a hell of a lot. That was the best way – or so I thought.

By now I'd become a bit of a connoisseur on the dining scene. I had completely and utterly fallen in love with food. I mean, it was unavoidable and for the past couple of years now I had been constantly eating out in the restaurants I was supplying. Five nights a week, and most lunchtimes too. Of course I was piling on weight, but I just couldn't resist eating vast quantities of rich amazing food. It was absolutely fabulous. The first time I ever tasted certain meals…I still remember them today, as they were so amazing.

Like foie gras. It was in Kensington Place, which opened in 1987, and was seen as Britain's first brasserie: I tried the dish for the first time there. It was on a sweetcorn pancake, and all that fat dripped into the pancake, making it melt like butter, and then you got the little sweet notes of the sweetcorn kernels, and oh baby!

I tried calves' brains for the first time in Blueprint Café. Oh, they are off the scale. So fatty – melty, buttery things. You don't know what's hit you. I didn't know such things existed.

I loved Stephen Terry's vanilla scallops ... Oh God, and his risotto. It was so beautiful, creamy, starchy, with drizzled oxtail sauce over the top which almost tasted of Marmite. Stephen is an amazing chef, one of Marco Pierre White's boys in his first place, Harvey's, with Gordon Ramsay.

The first time I had caviar was at Quaglino's. I knew this was an expensive dish, but had no idea it came so delicately served, with soft bellini and crème fraiche, and a chilled glass of vodka to complement. Oh God! I had affogato there too: that was the first time I tried this classic Italian dessert. I always think Italians know what they are on about with food of every sort. But again, this was another example of the brilliant simplicity of Italian food. Fresh, home-made vanilla ice cream, one big scoop, with a double espresso poured over the top. Wow! That's my second favourite dessert.

My first being my Nan W's rhubarb crumble. Now I was getting more and more interested in food, I asked her for the recipe, something she was happy to supply. That crunchy, crumbly sweet topping with that skilful blend of sweetness and sharpness is just the nicest thing I've ever had. If you get a good crumble I'd happily die with my head buried in it. It felt so good, too, Nan W seeing me make something of my life. I don't think she understood quite how far this had gone. She just noticed that the cars I was arriving in on occasional visits were nicer. The first decent car I bought was a convertible BMW – oh, how I loved the solid 'clunk' sound of that door closing!

Now I was eating out more and more I was discovering sticky toffee puddings too. What more can you say about this divine dish? The perfect sticky toffee pudding is a fine balancing act. If things are too sweet it gives you what I call 'itchy throat disease', when things get too uncomfortable, like ginger. The sweetness should take you to the edge of richness and stickiness and then, with a good pudding, you should be calmed back down very, very quickly, through either the cool moistness of the sponge or cream or custard. Now that is sticky toffee at its absolute best. If you find yourself almost scared of its sweetness, then it's overdone.

Pastry chefs call this 'over seasoning': when you put too much sugar in pastry. Gosh, desserts are a fine balancing act.

Then, then, after all this sensational stuff, I discovered Le Gavroche. Opened in 1967 by Michel and Albert Roux, this knocked my socks off the first time I went in, and it has done ever since. I'd been desperate to try it, and when we started to supply this amazing venture, I was so very proud.

Famous for classical French cuisine, it was the first ever British restaurant to be awarded three Michelin stars, under Albert, and it had two when I arrived. Actually I don't get the Michelin star system. I mean, I've been lucky enough to eat in the Waterside Inn, Bray, on the banks of the Thames, run by Michel Roux's son, Alain, and the Dorchester, run by Alain Ducasses, and Gordon Ramsay's restaurant in Royal Hospital Road, and I really don't understand why they all have three stars and Le Gavroche has two, but that's just my opinion.

Michel Roux Junior (son of Albert, who now runs Le Gavroche) is thrilled my favourite ever dish there is the first ever dish he got on his father's menu, and also strangely the first ever dish I tried there. I swear, if you don't want to eat it, just take it home and snog it, because this is something so special. Called Artichoke Lucullus, it's artichoke heart with chicken mousse on it, and inside the mousse are pieces of foie gras, and the whole thing is covered in truffle jus and finished with slices of truffles. Oh, my, God, it is delicious.

Michel Junior is also a pastry chef, and his pear and salted caramel millefeuille is to die for. You go through crisp layers of pastry to find slightly salted, sticky caramel, and then with all that honeyed pear juice in your mouth too it's the nectar of the gods.

Talking about desserts, the tart citron by Michel Roux at the Waterside Inn is the absolute benchmark of this pudding, the best ever lemon tart. It takes you to the edge of sharpness, making you suck air through your teeth with its tangy tartness, and then, whooaaaa, it brings you back down again into comfort and calm and cosiness. When food does that it's incredible; that's a true balancing act, and you need the palate of an angel to get it exactly right. I love it, although Le Gavroche has to be my hands-down favourite place. When I'm there I seriously consider giving myself over to gluttony, it's just so opulent. It makes me realise there is a supreme being up there looking after my welfare, because I just love, love, the food, the service, everything.

Denise was as happy as me to enjoy the high life too. She loved coming with me to official restaurant openings or out for the odd nice meal. One day she said to me simply, 'As long as you come home at night, get us a nice place to live and let me get on with what I want to do too, we can be happy.' It seemed so simple at the time, and as all my energy went into the business, I was content with that. But was I? I was drunk nearly every day. Drinking had slowly become part of my job, my living and then gradually my existence. It was less about running the company and more about keeping up with our contacts. I was now officially making friends with people for a living, and I was just a massive party animal, out with gangs of chefs at lunchtime and dinner and sometimes in between. I was waking up with a hangover, rolling into London and just eating, having a laugh. God knows what it was doing to my health, but it was fabulous.

I'd start my day early as usual in the market and then go to one of my favourite places, the Eagle in Farringdon Road, in Clerkenwell, the first ever gastropub, opened in 1991 by David Ayre and Michael Belben. As with many great ideas, it all started with a bit of a lucky accident. David wanted to buy a restaurant but he couldn't afford it, and pubs were failing a bit at the time, what with the recession and everything. So, using his mum's credit card, he bought the Eagle, a postman's pub, as it was near Mount Pleasant sorting office. He got rid of the pool tables, bought old mismatched furniture and set up a kitchen on one side of the bar. He cooked Spanish, French and Italian food, grilled chops, steak, fish, paella, and served it with big bowls of salad and hunks of fresh bread. None of the cutlery matched, and you had to order at the bar, but it was different, so, so cool and absolutely rammed day and night.

It was in the Eagle I first came across tiramisu. It used to be on every menu in the nineties but once something gets trendy and fashionable it tends to disappear again. Anyway, I was sitting at the bar and one of the lady chefs was ladling something intriguing into a bowl. It was all brown and creamy, and my antennae for brown wet food pricked up.

'What's that?' I asked.

'Here you go,' she said, grinning and handing me a big bowl and spoon.

I took one mouthful and oh God, I wanted to bath in it. 'What is *this*?' I almost shouted.

'Tiramasu,' she said with a smile. I had no idea what that meant but I knew I loved it. And that I could eat it with nothing but a spoon made it even better.

I loved David too: he made me laugh so much. He'd be at the grill, cooking, when customers wandered up to him. Now most people know not to disturb the chef, but some people weren't sure, as it was a pub.

Once a woman asked: 'Hello, er, hello, I am a vegetarian, what would you recommend?'

'A beef ana,' David shot back. 'It'll do you the world of good.'

Reminds me of a sign I once saw in a gastropub in north Wales: 'Vegetarian: Old Celtic word meaning useless hunter.'

Once I overheard David on the phone: 'Yes, yes ... we are a pub ... No ... no, we don't take bookings ... It doesn't matter how many of you there are ... You want a menu? Ah, OK, well, you stand by the fax machine and I'll try and get the blackboard in.' He did make me laugh.

I loved the whole area where the Eagle was. Clerkenwell has a series of old boozers and up-and-coming restaurants. Charlie used to call it 'Gregg's Clerkenwell triangle – he gets in there and comes out days later, and he doesn't know where he's been or what he's been doing.'

And he was right. I was overdoing it big time. One of the newspapers once photographed me carrying a box of veg into the Eagle pub and Charlie quipped, 'Well, that's authentic, isn't it? You actually carrying veg in there. Really it should be you staggering out again.'

One thing that was doing all right, though, was the money. For the very first time, I had so much that I could afford to move us into somewhere more decent, and we both plumped for East Sheen, a lovely suburban south-west London area, right near the Thames. I loved Bermondsey, but Denise wanted a bigger house, posh girlfriends and a better gym, the whole shebang, and now I could afford it, it seemed daft not to.

So when Tom was two years old we moved into a three-bed terraced house with a lush garden and nice neighbours. Tom used to wheel himself around our tiny flat, in his mobile walker, but in the East Sheen place he started going crazy, running like a maniac, laughing. He wasn't the only one to love his new home. For the very first time in my life, I knew I'd made it. Driving home and seeing my house come into view was a joy.

At first everything was hunky-dory. I mean, I wasn't sleeping with Denise much, but we were happy enough. I gave her a credit card and she made friends with our neighbours, nicely turned-out ladies with well-dressed kids. The warning signs were already there, though. Once I came home earlier in the evening and Denise looked genuinely surprised.

'What are you doing in?' she asked. 'Why don't you go out again to the pub?' I didn't argue with her: I just walked straight back out again.

CHAPTER 25

Angel Delight

*O*nce I appreciated how brilliant quality cooking was, I grew intolerant of bad food. I don't mean mass-produced food, I mean pretentious food. There is nothing wrong with simple things, but good quality is key. One evening I came home and suddenly had a craving out of nowhere for a Fray Bentos pie. So I told Denise.

She laughed. 'But, Gregg, I am a pastry chef. If you fancy a pie, I can make us a beautiful proper pastry one tomorrow evening,' she said.

'Nah!' I laughed back. 'I dunno why, I just fancy the idea of a Fray Bentos one. After all, I loved them as a kid.'

'OK,' she said, her eyebrows rising. 'I'll treat you to one tomorrow.'

The next evening, Denise handed me a steaming plate with my Fray Bentos dinner. 'Thanks, darling,' I said.

I was happy to eat again, to soak up some of the booze, so

I quickly got stuck in. Oh dear! It was horrendous. The pastry was like rubber, the sauce was gloopy and there was no definition of flavour whatsoever. My much loved pie from my childhood tasted like meaty sludge. What a disappointment!

That's not to say, though, that having access to nicer food has turned me into a complete snob. I don't think it has. Good food doesn't have to be posh or expensive: I stand by that.

Once I was in a pub with some of Denise's friends, Sarah and Dave, and the food was terrible. It was ordinary shop-bought pies and pâtés in a glass cabinet with uninspiring limp salads laid out next to it. Sarah looked at Dave with pride as he piled his plate high.

'Oh, my Dave loves his food,' she said.

'He doesn't,' I said with a laugh. 'He just hates to be hungry and that's not the same.'

Really, I am not snobby about where I eat. Take the Harvester, a good mid-range place that does good grilled stuff. I go about twice a month with my kids. Every time I mention it on Twitter, though, I get loads of stick. Recently I was in there with Mum and the kids, when a woman peered at me as I was helping myself to their salad bar and she whispered to Mum, 'What's he doing in here?'

'Having his lunch, dear, same as you,' Mum shot back. Good old Mum.

I have to confess my guilty pleasure is still butterscotch Angel Delight. I once sold it in a shot glass as a little pre-dessert in one of my restaurants I set up later. It's delicious and I love fast food. There is nothing as tasty or satisfying as a Big Mac or a KFC bucket; if the companies weren't any good, there wouldn't be millions of them all across the world. There are 'layers' of food people, I think. The ones on the bottom rung are those who are never exposed to good-quality food, and that's not their fault. When people say, 'Some people eat to live and others eat to live,' and claim people are not interested in food, I say that's just snotty cobblers. Everybody loves food. Show me someone who genuinely doesn't like food and I will show you a hungry corpse. You might not have the money to be exposed to quality food, but even someone who loves hamburgers and fried foods has a preference.

Some people think a so-called foodie like me should turn his back on the so-called 'lower standard' foods. But real foodies are open to absolutely everything. Raymond Blanc talks in his biography of how he went to McDonald's for the first time with his kids and discovered how delicious a Big Mac is, because he is comfortable enough to say that. It's only the people who are snobs who look down their noses. What people often really mean is that they don't want to sit anywhere near poor people when they eat their dinner, let's be honest.

While I am on this rant, I also get annoyed with silly descriptions on menus. Steak and chips is steak and chips, not aged cow hung for twenty-eight days, served with fried South American tubers. We don't need to know all the cooking methods either, or where it comes from. Chicken from Dawcett's farm in Durham whose family have just enjoyed celebrating their daughter's eighteenth birthday with friends in Castle Coombe . . . Oh, *come on*, it's chicken!

I champion seasonal eating, but we don't want to become food fascists. And if we do there are going to be repercussions that need proper investigation. I mean, what would happen to all the African bean farmers if we stopped eating French beans? I get asked to get involved with all sorts of food issues, from organic chickens to air miles, but I don't want to get political or be a food evangelist; plus many ideas are not properly investigated. Are we seriously suggesting the whole country just eats organic chicken? I am pleased about food being affordable in this country at the moment. Nobody starves in this country and it wasn't that long ago that malnutrition was common. I'm not sure we should tamper with that.

I love the purity of food. I love simplicity. I've been to the Fat Duck, I admire Heston Blumenthal and everything he does. I can wonder at his food and appreciate it but I don't think everyone should do it. It's like I can admire a painting that's won the Turner prize but that doesn't mean I want to hang it in my living room.

Anyway, back to the story. While I was making my living as a greengrocer, nouvelle cuisine was taking off and it started to get a bad name. There was a lot of food being placed carefully in tiny piles in the 1980s. I don't want to have to dismantle my food to eat it, thanks. It was supposed to be what the Japanese are so good at, doing lots of little elegant dishes but with European food. But too many chefs started to send out three tiny courses that weren't very good. It left a scar on our restaurants, unfairly really. Nouvelle cuisine was often abused by chefs who didn't have the talent and experience, just as some today try to pull off Heston-style meals, by serving up daft stuff like Rolos up ducks' bottoms, but without his expertise, talent and equipment. Nouvelle cuisine was bastardised in the hands of lesser cooks. People were feeling ripped off and leaving the restaurant hungry – something that should never, ever happen.

Simple food, well done, is still what I love. I loved the Vong in the Berkeley Hotel. It's not there any more – it closed years ago – but they did a dish called 27 Veg, and my goodness it taught me just how mentally brilliant veg could be on their own. It proved to me how incredible the European Asian mix can be. This was started in Vietnam, where the French chefs interpreted their own dishes with Asian ingredients. There were loads of baby veg, some crunchy, some sweet, all beautifully cooked and taken real care over.

Sashimi at Nobu is another favourite. What a brilliant idea – back to absolute simplicity again. Thin, delicate slices of raw fish, a little bit of wasabi, a little bit of soy – how divine and good for you it is! On another note, I am always fascinated by the French paradox too. The Japanese have the lowest rate of heart attacks and they consume the least amount of animal fats than any other nation. Yet despite consuming high amounts of animal fats, the French have the second lowest rate of heart attacks. How is that possible?

So, anyway, back to my business, which was booming, and although Denise and I were struggling a bit, we managed to conceive another baby. This was after a relaxed lunch in Sonny's in Barnes. Through Sonny's I ended up meeting Vernon, another restaurateur. His sister owned it and I got in touch with him through her. He was a little Indian guy who ran Cucina in Hampstead, well dressed with a cheeky grin. He was so much fun. We became good mates and whenever I was having a boring business drinks with chefs, I'd invite him along to liven things up.

Anyway, Denise and I ended up in the hallway and on the stairs making love, and bingo! We were expecting a baby girl and we called her Libby. I named her after Libby Purves on BBC's Radio Four, actually. I think it's such a pretty, clever name and thankfully Libby does too.

I told her that all the buses in south-west London stopped for three minutes and there were three sightings of Elvis that day she was born in 1996. And goodness, again I couldn't have been happier. A son and now a daughter – just perfect. A family of four. It was exactly as I wanted, and although my marriage wasn't in great shape, I felt a truly lucky man. A lovely house, wife, two cute kids, lots of money.

Not that I spent a huge amount of time at home. The business had expanded at such a rate we now had sixty staff and twenty vans. It was huge. And I felt I couldn't stop, not even for a weekend. Although we were doing well, it only carried on as long as we worked hard; we were not making huge profits, I had no assets, it was a case of just work hard and keep going and going. I was always on the look-out for more contacts, more friends in the business, more people to sell to, and I would attend every function, every party, just to keep up.

Then one day I bumped into two ladies who happened to edit a small magazine called *Chef*, which came free with *Hotel and Caterer*, a well-known trade mag. I got chatting to them about our Secrett's farm venture and told them how I thought seasonal and local was the new trend. I became friends with one of these women and she offered to help me and my business.

'We'd like to do an article for our magazine about you and your work with Secrett's, focusing on how you're championing local produce,' she said. 'Are you interested?'

Interested? Of course I was. More publicity was always good. So I found myself splashed over four pages about what we did and how we worked directly with the growers. It was great.

The journalist they used to interview me worked freelance and she also did stints at Radio Four, unbeknown to me – and also unbeknown was that this article in this small magazine was about to trigger something I'd never, ever have expected in a million years.

A few weeks later I got a phone call. When the lady said she was from Radio Four, I wondered if she'd got the wrong number. What on earth did she want?

'Sheila Dillon,' she said. 'Producer of BBC Radio Four's *Food Programme*. I would like to ask you to come in for a chat about the possibility of appearing on the programme.'

I nearly fell off my chair.

I went into see Sheila. Now I'd never listened to the show before but I knew all about it. It had been running for years with Derek Cooper fronting it, a man with a voice so smooth it could churn milk. Sheila wanted to do a programme on following a veg through from the grower to the wholesaler in the market to the plate of the customer. So I rang David Ayre to see if we could show that in his pub. I couldn't think of anyone better to do it.

'Yes, yes!' he cried. 'I love Radio Four.'

I also asked Charlie when I got back to the office. 'You listen to Radio Four,' I said. 'Do you want to help?'

'Marvellous!' Charlie said, his eyes lighting up.

To be honest I felt out of my league with this, completely so. I mean, David and Charlie were naturals, both terribly posh and funny. I just didn't see what I could offer, but I was definitely on for the ride.

And so we made this programme. We went and talked to Secrett's, and then went to New Covent Garden Market (we were the wholesaler); then we showed how chefs ordered and then how it ended up on the plates of the customers in the Eagle. I loved David's take on food presentation too: 'Cook it really well, hold it two foot above the plate and let go,' he said with a guffaw.

I'd no idea how us messing about with a microphone would go down with one of the most prestigious audiences the BBC has, but it was incredible fun making the programme and after it aired, Sheila got in touch again. 'We've had one of the biggest mailbags of support for a show we've ever had,' she enthused – and they weren't letters of complaint. It was brilliant.

But that, I thought, was that. My brush with fame was over and I just got back on with the serious task of trying to keep my business afloat. And what a task it was! Businesses went bust all the time in the market and things were getting tougher. We still had little to back us up, and we weren't small and trendy any more: we were mainstream and this was proving even harder to keep up. Now we were bigger chefs were more demanding than ever, pushing our prices down further sometimes, especially as we dealt with corporate companies who were only interested in price. We started making even less profit, especially with the outgoings we had: we had rent on a warehouse, office space and our vans to pay for.

Being a good greengrocer depends mainly on the cult of the personality and there is no brand loyalty there. Unless you are going to see those customers, maintaining regular contact, they will go elsewhere, except those who become true friends, of course. Some of the chefs were demanding second or third deliveries a day. When you're running a small business you can pander more to their requirements. We used to have time to find the right-sized tomato for the Ivy's galette, but when you have 400 other orders, you don't have time to find it. And it was getting ever harder to get exactly what people wanted.

Then one day Rushton, our best salesman, came to see me and Tel.

'I want to become a director,' he said crisply. 'I want some equity.'

I could understand this, to a point. I mean, it was thanks to Rushton's skills as a super salesman and buyer that we had many of the restaurants we did. But he was on £100k a year and I'd thrown a Merc in for him too. I didn't want to share a slice of the company, and neither did Tel. We turned him down and he went away, looking badly off.

Around this time, while I was in the office, Charlie rang me. 'You sitting down, Gregg?' he asked.

'Aw, gawd, what now?' I groaned. I had a big load of orders to get rid of and a ton of paperwork waiting for me when I got home. I was wanting to avoid any extra drama.

'I've just had a phone call from Sheila Dillon from Radio Four,' he said, 'and she wants to give us our own radio show.'

I started laughing. 'You what?'

If I thought he was kidding, I didn't five minutes later when he gave me details of where we needed to go for a meeting with the BBC. I couldn't believe it.

CHAPTER 26

Tomatoes

S o we handed over our everyday working jobs to others to hold the fort while we went off for a meeting at the BBC. Neither of us believed the proposed show was possible but we were up for the ride anyway. The producers wanted us to front a new show based on an American radio show idea, where two New York mechanics did a phone-in for people about cars. Radio Four wanted to do one about vegetables, and they wanted us to be the experts, using our skills as greengrocers.

Sheila was very enthusiastic, as was James Boyle, the head of Radio Four. 'I love the contrast in your voices,' he said 'I mean, I think this will be brilliant.'

Now James Boyle appeared to be so left wing he could easily meet himself in the opposite direction, and he seemed to love me. I took him down to Covent Garden Market into a caff for some bacon and eggs, and he lapped the whole place up. 'You have so much to give to this show,' he said, grinning and mopping up his runny egg with white bread. 'A real authentic voice. A real tradesman.' I wanted to believe him. I couldn't believe that Radio Four listeners would be happy to hear the likes of me when they tuned in, but if he was the big boss ...

Anyway, when we turned up at this meeting, we didn't realise it was actually a practice session for us. If we had, we might not have gone out the night before on a piss-up with a few chefs. We ended up in Stringfellows until 3.00 a.m. and were still drunk when we turned up at Broadcasting House the next day. Poor Sheila immediately realised something was awry.

'Are you boys OK?' she asked, as we probably turned the air of the small studio into the whiff of a distillery.

'Yeah,' I croaked. 'Just a bit worse for wear.'

'Is there anything we can get you?' she asked.

I shot a look at Charlie and read his mind as he said, 'A small vodka would be nice, thank you.'

'And I wouldn't mind a brandy,' I asked cheekily, not wanting to miss out.

And so, completely and utterly plastered, we managed to laugh, joke and chat our way through the practise session. By the time we left, we were still laughing, not really taking it at all seriously but hoping it had been good enough. And somehow it had been.

The next couple of sessions we would turn up and there would be a bottle of vodka and another bottle of brandy on the table. Obviously the thinking was that's what we liked. So once again we got a bit tipsy. Despite everything it felt brilliant to banter, with people listening at home, and to bring what we do to life. Suddenly I realised that what we didn't know about veg wasn't worth knowing. I loved Charlie's wit, which he brought along too. One episode somebody rang in to ask about tinned new potatoes.

'What an absolute British institution,' quipped Charlie. 'Readily available in public schools, hospitals and prisons, and between Gregg and me we've visited two out of the three of them.'

As James Boyle was, Charlie was fascinated by my early life, so very different to their own, and I got ribbed all the time. Once Charlie asked, 'Is it right you had an outside toilet, Gregg?'

'Yes, Charlie. Er, where are we going with this?' I replied.

'No, no, I mean, I just wanted to say we had an outside toilet too, you know.'

'Really, Charlie?'

'Yes, yes, my father had it built for the gymkhana.'

I couldn't help but laugh. Good old Charlie. Afterwards we found ourselves standing on top of the roof of the Radio Four building, looking out over London. 'This could be the start of a massive adventure,' I said.

Of course, though, as we recorded more episodes my old insecurities started to surface. My old fears of being out of place, of not fitting in, of not being posh or good enough, resurfaced with a vengeance. But just when my old demons started tapping at my door, Dixie Stewart stepped in.

Dixie was given the job of looking after our programme, *Veg Talk*, in its second year, even though it had only been expected to have one series; after she got hold of it we were given two series a year for six years. And she took me aside and saved my career before it was over before it had begun.

'Look, Gregg,' she said, seriously one day, 'don't let these bastards keep painting you as a cheeky barrow boy and stop playing up to it. You're just going to harm yourself. I don't want you to change your accent: that's fine, that's how you speak. But I do want you to give these listeners your fruit and veg experience. The joking has to stop and the knowledge start. You're far more than the cheeky chappie from Peckham.'

She was right. I had been playing up to that image, because that's what I thought was wanted. But actually I'd so much more to offer. Without this little bit of salient advice at the right moment, I'd have sunk into oblivion and been written off as a quirky cockney joker. With her belief in me, I could show I am more than that. Thank you, Dixie, thanks a lot, darling.

I loved doing that show. It was like one big long party and every Friday night after we aired the whole of Radio Four would go out to the pub. More drinking, more partying. It just never stopped. We quickly became known as the veg boys from the show. Charlie Hicks told the journalist Kate Adie once over a drink that her name was rhyming slang in the market for eight pounds eighty and I'll never forget the look on her face!

Life never stood still for long. Next thing on the agenda was another marriage. Mine to Denise. We booked the Richmond registry office, and Tom, now six, and Libby, four, were our special guests. Denise looked stunning on the day. I mean, she was so pretty, so delicate and elfin-like, and although we were living pretty separate lives, we were OK. I honestly believed I was doing the right thing. We had a lovely reception in the Dorchester in the Grill Room, and Mum was so happy for us. I was too. I hoped this would be the start of new things to come. We enjoyed an incredible honeymoon, going to Beijing, Hong Kong and Dubai, and spending three nights in the desert, in an incredibly expensive hotel involving stand-alone Bedouin tents, and having dinners overlooking a floodlit watering hole so that we could watch gazelle coming to drink there while we slurped our Chardonnay. It was the only time in my life when I have enjoyed complete silence. It was bliss.

After we married, we decided to move again, this time to Petersham. Oh my God, I loved that house. It was amazing. Four bedrooms, a front garden and a back garden 500 feet long, detached mock-Tudor 1930s: it was just so beautiful.

After the success of *Veg Talk*, I got another call and this time, I truly felt life had taken an unbelievable twist. I was asked to front a television show for the Discovery Channel called *Veg Out* and then one for the Food Channel called *Follow that Tomato*. Me on the telly? It really did seem extraordinary, but I just went along with the whirlwind, not able to believe my luck, and did what I was told. Luckily it was something I found easy to do: talk into the camera about food.

Follow that Tomato was most memorable. It was a series about Italy, a place I'd admitted I'd never ever been to, and now I was going there, with Charlie Hicks in tow, of course.

Now I knew nothing about Italy, and to go and travel around the country for a few weeks, region by region, south to north, and sample the delights was some mindblowing way of discovering the place. Wow, the country is incredible if you want to learn about food.

The cuisine of the south of the country with its love of veg and its stunning simplicity is my favourite. There they elevate veg to a regal status. There are three types of people who love vegetables: Hindus, southern Italians and me!

There are also only three original pizzas and only two necessary ones, in my opinion; everything else is just crazy. The Neapolitana (tomatoes and cheese), the Margherita (just simple mozzarella, tomatoes and basil) and the Marinara (same thing as Neapolitana, except with anchovies mixed in).

The Margherita pizza was named after Margherita of Savoy, the queen consort of Umberto I of Italy. With its colours – red tomato, white cheese and green basil – representing the Italian flag, it was made in her honour when she visited Naples in the 1880s. The people were thrilled she'd arrived to visit them and thus made up this pizza, but actually the Queen was just escaping a massive cholera epidemic in the north and going as far away as possible.

Yes, the best pizzas in the world are in Naples for sure. Be careful of your wallet and take off your expensive jewellery if you're visiting, but go if you can. The basic premise of Italian food is extreme simplicity. Like buffalo mozzarella: all you need is a few sliced tomatoes and salt, and that's it.

During one filming sequence I had broad beans, chicória and a wedge of lemon, and I couldn't believe what was happening in my mouth. I had the bitter chicory, then the sharpness of lemon, all eased down with the sweetness and texture of the broad beans – a flavour combination I'd never experienced before and one I'll never forget. I also fell in love with bruschetta, which is lovely bread rubbed with garlic and topped with raw tomato. I mean, really – who thought of that?

The food of Italy is translated around the world amazingly well because it's not difficult to replicate. I also learned we interpret things slightly differently too, as I discovered in Emilia Romagna in the north, famous for balsamic vinegar, Parma ham, tortellini and of course Bolognese sauce, a *ragù* from Bologna. The Italians don't understand why we serve it with spaghetti, as it's the only pasta that won't pick up the sauce. They think we're crazy serving it as we do. They also think we're mad for having cappuccino at any time of the day other than for breakfast.

We visited Calabria, the pointy toe of Italy, with its

mountainous rugged countryside, where they love really strong salamis and hard salty cheeses. They love dried chillies as well, calling them little devils and hanging them on their doors, and sprinkling them over their food as the rest of Italy sprinkle Parmigiano-Reggiano.

We went to Modena, where the singer Pavarotti used to live, the whole place looking like a big Knightsbridge to me, and saw how balsamic vinegar is made. Real balsamic goes through seven different wooden barrels over seven years, one a year, before it's ready. The liquid picks up the different residues from the wood, and the barrels are never cleaned, so the flavour just gets deeper. When chefs reduce balsamic vinegar I think: nooo! What's wrong with you? Don't reduce it, just buy a good aged one. I once paid £40 for an ice cream with 100-year-old balsamic vinegar drizzled across the top, and my God, it was delicious and worth every penny.

I had the most unforgettable experiences as we filmed. We went with grape pickers on the little island of Ischia, with wild rabbits everywhere. The place is the shape of a witch's hat, and traditionally people lived on the flat bit and the grapes were grown on the steep slopes. They'd work in the morning, and because it was too far to come back down for lunch, they'd trap rabbits up there and cook them there and then. I found myself sitting with a bowl of brown wet food, my favourite, in a paradise. I wanted to say: 'Do you people realise you're living the dream?'

I love the passion of the people. You'd see them in the mornings, and think a fight was going on, but they were just so animated, talking about football or what the best sauce for a tomato was or something. I loved their philosophy on booze too. It was absolutely all right to drink whenever you liked, even at 9.00 a.m. as a pick-me-up, but it was absolutely not all right to be drunk.

The most amazing meal I have ever had was in La Marche, next to the Adriatic Sea, on the coast opposite Tuscany. We went and saw a farmer and his family, eight of us having a lunch of six courses. And we didn't eat anything at all that didn't come off this man's own land. The water, the wine, the liqueurs, the nuts, the veg, the meat – absolutely everything. The mum and daughter cooked all day, they ran a farm downstairs and the grandparents ran the shop. It was incredible.

Food out in Italy is your birthright. They don't have the celebration of the chef as we do here and in France. To the Italians, the best food you can have is in your home, and it's nothing to do with the money you earn: they are just inventive, clever people. Look at what food they've come up with, with big families and no money, and how incredibly it translates all over the world.

We filmed with some farmers working up on the slopes of Vesuvius, where they'd been growing big juicy tomatoes, the San Marzano, for centuries, thanks to the rich volcanic soil. They'd also scatter basil, rocket and parsley seeds as they tended them. We watched as they went off, taking a small simple bag of food with them. Then at lunchtime, they sat down in the sun, sliced some tomato and sausage, rubbed their pieces of bread with garlic and picked up some basil as they glugged from the wine. Watching them, I thought: now this is what God meant. Once I heard somebody say, 'French food at its best shows the genius of a chef, Italian food at its best shows the genius of God.' Too right.

By the time I returned from filming I was truly in love with this fabulous country and I go back at least once a year. Back home, I heard on the radio the Italian ambassador to London (leaving after twenty years) being asked what he'd missed most about this country and he went quiet for about three seconds. Then said: '*Agnello*.' Your lamb. And I felt proud, as one thing the Italians don't have which we do is lush green pastures and lots of rain. Their lamb is a bit scrawny and it was nice of him to give ours the thumbs-up.

A few months after it aired, we were absolutely thrilled when *Follow that Tomato* unexpectedly won a Royal Television Society award. It was so much fun making it and it was so educational: I guess it was great entertainment and I was very proud to have been part of that.

While my media career was kicking off, I was starting to get very worried about George Allan. After doing *Veg Talk* and filming I'd go straight to the office and stay there till 1.00 a.m., as I tried to work out what to do. The accountant had called me with bad news: 'The books are not adding up,' he'd said and something needed doing about it.

To top everything off, after we refused to make Rushton a director, he decided to leave. This, I knew, was going to make life hard, but when 25 per cent of our customers went with our star buyer, I knew things were going to be impossible. We needed to restructure our whole business. We just hadn't got the money in our coffers to cover big losses now. And we had so many outgoings. Like me, Tel was pulling out all stops to keep it from sinking. All his warnings had come back to haunt us. We really had grown too big now. There was so much to keep up with. I felt like a rabbit caught in headlights. We were getting monthly management reports and losing money every single day.

Then I got another call, which took me off into another direction. This time I was wanted to front a BBC show called *Saturday Kitchen*. This was before it was on live TV. I was going to be inviting chefs and they needed a presenter to link the cooking bits together.

This, to me, was yet another miracle and I was made up, but I also felt out of my league. That evening when I was down in Soho, meeting some of the chefs, they couldn't believe it any more than I could. I was so nervous, but once again I had real fun. The producer was a lady called Koz and she was naughtier than me, although a great girl, and encouraged me to be naughty as well. I love my innuendoes, and I would make jokes all the way through, making such quips like: 'I've got a Korean cookbook at home called *100 Ways to Wok your Dog*' and 'Henry VIII liked getting head from his wives', and of course anything with nuts or melons brought a smile to my face and a few cheeky words.

As much as I loved having my face on the telly and feeling all the more accepted for it, I started to feel real fear when it came to my business – the business that was now making me famous. It was collapsing around me and I couldn't keep up. One morning at 2.00 a.m., I arrived at the office to find Tel with his head in his hands, swathes of papers all around him.

'Gregg, this ain't working any more,' he said, waving them in front of me. 'I want to go.'

I felt hot and sick. 'Really, Tel? Is that what you really want?'

His face said it all. He'd had enough. We'd already let about half our staff go, our vans were on HP and we were struggling to find the cash even for that. It seemed that we were suddenly going the way so many businesses in New Covent Garden Market had gone before us. They start small, get medium sized, then get big and go bust – we just thought we'd be different. At our height we'd been turning over £7.5 million a year. Now it was a very different picture. There was no way I was going to generate enough money to pay the leaseholders on our offices and vans and everything. I still hoped I could save the company, though. I thought I'd be able to soldier on. Somehow.

I carried on, worrying, filming, worrying, working, filming, worrying. I couldn't sleep. When I wasn't doing telly stuff I just wanted to work and drink. In the end I gave £25k to Terry to leave the company, and he couldn't get out fast enough. Another partnership failed. It was over.

CHAPTER 27

Courgette Flowers

By now, I was struggling. I felt so broke without Terry. I had trusted and relied on him, and I didn't have the fight and energy to sort this thing out on my own. I was way, way out of my depth. I managed to raise £70k from our new mortgage and I sank it into the company, but it was a drop in the ocean. We were owed millions and we owed millions too to wholesalers in the market. It was starting to all look a bit mental. I suppose, looking back, it seemed that I was swanning around, cock of the walk, now that I was on the telly, but actually behind the scenes I was working my nuts off to stop this thing sinking.

There was nobody to turn to any more. I was also still contracted to *Saturday Kitchen* and that took up so much time too. I felt I had little to give the company now; I felt frozen and impotent in the face of a real disaster. This TV lark was a major project; I had no time to see customers, reassure them, run the warehouse and sort the deliveries out. I wasn't Superman.

A few weeks later, I came into the warehouse after a long day filming and asked to speak to Paul.

'Where is he?' I asked one of the lads.

'He's gone to work with Terry,' he replied, not meeting my eye. I felt my heart almost stop beating, as I nodded and tried to smile, walking quickly into my office to catch my breath. Gone with Terry. Oh my God! I knew what that meant. They'd be hitting my customer base, good and proper. I sat down at my desk and looked around. It was so quiet, except for the few cries of some early morning deliveries starting up outside. I couldn't believe this. What a mess! I knew then and there, though, there was nothing I could do. I was sunk. I sat there for hours, thinking of what I could do next. All I could see were reports of money we were losing.

At 9.00 a.m., with trembling fingers I dialled the number of the bank. 'I am in big trouble here,' I said, trying to keep my voice even. 'You'll need to bring in the receivers.'

The manager put on one of their financial people and he talked me through the options. Which were truly limited.

'Do you want to try to keep the company? Sell it on?' the manager asked.

'No,' I said. I knew very, very soon I'd have every man and his dog on my back, chasing me for money. I felt as if I'd taken a running jump straight into the nothingness I'd been trying to avoid.

My mind was in overdrive as I tried to work out a plan to survive. I had the mortgage to pay, I had the lifestyle now. The mock-Tudor house, the Merc, the wife, kids in private school: I was the boy from Peckham who'd done good. Was I really going to lose everything? This fast? It just didn't seem possible. Except it was. And it was happening. And there was nothing, nothing, I could do except watch.

Luckily, we were a limited company so I had limited personal liability and therefore didn't have to pick all the bills up personally. The next step was for the receivers to come in and sell up my assets like the vans at auction. The creditors would book all the money I owed. The bank had what's called preferential creditors, who were paid off before anybody else; then every man and his dog who wants money from you queues up and waits.

How did it go so wrong? Well, many people have asked me this. And it's easy really, except we didn't realise it at the time. The biggest mistake we made was not having really brilliant up-to-date management accounts. You should always know exactly how much money you have at all times. Cash flow and profit are very different things. Cash flow projections are very important. You should have a business forecast for every four, six and twelve months, and a budget to show where you are and exactly what your margins are. We weren't doing this well enough. Oh, for a proper mentor at this time! We'd had none; we were learning on the job. And we'd succeeded on that job. But now we'd failed. Since then I've seen and realised it happens time and time again. Big companies in New Covent Garden get too big and splinter into smaller ones. It's par for the course, but hindsight is a beautiful thing.

When the crash came, I just fell into a numbness. Suddenly I had no earnings. Except for the bit of telly work. I'd finished filming *Saturday Kitchen* by now, thankfully, and I knew they wanted to do a second series.

But then in a brief meeting I was told a third series had been commissioned, but on live TV with Antony Worrall Thompson fronting it.

I laughed, loudly. Except it was from a place where nothing was funny. This was like a horrible joke, though. After losing everything I'd built my media career on, being Gregg the Veg, I'd lost it. So from running a multimillion-pound business and being a fledging telly presenter, I went to nothing, Mr Unemployed, almost overnight.

As I cleared out the office, I locked it up and somehow managed to get myself home to Petersham. I opened the front door, it was dark, Denise was in bed. And I just sat in the living room, in silence, alone, unable to move. I was still there hours later. Just sitting there. I went to get up to get a drink, but my feet moved as if they were set in concrete. I couldn't even walk properly. The house, our lovely house, all our lovely furniture – it just looked as if it was made of sand now. I almost expected it to disappear before my eyes, as if it had never existed. A day or so later, our Merc did just that, when the receivers came. I couldn't bear to watch them drive it away, I really couldn't. What was I going to do?

On top of that Terry rang me and was furious. He'd been chased by creditors after the vehicles were put up for auction as, like me, he'd signed personal guarantees, which meant that if the vehicles didn't come up with enough money we'd be chased for it. 'I've left the company, so why should I pay?' he raged at me.

I did have some sympathy, as I was in the same position. But also I could not help feeling that if he had not left and attacked our customer base with Paul, perhaps we could've even had a company still.

It was a nightmare. And incredible, how many hours, how much dedication it takes to build up a company, yet when the end comes, how quickly it disintegrates. Meanwhile, I just tried to get through the next few days. I couldn't eat or sleep.

Life was a mess. Denise was also very upset.

'What are you going to do, Gregg?' she kept asking. 'What?' I could see how fragile she was. In the morning, I watched Tom and Libby running off to their posh school and my heart nearly broke. I knew I had to sort this for them too. I'd built this all up, it'd come crashing down and it was only up to me to build it up again.

One business acquaintance happened to ring at this time, a bloke called Vince O'Brian.

'Blimey, Gregg,' he said. 'How are you going to get out of that one, then?'

'I dunno,' I said. My words came out thick and slow. 'I really don't. I set up a business. I gave it a good go. I failed. I mean, what can I do? I'm done. Finished.'

'Nah, don't talk like that. That's not like you, Gregg,' he said.

He was right: it wasn't. I moped for another day, my brain in overdrive as I desperately thought of ways to get out of this. Then the next morning, I decided to catch a train and go to Borough Market. I needed somewhere to think, and I needed inspiration. I ended up wandering round there for a few hours. I missed the buzz of a market – the stalls, the selling, the life, the fruit and veg. It was so simple. I'd already thought about going back to New Covent Garden and starting all over again, as a salesman, but many of the traders had joined forces and said they'd refuse to employ me. It wasn't fair, but they blamed me for George Allan's closure; they thought I'd got too fancy and big for my boots, being on telly now, and I'd let it all go to pot. Nothing could've been further from the truth, though. It's always the way: the last one out to turn the lights off gets the blame.

As I wandered round, my mind was whirring. What was I

going to do? What? I could be a salesman again, but where? For whom? As I walked past the piles of fresh fruit and veg, fish and cheeses of Borough, soaking up the atmosphere, I started to think properly. Then, surrounded by the lettuces, tomatoes and apples, it occurred to me. I could be a salesman for another company, but not one in New Covent Garden Market. And there was someone I knew who could help.

I dashed home and rang the number of Charles Secrett. 'Can I come down today and speak to you?' I begged him.

A bit bemused, he said he'd be around that afternoon on the farm, so I agreed to drive down. For the first time in weeks, I felt a huge hunger again, and not just for work but for food. So I went down to Bermondsey, walked into Manze's and ordered two large meat pies with two scoops of mash and drowned in lashings of green liquor. I covered it in pepper and vinegar, and had a feast. As I sat back in the seat, I began to feel the magic effects of the pie, my belly feeling full and warm again, just it did as a kid. And suddenly, I was much, much better.

I rushed back home as fast as possible, jumped in our BMW, the only car we had left, and zoomed down to Secrett's straight away.

I was almost out of breath with excitement when I finally saw Charles.

'Listen,' I said, 'I've lost everything, everything … but I have a proposition for you.'

In one long breath I explained how I still had my customers, the chefs, I could still drive a van, and I could still sell his produce and only his produce.

'You grow it, I'll sell it,' I said. 'I can do that. Yes, I can do that!'

Charles listened, rubbing his chin. I knew it was a bit of a gamble asking him. After all, George Allan still owed him money and I had none to offer.

He thought for almost a minute. Then he nodded. 'I know you can sell. I know you will work hard. I know you will sell it to the right places. You're on,' he said.

I could've kissed the man.

Later on Vernon, my restaurateur friend, rang me up to see how I was doing. Thankfully my friends hadn't turned their backs on me.

'What you gonna do?' he asked.

'I have this idea of working for Secrett's farm,' I said. To my surprise Vernon sounded interested.

'Right,' he said. 'I want to get out of the restaurant trade and would love to go into a business. Can I give you some money to join in after I sell up, if you pull this off?'

'You're on.'

The next man I went to see was Howard, my accountant. He'd become a friend too, and is now a partner in Wallace and Co., my restaurant in East Putney.

'I've got this germ of an idea,' I said, going on to explain.

Howard stared at me intently. 'Where are your clients going to come from?' he asked.

'George Allan's customer base,' I said.

'You still have a customer base?' he said, arching an eyebrow.

'Yes!' I cried.

'They don't care you've gone bust?'

'We owe money to the people on the market,' I said. 'But chefs don't care.'

Howard reached into his bag and started writing a cheque. 'OK, I will give you 10k for 10 per cent of your business,' he said simply.

Later on Vince rang again to ask me how I was doing.

'Oh, hiya,' I said. 'Well, I have this germ of an idea and two backers now to work directly with growers on a brilliant farm George Allan worked with for years.' I rattled on.

'Bloody hell,' said Vince, laughing. 'Good man. That's better.' He couldn't believe how fast I'd turned things back on the up again. Just twenty-four hours later the broken man was back in business. That's when I knew this would work; people believed in me still. It was such an amazing lesson. Everything had disappeared – the TV work, my Merc, the expense account, the business – but somehow I had stopped being scared, because the one thing I was most frightened of had happened. When you've lost the lot you only have your balls and your brain left to rely on, and that's when you can go back out there and do it again. Sometimes we're at our very best when facing adversity.

Within six weeks of going bust, I was up and running around London again in a van, doing what I did best: selling fruit and veg. To begin with I was an employee of Charles, but he knew nothing about supplying and I was still a novice in growing, so I asked him if I could keep his name but run my business myself, along with Vernon and Howard. He agreed and off I went. Secrett's Direct had been born. On £70k a year again straight away. I'd learned the lesson that a greengrocer can never be big. You should never have more than four vans at any time. Keep it small, keep it manageable. Just as Tel had suggested all those years ago.

Never afraid of hard graft, I was back on the phone, all hours, trying to drum up business and get as many of George Allan's clients back on board as I could.

One Saturday I was at a barbecue with Denise at one of our posh neighbours' houses and everyone was toasting the owners of the house, but I couldn't relax and join in. I had so many orders to check and work to do. Setting up a business again was nothing but hard work.

'I need to make some calls,' I whispered to Denise. It had been so hard since we'd lost everything. Denise had told me how humiliated she had felt alongside the other wives, standing in their designer clothes discussing new conservatories, while everyone knew I'd gone bust. Now with this chance, I was determined to grab it, even if it meant interrupting our weekends.

CHAPTER 28

Poires Belle-Hélène

*O*f course I still hadn't lost my touch with sales and it was just fantastic. With my new venture of Secrett's Direct, I soon got the River Café back on board. A few years earlier John Torode had started Smiths of Smithfield, and he was on side, of course. Then Anthony Demetre, who runs Wild Honey, joined and Le Gavroche came back, along with Alistair Little's place and the Eagle, and a Tom Conran place in Notting Hill. I never got all the Conran joints back, though. The buyer in Quaglino's couldn't stand me, as he'd spent all his time building up a relationship with George Allan only to see us go bust and, unlike the others, he couldn't quite forgive that.

I did all the deliveries with Vernon. We had a van each and worked our socks off, often from midnight till 3.00 p.m. I'd snatch a couple of hours' sleep and then be back on the phones till 7.00 p.m., taking orders. Then I'd get a few more hours' sleep before getting back to the farm.

The last delivery would always be at Putney Bridge in Demetre's place. He used to feed me there too. I'd sit there, in my dirty tracksuit bottoms, knackered and grateful for something good to eat.

This was the start of yet another new venture. As our customer base burgeoned, our ideas did too. Now I had somebody to grow the fruit and veg, I wanted to grow our range. I found inspiration everywhere. Once I happened to be in a tiny restaurant in Oxfordshire and found baby salad leaves on my plate. I asked where they got them from and went to see the growers. From then on, we planted all kinds of salad leaves at Secrett's, including mizuna, Bull's Blood beetroot leaves, amaranth and red sorrel. We ended up finding a restaurant, Asian de Cuba, which couldn't get enough of the stuff: they ordered between 30 and 40 kilos of it, as opposed to the usual 3 kilos others wanted.

Another food we brought to the tables of London was sprouting seeds, such as pea shoots and onions. We grew a few and then took them direct to chefs' kitchens, asking them to try them. The sweet, savoury taste and texture were so unusual, with an explosion of flavour, and they loved the stuff. All the best places started sprinkling sprouting seeds on top of the salads on their menus and diners loved the idea: they were so wholesome and different. What a world away from the iceberg lettuce! We sold them at £8 or £9 and, yes, we made a fortune out of them. This was because if chefs could put the 'back story' of their food on the menu they could charge a premium to the customers. Although, as I say, there isn't always a back story. Once I saw a menu that read 'Orchard apples' and laughed my head off. I mean, where else are you going to get apples? The difference was that the ingredients we provided for these places really were cutting edge and experimental, exciting and different. One food critic described Secrett's Direct salads as being like the Gucci handbag of food. Result!

The River Café taught me that food could be very, very simple but still very, very good. I'll never forget when I had their carpaccio on roasted beetroots and horseradish. So fresh, so delicate and absolutely delicious. I loved Rose too, although she terrified me, always so dry and quick-witted. I remember the pride I felt in some of the produce I was getting for her, and impressing her meant everything. Once we grew some Violetta aubergines. Now these were big, heavy and dense, and their colour was much lighter than that of a normal deep purple one. They had no seeds and the flesh was as thick as a paperback book. And at Secrett's we had managed to get them to grow ourselves.

Anyway, I turned up at the River Café with some and showed them to Rose, and her eyes nearly fell out of her head. 'These,' she said in her raspy voice, handling them as if they were jewels, 'are beautiful, Gregg.' Her eyes narrowed. 'Where did you get them? Did you grow them?'

'Not me,' I said. 'But a guy I commissioned to grow them.'

'Honestly?' she said, arching an eyebrow.

'I wouldn't lie to you,' I said.

'Right, how many have you got?'

I called Vernon and he told me we had 30 kilos.

'Right,' Rose said. 'I'll have the lot.'

She ordered boxes of them. The next time I walked into the place there were bowls of them, all glossy and colourful, used as decoration, as well as on the menu. I glowed with pride.

Since I'd lost the George Allan business, I knew I had to work hard to keep ahead of the game and I'd learned my lesson about making the business too big. This would be kept small and high quality. And quality became our middle name.

We were pushing the boundaries, providing amazing ingredients no other veg firms could get their hands on. And we were actually growing the stuff.

Once we grew courgette flowers in raised beds in our greenhouse down on the farm. The River Café wanted these beautiful, delicate star-shaped, vivid yellow flowers too. They were a delicacy to be dipped in flour and then gently fried. Delicious. But the flowers only open when the sun comes out, and then they close again. There was only one way of harvesting them, and that was by hand, very, very gently and when the sun rose. So Vernon and I set off early every morning that summer. We arrived at 5.00 a.m., in time for the magical sight of these flowers gently unfurling to soak in the rays. I handed Vernon a Stanley knife.

'C'mon, then,' I said, winking. And we set off, wading chest deep in these lush plants, gently slicing the flowers off at the stems and placing them one by one in polystyrene trays, to be whisked to London safely. You really couldn't get fresher than that. I got such a buzz from this side of the business. I mean, I loved being a wholesaler, but a grower? It's even closer to the food.

Actually freshness is key to proper-tasting food. It has nothing to do with being organic or non-organic, and anyone who says using pesticides impairs flavour is a lunatic in my opinion. The only thing that affects the taste of your food is the speed with which it is transported from the ground to your gob. End of. As soon as you cut fruit and veg it's dead and dying, and the trick is to race it to the table as fast as you can.

We started to prove this to our chefs. We told them that what they ordered we would grow and could get to the plate quickly, sometimes even on the same day, and the taste difference was incredible. And I started to invite some of them down to the farm. Once I got a Bunsen burner going to boil up some water and salt just outside the field. Then I stripped a sweetcorn plant we'd been growing of its cobs and flung them in the pot. Ten minutes later they were cooked and I handed a chef a plate.

The look on his face said it all. 'Incredible, isn't it?' I grinned. 'Didn't really think corn on the cob tasted like that, did you?'

I have never supported using chemicals to enhance growth. That's nonsense. I agree with using pesticides sometimes, though. I mean, what are you going to do? Sit and watch your crops being eaten? It's either man or insect, and the insect will win if you let it. When we grew Opal plums, a really delicious fruit that eats like a peach, we found an infestation on the trees. I didn't hesitate to sort it out with spray, not for a moment.

We'd bought in mature strawberries plants too, all of subtly different flavours, and the top chefs appreciated this. The pastry chef at the Ivy once said to me, 'Gregg, you do the best soft fruit ever,' and I was so proud.

We started growing Mare de Bois strawberries, which are the closest cultivated strawberries you can get to fraises du bois, the wild strawberries that grow in the Alps and on forest floors. They were on the farm's 'pick your own' site and obviously we wanted punters to stay away from them, so we cheekily stuck up a sign saying 'Just sprayed' and nobody touched them.

I feel as strongly about chilling food. A lot of the time it can be unnecessary. If strawberries were meant to be cold, Eskimos would grow really good ones. We're obsessed with chilling stuff in this country and it annihilates flavour. In Spain and Italy you see food being bumped around on the open backs of trucks in the roaring sun. They eat outside, slicing warm ham on to warm cheese and bread, and nobody gets ill. You don't see them dying of warm sandwich disease, just as you don't find husbands ringing up their wives as they leave work: 'Oh, darling, put that sandwich in the fridge for me, please, will you?' Why do we do it? It kills flavour.

While things were finally on the up with the business, my personal life was falling apart. I split up with Denise and moved out. It was all heartbreaking but it wasn't working, and to be honest with myself, it hadn't been for a long while. But my burning desire to have this family and to give them what I never had was at odds with that.

I moved to Hampton Wick, into a one-bedroomed flat, and kept in as close contact as possible with the children. I couldn't even bring myself to tell them I was leaving for good – we never had that conversation; in my mind I would see them as much as possible anyway. It was never them I was leaving. By now Tom was old enough to play rugby and I took him to a local team where he lived, so we spent lots of time bonding over that. Eventually he got into the London Welsh's under-seven team and I was a father always on the pitch side cheering him on with enthusiasm, come rain or shine.

As soon as Libby was old enough I got her to join in too. Just because she was a girl didn't mean she had to miss out.

By the time Tom joined the under-tens, I was hooked on watching the kids' games as well as adults': they could be just as exciting. The team's coach spotted this and after a few months asked if I'd be interested in doing a coaching badge to coach kids.

'You betcha!' I said.

This was another big love of my life. I just loved coaching kids and teaching them the basics. It was brilliant fun. They'd arrive all timid and I would take real pride in building their confidence. As they got older and the game became full contact I'd do a big talk to try to inspire them. 'Listen. I can't coach you to play rugby without it hurting, but I can teach you not to care that it hurts. Those bruises can be a badge of honour. I want you to fly into tackles and I will teach you properly, so you don't have to be scared. We'll practise, practise, practise, and I will turn you into a fantastic rugby player.' It's a speech Tom has heard many times.

I once met Matt Dawson, England's most capped scrum half, on *Celebrity MasterChef* and I told him I watched games in slow motion, and we ended up discussing the game. I was thrilled he was on the show, in complete awe. 'You're a proper rugby anorak,' he said, laughing. He loved the fact I was so passionate about what he did, and I loved the fact he watched *MasterChef.*

I love the fact Tom still plays. It's one thing we always have proper father-and-son time together with, and we go to matches all the time. He's gone from London Welsh to Whitstable to Blackheath and had a senior year in Thanet, playing scrum half. He's quite a small chap, but ferocious on that pitch, with a good side step. He'll tackle anything that's coming. Although that's not always easy for a father to watch. Once I was watching him play for Blackheath and the opposite kicked the ball on, and the fall back and Tom were chasing it when this enormous flanker cheekily kicked the fall back after he got the ball. Tom saw this and punched him in the guts, doubling this big lump over. I shuddered, thinking: wow, Tom is going to be stamped on for the rest of this game. But he didn't touch him again and Tom shook his hand as they left the pitch.

'Did he say anything to you?' I asked, ever the anxious dad.

'Yeah,' said Tom with a grin. 'Great punch, Titch!'

Around this time, I took Tom back to wander round my old Bermondsey haunts. I took him outside my old flat and into the Queen Vic. I still took him to Millwall whenever I could as well, something I was desperate to do. I mean, to me it is like a homecoming every time I approach that stadium and find myself standing there, and to be doing it with my son by my side is an amazing feeling. Tom really is everything I'd ever hoped to have in a son.

Once, on the way back, we came across an old friend, Kenny, a painter and decorator, and he was so pleased to see me.

'This is my boy,' I said proudly. Then Kenny asked which school he was going to and Tom told him the name of his private school. Kenny jumped backwards as though he'd had an electric shot. 'Nah way!' he cried as he heard Tom's rather posh accent. 'What you done to him, Gregg?' I laughed. I didn't mind.

Just as things were going well with the business, the possibility of working in front of the camera again came up. I still couldn't quite believe my luck, but actually, as I've said, I found talking on camera fairly easy (well, I find talking easy wherever), my love of food was genuine and I was learning as I went along, so all was good. One day my agent, Rosemary, gave me a bell.

'There's a big new cooking show the BBC are making and they're looking for a new presenter, so I've put you forward.'

'OK, great! Thanks!'

I found myself going down to an office in a disused church in Notting Hill, without a clue what to expect. There I met Karen Ross, a wonderful scary lady, the big boss of this new project, and I was told to sit in front of a camera next to a desk with a few people around.

'Right,' said Karen, nodding at the camera assistant to start the camera rolling. 'I want you to tell me about food, Gregg.'

'Er, anything?' I asked.

'Anything at all.'

'OK.'

I spoke for forty-five minutes without taking a breath, spinning from restaurants to waiters, to fruit and veg to the disconnection between meat and beasts, from people's fear of fresh fish to my hatred of barbecues. Finally, as I realised my mouth was going dry and actually it'd been rather a long time since anyone had said anything aside from me, I stopped.

'Er, is that enough?' I asked.

Karen was beaming. 'Yes,' she said.

We went outside and she said, 'We're making a revamped version of *MasterChef* and it's a big project. It's going to take three months to film and it starts in six weeks. Can you do it?'

'You want me?' I asked, flabbergasted. I mean, *MasterChef* was presented by Loyd Grossman asking Mrs Corgi Trouserpress from the Home Counties what ridiculously named dishes she'd cooked, and I wasn't sure how I fitted into that.

'Yes, we do,' she said, laughing. 'You'll be one of two judges.'

'Who is the other one?' I asked.

'An Australian chef who's done a few things on TV before,' she explained, 'called John Torode. Do you know him?'

'Yes.' I laughed out loud. 'Yes, I know John.'

As always, life is what happens to you while you're busy making other plans. I don't want to go into details, as I hate saying derogatory things about exes, but one day Tom and Libby came and lived with me and I got custody of them.

It wasn't expected, and as we started filming *MasterChef*, I found myself looking after them and having to bring them into the editing suite to watch *Star Wars* after a runner had gone and got pizza and burgers for them. Despite being a ferocious boss, Karen Ross was extremely supportive around this time. It was a struggle, and for the first three months we lived in my one-bedroomed flat, me on the sofa bed. Then I bought a house in Whitstable, where Mum had moved to. She desperately wanted to help and my goodness she did.

A little while later I got a place in London too, so that I could work and stay some days. At one point I lived round the corner from John Torode's restaurant, Smith of Smithfields. A few years earlier I'd sat down with him and had a scout through his new menu.

'What's this, John?' I said, laughing. 'You've got fish finger sandwiches down for breakfast. Are you gonna do goujons or what?'

'Nope,' he replied cheekily. 'Actually it's going to be Birds Eye. On white bread, all pressed down to perfection.'

Now that took me back. A fish finger sandwich, no getting away from it, is a wonderful thing. You bite through soft white bread, soft white cod, and there's that crispy layer in between. The flavour is neutral, so you need the brown sauce or ketchup, although John had tartar sauce on it, and to me that's just 'poshing' up a fish finger sandwich beyond its natural state. Yeah, even back then we didn't always agree on flavours and food!

I love John, though, and filming *MasterChef* was brilliant. We had more to genuinely disagree on and maybe the fact we each bring something so different to *MasterChef* is one of the reasons for its success. Just like Michel Roux Jr, John watched how people cooked and the process and how they worked, whereas I didn't care. I just wanted to know what it tasted like. I could never say, 'It's all right apart from . . .' Well, there is no 'apart from': it either tastes good or it doesn't, regardless of how someone has made it. If something tastes like Satan's armpit then what's the point?

Everyone knows, though, that I cannot hide my delight on *MasterChef* when it comes to puddings. I've never lost my sweet tooth and certain dishes and flavours give an instant blast of childhood memories. In 2007, *MasterChef* winner Steven Wallis served up a Poires Belle-Hélène, poached pears with vanilla ice cream and a chocolate sauce, an absolutely outstanding dessert. Straight away I was looking forward to tasting it. I picked up my spoon and got a good dig in the pear, and then dipped it in the sauce. I closed my eyes, and as the juicy pear grabbed me I was sent straight back to Wimbledon, fruit and cream, sitting next to Grandad W, all served up by Nan W, smiling. Then, tasting the chocolate, I was back dipping my hand in Grandad's jar of doings. With that one dessert, with all its sticky sweetness, Nan in Wimbledon and Grandad in Peckham were suddenly there, with me, patting me on the head, giving me a kiss with their arms around me.

There was a pause as I opened my eyes to see the crew in silence, John staring at me.

'For me,' I said slowly, my voice breaking a little, 'this dish tastes like a winner.'